The Swiss Cookbook

THE
SWISS
COOKBOOK

Nika Standen Hazelton

Atheneum

NEW YORK

1973

FOR *Heidi* AND *Gerold Albonico*

BEST OF FRIENDS

Foreword

I CHOSE the recipes in this book because to me they seem to represent Swiss cooking rather than French, German or Italian cooking transplanted to Switzerland. This is the reason why my readers won't find the standard recipes for omelets, sauce Béarnaise, sauerbraten, spaghetti, etc., which are eaten as much in Switzerland as in their countries of origin. If some categories of dishes are not fully represented, it is because they would, to my mind, be of foreign origin, though through constant usage they have become part of Swiss cookery. I have also tried to keep to dishes that American cooks are likely to make and that appeal to the American taste, which, in many cases, is simpler than the Swiss taste.

As all cookbooks must, this one reflects the author's taste. But I apologize to the readers who may miss a favorite recipe, and if they will write to me in care of my publishers, I will do my best to get it to them.

I have collected these recipes over many years from all kinds of Swiss sources—town and country homes, rural and city restaurants, hotels, old manuscripts, books and from my own childhood Swiss home. I've been back to Switzerland many times, and the recipes are authentic. Very few of them have ever appeared in English, to the best of my knowledge.

The recipes were tested with standard American kitchen equipment, and, unless otherwise specified, they make 4 to 6 servings, depending on how they are served. I want to express my thanks to Helen Feingold, the well-known home economist, for her invaluable assistance in helping me to test them.

N.K.S.

Lugano—Zurich—Geneva—New York

Acknowledgments

MY HEARTFELT THANKS go to all the people in Switzerland who gave me so much of their time and advice; I shall never cease to be grateful to them.

Among them, I particularly wish to thank the following: Mr. Hans Baertschi, Managing Director of the Swiss National Tourist Office in New York, and Mr. Max Lehmann, its Public Relations Director; Mr. Fred Birmann, Director of Press and Public Relations of the Swiss National Tourist Office in Zurich; Mr. Jakob Baumgartner, formerly Assistant Director of the Zurich Tourist Office; Mr. Armin Moser and Mr. Werner Boos, respectively the Director and Assistant Director of the St. Gall Tourist Office; Mr. Paul Braun, of the Emmental Tourist Office; Mr. and Mrs. Gerold Albonico, Mr. and Mrs. Rudolf Laber, Mr. and Mrs. Urs Schwarz and Dr. and Mrs. H. Scharer of Zurich; Mr. Max Baumann of Berne; and Mr. Heinz Hofer and Mr. Willi Bühlmann of the Schweizerische Kase Union.

Special thanks go to Mr. Charles Sandmeyer, Manager of Pan-American Airways in Zurich, for all his kindness.

Finally, I want to thank my publisher, Mr. Alfred Knopf, Jr., for his patience, and my dear father and mother for their wisdom in bringing me up in Switzerland.

Contents

The Swiss Cookbook

I

Introduction

SWITZERLAND lies in the heart of Europe, surrounded by France, Germany, Austria and Italy. It has an area of nearly 16,000 square miles, about twice the size of New Jersey. There are about 5.5 million Swiss. Instead of a common language, they have four national languages. German is spoken by 693 per 1,000 Swiss; French by 189 per 1,000; Italian by 95 per 1,000; and Romansh, a variety of Latin, by 9 per 1,000. In addition, the Swiss speak many local dialects. The German-speaking Swiss of even the highest social classes attach the greatest importance to their Schwyzerdütsch and speak it constantly. Schwyzerdütsch breaks down into many local dialects, and these vary from valley to valley and canton to canton; they are the mother tongues of the German-speaking Swiss, while literary German is learned at school, like a foreign language, and used only in writing and for formal occasions.

Switzerland is a democracy, and it has survived as an independent nation for 675 years. The country is divided into 22 cantons or states, with a federal government residing in Berne, the nation's capital. The cantons enjoy considerable independence, and the Swiss are the only people in Europe who understand what an American means when he speaks of states' rights.

Of every thousand of the population, 526 are Protestant, 456 Catholic, and 18 belong to other faiths.

There is no distinctively Swiss physical type. The Swiss may be tall or short, heavy or thin, fair or dark. But there are considerable emotional differences between the Swiss of the various regions.

Switzerland is still a man's country, but though the women don't have the vote, they are by no means oppressed. All the girls are well educated and very polite, and most of them, regardless of social status, go abroad to learn foreign languages while working as mothers' helpers or in some other expense-meeting capacity. It is taken for granted that girls will work until their marriage, and afterward until they have children; then, in middle- and upper-class families, they stay home. Family life is conservative; in the smaller towns and villages Daddy still has the upper hand and it doesn't do for a girl to get herself talked about.

The Swiss are reserved, even among themselves, except at Carnival time. With the constant influx of millions of foreigners, their reserve resembles the fence a home-owner puts up to ensure privacy from even a friendly neighbor. But once you have a Swiss for a friend, he is your friend for life.

Switzerland is a hard-working country, and the Swiss mistrust any kind of *dolce vita*. They start working early, stop late and are even proud of it. They are well paid, and they subscribe to the old-fashioned notion that it is fair to give value in return. Their honesty is great; frauds are reported by the newspapers with a kind of awed wonder that such a thing should be possible. In Switzerland it is rare that a waitress will add the day's date to your bill, and there is no bargaining on prices. These traits, plus the natural secretiveness of the Swiss which led to the unique institution of the numbered bank account, have made Switzerland a repository for the world's money.

Switzerland has always had a pronounced cultural and artistic life expressed in the architectural treasures of her towns and villages, the excellence of her universities, the quality of her music and the way the country has encouraged native and foreign painters and writers.

Of the 15,941 square miles that make up Switzerland, only three quarters can be cultivated. Only about three fifths of the food needed to feed the population can be produced from the soil, so Switzerland is permanently dependent on food imports. This helps to explain the Swiss people's familiarity with a great many foreign food products.

Switzerland has no mineral wealth to speak of. Its only natural resource is hydroelectric power, which is manufactured in thousands of power stations, some on the grandest scale. These power resources have helped to make Switzerland a manufacturing nation, specializing—quite apart from watches, chocolate and cheese—in precision machinery. Today more people are employed in industry and manual trades than in any other branch of the economy. The labor shortage in Switzerland is profound and chronic. The country imports about half a million foreign workers, ten percent of its total population, from as far as Turkey and Greece, which makes for special problems in this small country.

Switzerland is not, as many people think, all Alps. Not all Alps are in Switzerland either, though the most important ones are there. Switzerland's mountains give the country an astonishing variety of climates. South of them, in the Ticino, spring is in full flower while in the north the snow covers the ground. Or you can suntan in one valley and ski a few miles away. Over fifty lakes and over forty rivers are to be found in Switzerland. Two of Europe's most important rivers, the Rhine and the Rhône, have their springs there.

Swiss ingenuity has turned her landscape of high Alps and barren rocks into a paradise for visitors. The quality of the highways, though they are often jammed, is a joy to the motorist, and the trains are the world's cleanest and most efficient. Swiss funiculars, cog railroads, aerial tramways and ski lifts lead to improbably high belvederes with a staggering view, a hotel and a flagpole flying the national flag.

For those of my readers who may wonder, as I did, if it is possible to buy a Swiss Alp, and if so, how to set about it, I quote a communication from the General Consulate of Switzerland in New York, who certainly ought to know:

> . . . The right to private property in Switzerland is guaranteed by cantonal (state) constitutions. Public law may limit the right to property in the public interest. In this case, however, expropriation proceedings must take place with full indemnification. The prerequisites for an expropriation are that the purpose of the project be in the public interest. This is the case, for instance, in the building of roads, public facilities, installations of public utilities, etc.
>
> Private property cannot include land that is not usable, as, for example, rocks and glaciers. These cannot be the object of property rights, but come under the sovereignty of the state.
>
> Given these two principles, the Swiss Civil Code sets forth the framework of private property

ownership in Switzerland. Ownership implies all that is above and below the surface to such a height and depth as the owner may require as stated in Article 667.

There is also the right of access to another's property. Every person has, according to Article 699 of the Swiss Civil Code, (to the extent allowed by local customs), free access to the forests and fields of another person and may pick wild berries, mushrooms and the like.

With regard to hunting, shooting, fishing, the cantons are allowed, however, to make special regulations.

As to the use of land for military purposes, an expropriation must take place if the use is permanent. For usual military exercises, the Swiss armed forces are entitled to use the land but are under obligation to avoid any damage or, if this is not possible, to make arrangements beforehand with the owners under guarantee of indemnification. If the owner is a municipality, the agreement will be obtainable under public obligation, but for a privately owned piece of property, the owner might refuse and will be protected in his decision.

II

About the Swiss and Their Food

Y ou always eat well in Switzerland, down to the most rural of inns. But there is more to Swiss meals than good food—you have the feeling of taking part in a pleasant occasion. A Swiss headwaiter, sophisticated to the point of weariness, explained this to me. "We Swiss are a practical people," he said. "Anybody who spends money on anything wants full value for it, so that food, both at home and in restaurants, is expected to be good. But our people want something else besides what's due to them. They want to be happy when they eat. And making customers happy is an art at which we Swiss excel."

The variety and character of Swiss food is a revelation to all who break away from the international hotel cuisine (on whose excellence I cast no aspersions). Swiss food does not have the ultimate finesse of French food, but it still retains a quality that today is well-nigh unique: it is prepared with care and with love, with what the French call *soigné*. The meals in Alpine climbers' huts, in working-class homes, in remote little mountain inns, in the inexpensive vegetarian and temperance restaurants are prepared with the intention of pleasing, just as they are in the hotels and restaurants de luxe.

Swiss food, like Swiss life, has been influenced by the countries around Switzerland—France, Germany, Italy and even Austria. There is no Swiss cooking as radically different from that of its neighbors as, for instance, Dutch cooking is from Italian. What Switzerland abounds in is endless specialties from the various cantons, regions and even towns and villages, all referred to with their place of origin since the Swiss have the fiercest local pride possible. Many of these dishes are extremely old, and are now obsolete because they are far too substantial for modern living, even in the country. Their pattern, however, is still to be seen in today's Swiss eating: the stress on soups, the secondary importance of meats, the simple meals consisting of home-fried potatoes, a bit of cheese and *café au lait*, or a supper of fruit tart and tea—in short, the frugality of daily Swiss living. In another country this frugality might lead to carelessness and insipidity, but not in Switzerland.

The Swiss like variations on a theme; the many and interesting ways the basic Swiss house, the chalet, is interpreted in the various regions of the country are proof of their inventiveness. They ring changes on basic dishes, such as the home-fried potatoes, the cabbage-and-meat combinations, the things made from cheese. Nowadays foreign travel has also influenced Swiss cooking, and I would say the nation is on an exotic kick, but a cautious, rather bland one compared to our tastes. The Chinese and Malayan food I ate in Switzerland was very good, but it had a definite Swiss anchorage.

Another factor which has strongly influenced Swiss eating is a food-reform movement which taught the Swiss to include and even to start their meals with uncooked salads, to prepare vegetables so as not to lose their vitamin content, to use whole wheat grains and to adopt a more modern and rational diet. There isn't a Swiss family today, even in the most remote parts of the country, which has not incorporated some of these sound eating principles in their daily living, or one which is not familiar with the founder of the movement, Dr. Bircher-Benner of Zurich. He created a new national dish, the *Muesli*, or porridge, a combination of uncooked oatmeal, water, condensed milk, lemon juice, grated apples and nuts—an excellent breakfast or supper no Swiss will ignore (all restaurants serve it). The *Birchermuesli* has found its way into the United States in package form under the name Swiss Breakfast.

A characteristic of the Swiss is their matter-of-fact approach to food. Dishes are honestly described, but then honesty is as Swiss as the Jungfrau, and so is the insistence on quality. The first thing a Swiss will ask when he's out spending money is: "Is it true what you say about it? Is the quality good and will the thing last?" The stress on and pride in the quality of things Swiss, a very justified pride, comes up constantly in all dealings and conversations.

An aspect of Swiss food which floors the foreign visitor is the size of the helpings in the restaurants. A portion of *Berner Platte* is a monumental platter of several kinds of smoked and salted pork, sausages and a bit of tongue, accompanied by a mountain of sauerkraut, green beans and boiled potatoes. A waitress will serve you what you consider a hefty veal cutlet, and a few minutes later, with a dazzling smile, she will serve you another, equally hefty one, as part of your portion. A piece of cherry cake is a yard long, and the whipped cream alongside it is a veritable little Matterhorn. And then there are double portions that you can order, especially in the rural districts, but let us not go into these.

II (*About the Swiss and Their Food*)

Another factor in the high happiness quotient of Swiss food is the kindness and politeness that come with it (see Chapter VIII). This is true of most Swiss life, as expressed in the Swiss habit of greeting each other and even strangers with a gently chanted "*Gruezi*" or a "*Bonjour*" or a "*Buon giorno*." When you come into a local restaurant, you greet the assembled guests with a "*Gruezi miteinand*"— that is, greetings to all of you. In the French-speaking parts you murmur a "*M'sieu-Dames*," and in the Italian ones you just pass the time of day. By the same token, when you depart, you gently chant goodbye with "*Adieu miteinand*," which combines French and German in a very Swiss manner.

A Swiss habit that has been said to drive foreigners mad is the continuous use of "*Bitte schön*," meaning please, and "*Danke schön*," "*Merci*" and "*Grazie*," all meaning thank you. Whatever a Swiss aims to say or to do is inevitably preceded by several "*Bitte schöns*" and followed by "*Danke schöns*" with an occasional interpolated "*Ja Gern*"—yes, gladly—if he's asked to do something, or their French or Italian equivalents. You really can't say please and thank you too often. The fact that the Swiss really care about this polite kindness is borne out by the classified ads in the newspapers. Every situation-wanted ad tells you that the person sought or available is "*freundlich*"—that is, pleasant. I remember an incident in a stationer's shop in Zurich, where a customer protested that I had been waited on before her because I was an American. What with the pronounced Swiss sense for fairness, this was not true. All the other customers participated in the incident, stressing equally that this was not *freundlich* behavior at all on the part of the lady, and that the suggested favoritism was quite inconceivable.

I know that many foreigners think the Swiss far too

reserved toward them, and that some regard this reserve as unfriendliness. It is certainly true that there are two Switzerlands, that of the Swiss and that of the tourists, and that the Swiss will not take strangers into their homes as readily as Americans do. It is also true that the Swiss often consider themselves superior to others. This, to my mind, is balanced by the other side of the coin of their rectitude—their sense of fairness and their reliability.

SWISS FOOD OF THE PAST

The Swiss have food on their minds, because they like to eat well and also because of their tourist industry. The world's fanciest chef schools are in Switzerland, but the people who prepare and serve boned chickens stuffed with truffled *foie gras* choose for themselves food that is tasty and plentiful but very simple. Even the everyday diet of the rich Swiss—and there are a great many of them—is remarkably plain, if you compare it to that of Frenchmen or Americans.

The reason for this dichotomy lies in the history of the Swiss. The Swiss started out as a rural people in a country without natural resources—except for water power, which could be harnessed only in modern times. To produce, they had to import raw materials. The watch-making of the Jura, the textile industries of Glarus and St. Gall, the ribbon-weaving of Zurich started as cottage industries in the late sixteenth century, and Swiss goods were exported as far as China long before Switzerland became industrialized in the nineteenth century.

Swiss industry, to this day, is founded on an industrious and skilled people rooted in their rural surroundings. Smokeless modern Swiss factories rise in the middle of tilled fields, where the workers can keep up some of their farming while turning out the high-precision machines which form the country's major export. Every Swiss has relatives in the country with whom he keeps in close contact, and there is none of the sharp division between rural and urban life found in other industrial nations. Switzerland does not have an urbanized proletariat, nor has she any slums.

In a country that speaks four national languages there is bound to be a great deal of local pride and competition. The two greatest rivals are the German- and French-speaking Swiss, who say horrible things about each other. The people of the Ticino do not mince words about their brothers across the Gotthard. The people of the Grisons felt so strongly about their own identity that they managed to have their language, spoken by about only nine percent of the population, adopted as the fourth national language along with French, German and Italian.

German-speaking Switzerland is without doubt the strongest part of the country, the one that has given the world the Swiss image. The educated German Swiss are usually fluent in French, but the German of the educated French-speaking Swiss is usually rather poor or even nonexistent. Girls from the best-connected German Swiss families are often sent as voluntary workers to French Swiss families to learn the language, but the reverse is not true.

This interfamily bickering goes much further and deeper. A Swiss once told me that there were no Swiss, only people from Lausanne or Berne or Chur or Spiez or Appenzell, and that every one of them was utterly and irrevocably convinced that his town or village or hamlet was the best. A marriage to anybody outside the immediate neighborhood is considered a mixed marriage, and much shaking of heads goes on when one takes place. A young friend of mine who is from St. Gall became engaged to a man from Zurich. Her mother kept phoning her long distance to warn her about living in this den of iniquity. A story is told about the three qualities needed by the Bishop of Chur. First, he should be a Catholic; second, a priest; and third, he should be a native of the Grisons. But if necessary, it is said, one could do without the first two stipulations.

Every Swiss belongs emotionally first to his home town, then to his canton and then to Switzerland. Legally, regardless of where he resides in Switzerland or abroad, he remains a citizen of his home town or village. If he is in need of help, it is to this place he must go; and the descendants of Swiss who lived for generations in Bulgaria or Argentina have come back to the village of their fathers when their adopted country has failed them. These intense local connections make for an unattractive, excessive parochialism on one hand. On the other, they also make for a great Swiss virtue: tolerance. If you don't like your neighbor, yet manage to live in peace with him, and even cooperate smoothly, you are a thoroughly civilized person and one who practices democracy. And who knows whether this letting off steam about neighbors has not worked as a safety valve, benefiting the world in general? The Swiss invented the Red Cross, they have put themselves out helping the victims of wars, and they have kept the integrity and inviolability of their nation without hurting anybody else.

Well into modern times, life in much of Switzerland was poor and harsh indeed. Until the nineteenth century, Switzerland's greatest export was men. The Swiss Guard at the Vatican, delight of tourists in their Renaissance uniforms, are the last institutional survivors of the formidable armies of mercenaries who won so many of

Europe's battles. However successful they were, home-
sickness never left their hearts, as we know from the
moving old folksongs like "*Zu Strassburg auf der
Schanz.*" Now the tables have turned: Swiss industry
could not survive without importing foreign workers
from as far as Spain or Turkey.

The Switzerland of the past was a nation of peasants
and herdsmen, but it would be a mistake of the grossest
kind to think of the Swiss as nothing else. The very
contrary is true. From the Middle Ages on, Swiss society
was highly organized in many layers and sublayers. Basically, there was the division between country and city.
In the country at the top were the *Ritter* or *seigneurs*,
the noble lords of the Middle Ages who warred with
each other from their hilltop castles in the complicated
mosaic that is Swiss history. Time changed them into
patricians, soldiers and merchants. We see their big
proud houses in some very small towns; I am thinking of
one especially, the Freuler Palast in Näfels in the canton
of Glarus. Below them lived a hierarchical and very rigid
society of big, smaller and very small farmers, their
tenants and their hired help. The big farmers lived almost
like rural kings in their enormous, splendidly gabled and
carved wooden houses, of which perhaps the most sumptuous ones are found in the canton of Berne.

In the cities, the big patrician merchants, bankers and
members of the legal profession dominated urban life as
they did in Germany. Their palatial Renaissance, Baroque and Rococo houses are the glory of Berne, Zug,
Basle, Sion, St. Gall and any number of other cities. The
houses are still lived in, often by the families that built
them. Such is the consideration of the Swiss for their
artistic inheritance that when a house suffers from the
malaise of old age, its front must be restored or rebuilt in
a style which fits in with the architectural unity of the

other buildings. The exquisite old part of Berne bears witness to this official wisdom. The opulent interiors of these patrician palaces can be studied in the many that are now museums and open to the public, or in the furnishings of the Landesmuseum of Zurich. Americans will be amazed at the wealth of exquisite carved paneling, the rich furniture, the decorative porcelain stoves, the noble pewter dishes and drinking vessels as well as the lovely china, faience and glassware made in local factories that were part and parcel of Switzerland's patrician life.

Cornerstones of urban life were the artisan guilds, each one with its own rigid social code and place in the social landscape. These guilds were the forerunners of industrial and bourgeois society, and they still play a part in at least the social life of modern Switzerland. Their magnificent old mansions now often house equally sumptuous restaurants; the ones on the Limmatquai in Zurich are splendid examples.

In the old days there was a definite distinction between country and city food, as well as between the diets of the various classes; we must remember that we are concerned with one of Europe's strictly ordered civilizations, unlike anything in American history.

Until the nineteenth century the peasants' economy, depending on soil and climate, was roughly divided into dairying, cattle-raising, agriculture and wine production. Milk and meat dishes predominated among the cattle people, foods made with oats, barley and the prized wheat among the farmers, whereas the grape growers' children drank wine rather than milk. Gruels and soups, made from grains or milk, were the habitual breakfasts and suppers of all the Swiss. The peasants raised chickens and had eggs, but only the well-to-do ate them frequently; the poorer ones sold them. Fried eggs—

"*Stierenaugen,*" or bulls' eyes—were the most common, and scrambled eggs were company fare. Butter, produced for the cities, was a luxury among all rural people; to show esteem for visitors, a large cake of butter would be dished up, to be spread on braided breads made from the luxury of luxuries, fine white wheat flour. Lard and suet, not butter, were used for cooking, as well as oils made from nuts and locally grown poppyseed.

Even in early times the Swiss peasants relied very heavily on vegetables of all kinds, especially cabbage, turnips, carrots and beans. Dried apples and pears were often used as substitutes for the more costly bread, and were as much part of the daily diet as fresh salads. Potatoes, without which the modern Swiss could not exist, did not reach Switzerland until the beginning of the eighteenth century. In spite of official sponsorship—it was hoped that potatoes would abolish the periodic famines—the population resisted them. The peasants thought this "devil's weed" poisonous and fit only for pigs. An old chronicle tells of a schoolboy who refused to sit next to another boy because this other boy's family ate potatoes.

Bread differed greatly in the country and in the cities. Rural loaves were dark and coarse, and often made from rye, barley and other grains. We still find these wonderful-tasting breads in the more remote communities; among the best I have eaten is the ring loaf from Poschiavo. City bakers made the fine white bread, called "gentlemen's bread." They also made a great variety of small bakings, working under very rigid official conditions to ensure their honesty and the bread's purity.

Meat, generally speaking, consisted of pork—fresh or, more usually, smoked. Slaughtering day, the *Metzgete,* was an incredibly joyous and also bibulous event. Beef, from milk cows or field-tilling animals, was tough and not highly regarded. From early times the Swiss produced an enormous variety of sausages, head cheeses and similar pork products, and to this day these are part of the nation's basic nutrition. Butchering and good food remain closely allied; many excellent Swiss restaurants in the smaller towns and the country are run by local butchers, and their monumental dishes of first-class meats have to be seen to be believed. But meat was for Sundays only; the poor ate it maybe once a year.

Fish and game also played a great part in rural and urban eating as a delicacy. Game was considered gentlemen's fare, and most of it went to the cities; as in the case of all foodstuffs, its distribution was regulated by the authorities. To this day, fish and game are very highly prized by all Swiss, and are treated in quite a formal manner.

Cheese was a standard food as early as in the thirteenth and fourteenth centuries. The early cheeses were simple products made from soured milk, such as homemade cottage cheese, and well into the nineteenth century many rural households relied on no other. The solid, lasting cheeses that we know as Swiss cheese turned up in the fifteenth century, when they served for travelers and soldiers as one of the earlier kinds of convenience food.

In the cities, in the seventeenth and eighteenth centuries, food became more varied and sophisticated. The poorer people still relied on their gruels and milk dishes, but the better-off ones adopted sugar, coffee, rice, and cornmeal, products of the New World and improved communications. Sugar especially made a great difference in daily life. Before it became readily available, all sweetening was done with honey, and the goodness of a sweet depended on its spicing. When sugar became common, the whole Swiss nation embarked on an orgy of desserts and pastries which resulted in many strange and decorative bakings current to this day. As importantly, sugar was the father of professional Swiss dessert- and cake-making. This took Swiss bakers—especially those from eastern Switzerland, the home of the fanciest of all baking—to the courts of Europe; today it takes them to the most *recherché* of hotels and restaurants. The fame of the Swiss pastry cooks has never dimmed.

Even more far-reaching in its influence than sugar was the advent of coffee, which turned Swiss eating habits upside down. *Café au lait*, taken with sugar, is part and parcel of domestic meals such as supper, and is considered a food rather than a stimulant. *Café au lait* with home-fried potatoes, *café au lait* with cheese and/or cold cuts and salad, *café au lait* with cheese or fruit tarts— that's what many Swiss live on. Coffee and milk took the place of the breakfast or supper soups and gruels, even in the country. One old chronicler relates that the peasants served *Milchkaffee* in the evening. Since coffee was extremely expensive, it was stretched with local produce such as dried chicory, turnips and even acorns. These were bitter, but the hot milk made them palatable. In the Zurich countryside four coffee beans were reckoned as necessary for one person. Making coffee was the extreme accolade for visitors, and then as many beans as the hostess could afford went into the brew: strong coffee was looked upon as a sublime treat. And this attitude still exists; many a time, when I've visited Swiss friends, the lady of the house greeted me with the promise that she would make me a good, strong cup of coffee.

Throughout their history the Swiss have drunk much tea, albeit made from local plants. Rose hips, dried apples, elderberry, the flowers of the linden tree, camomile, yarrow and other herbs and flowers have yielded endless tisanes, all considered salubrious for one ill or another. The tea-drinking habit, including Indian tea—*Schwarztee*—is ingrained. Interestingly, many old-fashioned Swiss devotees of the fondue claim that the only healthy thing to drink with it is tea, since tea will further the digestion of what, after all, is hardly a light meal.

From early days the food of the city's upper classes was remarkably sophisticated, due to the cosmopolitan connections of the Swiss merchants and soldiers. Duck, grouse, ortolans and assorted songbirds, cooked with heavy spicing, were the joy of the sixteenth century. People also esteemed pike, and crayfish was cooked in a very modern way: first boiled, then shelled and either broiled or sautéed in butter. Equally up-to-date was the high consumption of vegetables, including asparagus. Those who could not afford it ate hops instead, as people do to this day. The use of salads—made from watercress, for instance—also spread; a 1580 chronicler recommended that these salads, with a vinegar dressing, be served before the meal proper to tease the appetite.

Professional bakers produced astonishing quantities of fancy cakes flavored with a large variety of spices, as well as macaroons, marzipan and honey cakes. I am inclined to think that their popularity was also due to an instinctive desire to compensate for food that was not always the freshest, most interesting or most nutritious. An interesting Zurich specialty was a sweet called *Crème de Roses*, the recipe for which directed the baker

to collect the fully opened morning roses, after the sun has dried the dew, and to separate the petals from the rest of the flowers. The petals of one hundred roses should be minced and creamed with two egg yolks. After this, sufficient white flour is to be kneaded into this batter to make a dough as solid as noodle dough, which is rolled out to the thickness of half a finger. This dough is to be baked in an oven, after the bread has finished baking [that is, I imagine, a moderate oven] until golden yellow and then dried out in a slow oven until so dry that it will easily crumble. The cake is to be ground to a fine powder and kept in a well-covered glass. A few spoons of this powder, softened in milk and cooked with a little sugar over slow heat, will make a delicate cream which has the flavor of roses and which will be as nourishing as strengthening for weak persons and convalescents.

MODERN SWISS FOOD

Even a hurried traveler to Switzerland should take time for a look at the local food stores; their cleanliness and sophistication and the friendly service will be eye-openers. The stores are still specialized; there are self-service stores, but enormous supermarkets like our American ones are not common. The meat shops, even in small towns, are especially remarkable and even elegant. What strikes an American most is how appetizingly and conveniently the meat has been readied for cooking. Chickens are already boned; veal, for the famous minced veal, is cut by machine into wafer-thin julienne strips; stew meat is cut into orderly pieces, free of fat and gristle; liver sits neatly on decorative skewers; *tournedos* and veal birds are tidily wrapped in bacon. You buy all this by the pound or the portion. Everything is displayed so that it looks attractive rather than meaty. Nothing is piled up; there is greenery and even flowers. The butcher shops also offer delicatessen, not in our American higgledy-piggledy manner, but as gourmet displays of decorative aspics and pistachioed galantines, *pâtés* in and out of *croûtes,* and a wealth of the noble eating and cooking sausages at which Switzerland excels. Meat (including chicken) is very expensive, far more so than in the United States, and is treated with due reverence. The *Berner Kochbuch,* a home-economics manual used in schools, starts the meat chapter with: "Meat is a very expensive food. But even small portions, with plenty of vegetables, salads and fruit, are sufficient for good nutrition." These words are faithfully followed in family meals. By the same token, restaurant meals, festive occasions, glory in large helpings of meat.

The spotless little milk shops sell thick cream in little jars, and slabs of wonderfully fresh butter decorated with imprints of cows or flowers. There is more to cheese than Gruyère or Emmentaler (pages 126–128). I think with special tenderness of the lovely little cream cheeses that nestle on glistening grape leaves.

The vegetable markets reflect the Swiss love for orderliness. Instead of gargantuan heaps of greens or fruit in the American manner, there are tapestries of succulent cauliflowers, tiny green beans, marble-sized potatoes, tender peas, little carrots, and small salad greens (the cress is especially delicious) with the delicacy of ferns. The fruit, imported from all over Europe and even, in the case of apples, from the United States, is unblemished.

As in the past, much bread is eaten. I imagine that a baker's shop carries one to two dozen different and differently shaped white and dark breads for daily use, all superb. The long French loaves and the unbelievably good crisp breakfast rolls and croissants are fetched fresh from the baker each day, and sometimes more than once. Especially in French-speaking Switzerland you see children in their school aprons hurrying home with long loaves under their arms. Baking is still the art it always has been. For their master's exams, the Swiss bakers' apprentices will create braided loaves with six, nine or even twelve strands, and bread figures several feet high. Interestingly, the Swiss also use a great deal of ready-to-bake pastry, and they were doing so long before Americans. Pastry dough and especially puff pastry, which is complicated to make, are commonplace in the Swiss bakers' shops, and I wish they were in ours. Puff paste is part of the *haute cuisine,* and it is especially good in *vol-au-vents* and their little sisters, patties, which the Swiss fill with delicious mixtures of fish, chicken, sweet-breads and mushrooms cooked in white wine and smoth-ered with cream and eggs. Puff paste, wrapped around a loin of pork, or around a beef fillet to make the elegant Beef Wellington, or encasing a goose liver or a game pie, is much used for festive household occasions. I remember dining in a Swiss home where the lady of the house had interests more urgent to her than cooking. Without a cook, she served a superb Beef Wellington, and I congratulated her on her light hand with the puff paste. She smiled, and that's when I first learned that buttery, feather-light puff paste is a Swiss convenience food.

All the Swiss have a sweet tooth, and, to be honest, several. There are two basic kinds of cake: those made by the bakers, such as the simpler coffee cakes and open fruit tarts, made with bread dough, considered food rather than a treat; and the rich, fancy cakes made in the *confiseries.* The *confiseries* are the worthy descendants of the famed Swiss pastry cooks of the courts of Europe. Downfall of native and foreigner alike, their variety of cakes and goodies must be seen to be believed. House-wives don't have to be fancy bakers; for parties and special occasions, the dessert is ordered from a good pastry shop. This makes for a far more elegant goodie, and besides, for one considered far classier than anything that could be made at home.

But I think that the high standard of Swiss living is

most apparent in the grocery stores, especially in those of
Migros, a cooperative that is part of the national economy. They are extremely well stocked and include many
foods we would consider gourmet. In many cases, Swiss
food-packaging is far beyond ours; the many flavored
mustards, mayonnaises and jams in plastic tubes, with
intricately shaped nozzles so that they can be squeezed
out in decorative patterns, remain especially in the mind.
The Swiss invented many convenience foods, such as a
great variety of gravies and sauces in cube form, soups in
cubes and bags, dried vegetables and flavored sugars.
Both in home and in restaurant cooking, the Swiss use
spiced monosodium glutamate (under the trade names of
Aromat and Fondor) to an inordinate extent. I think that,
just as in Chinese cooking, it gives a very boring same-
ness of taste to foods. It's not horrible, but you can tell it
is there.

Frozen foods of good quality exist, but they are not so
generally accepted as in the United States. The Swiss are
conservative, the frozen foods are on the expensive side,
and, furthermore, Swiss refrigerators have little if any
provision for storing frozen foods. It does not seem to
have occurred to the Swiss frozen-food people that there
can be no widespread acceptance of their products without adequate storage space. Canned foods on the other
hand, are cheap, good and very popular.

Swiss women are used to shopping every day, and this
habit is only just beginning to change. The reasons for
the change are that more women now work outside the
home, and that there are more foods which can be
bought in advance, and more storage possibilities, such as
refrigerators (small though these are).

Wines and spirits are also sold in the grocery stores,
and the labels are very respectable. And of course there is
the onslaught of all the familiar American package goods

such as cereals and canned goods, as well as the detergents of American makers, though they sometimes go under a different name.

Swiss food merchandising is just as aggressive as ours, but it runs more along service lines. The two leading manufacturers of soups, sauces and similar products, Maggi and Knorr, spend fortunes on home-economics and recipe work which reaches the most distant Alpine hamlets and schools. They advertise constantly and heavily, though with more plausible claims than American food manufacturers. The Swiss promise a good meal and plenty of savings where we promise the sexual millennium. Migros, a *Konsumverein* or cooperative, sends fully equipped food trucks up and down those parts of the country where isolated peasants and villagers do not have a Migros store handy. In short, the Swiss food world is not unlike ours except in one regard: the Swiss housewives shop with a carefulness which makes New England housewives look wanton.

SWISS HOMES

By European standards, the Swiss standard of living is high. So are wages and prices. The country is so small that in Zurich, for instance, the cost of land and rents are often higher even than in New York. The mass production of washing machines and other electrical appliances is just beginning, and they still cost much more than in America. Furniture, linens and clothing are also expensive, since they are not produced on the same large scale as here.

Generally speaking, the prices for many foods are about the same as in the United States, but since wages are not, people have to live much more simply. Meat is far more expensive than here, and so are coffee, tea, sugar and all the other imported staples. Wine costs less, liquor more; a bottle of whiskey is a handsome gift indeed in Switzerland.

The Swiss are a house-proud people, as you can see by glancing at the painted and flowered peasant houses and at the home-furnishing stores. Everywhere the stress is on quality and more quality. All homes are comfortable, and those of the middle and upper classes very beautifully furnished, with antiques and the best modern. In one house I know, the radiator is built into an antique painted porcelain stove. Kitchens have built-in storage walls, built-in wall closets with pull-out drawers for staples, blenders, grinders for coffee and all sorts of extremely well designed appliances. Small gadgets such as cherry-pitters, food mills and graters for potatoes and other vegetables are common and very practical. People cook on gas or electric stoves of excellent quality, though not as gadgety as ours; the Swiss don't go in for the unnecessary. In rural districts an electric stove (the country is completely electrified) is the first thing a farmer buys his wife when he becomes affluent, discarding the old wood-burning one. It is a status symbol.

Refrigerators, though not as large as ours, are common, and in the rural districts people who don't have them share communal freezing lockers. Deep-freezes are on the increase, and in a few years the Swiss women won't have to shop daily with their baskets or string shopping bags.

The standard of cleanliness is extremely high. Swiss women are demon scrubbers, as anyone who has observed the laundresses at the village fountains or washhouses knows. I've never seen any Swiss children who weren't freshly scrubbed and in clean aprons—all the girls wear aprons, and the little boys as well, at home and for school. Their hair is slicked down, their cheeks shine like apples, and they are gay and lighthearted, but not naughty.

Any American woman could move into a Swiss home and keep house with some adjustments, though not traumatic ones. The major ones might be the daily shopping, and the scrubbing.

SWISS MEALS

The standard modern Swiss breakfast consists of coffee with hot milk and sugar, bread, butter and jam. This is called a *café complet*, with the variations of *thé complet* and *chocolat complet*, all to be ordered with these words at all hours of the day. Many impecunious students have been known to live on them. The coffee and the milk, both very hot, come in individual pots, which usually wear gaily printed paper holders on the handles to protect the pourer's hands. The butter is daintily shaved into curls, and the jams are housed in little pots. An ode of unabashed adoration could be written about Swiss jams, pure and succulent affairs of nothing but superlative fruit and simple sugar. I urge my readers to hasten where imported Swiss jams are sold and sample them. Few joys in life are as easily within the means of all of us.

There is a special joy to a Swiss breakfast, and it hit me first when I was about eight years old and summering with my mother on the San Bernardino, an Alpine resort in the Grisons. Another little girl and I used to get up at the crack of dawn to dam a brook that flowed through the vivid meadows. We fetched stones from a little ravine for our task, climbed over fallen trees and picked the dewy blue gentians and wild red rhododendrons for our mothers. Then we raced each other to the terrace of the staunch old mountain hotel, where the tables were set

for breakfast under the brilliant sun of those high altitudes—we were at about five thousand feet. The hotel
baked its own bread for each meal, and I've never again
.eaten such delicious rolls and croissants as in the old
Hotel Victoria on the San Bernardino. Their crisp crusts
shone with a glossy gold, their insides were snowy and
soft, and I can still remember the buttery scent that
wafted out when they were split open to be spread with
the curls of golden butter that were piled high before us
in little ice-filled glass dishes—butter that an Alpine
herdsman brought down daily from an even higher Alp.
On the table, too, stood jars filled with delicious jams
made from dark cherries, from chunks of golden-red
apricot (my favorite), from golden mirabelles and
purple plums, and from all the lovely berries—
gooseberries, raspberries, currants. The choice was made
even more difficult by the presence of dark mountain
honey in which one found the echo of all the scented
flowers that grew around us. With this I drank fragrant
chocolate, made even dreamier by a dish of sweet whipped cream. I could never understand my mother and my
father, who resisted the irresistible in favor of toast and
tea, cold roast beef cut into transparent slices and a bit of
cheese. I see the wicker furniture and the red-and-blue
tablecloths on the terrace of that mountain hotel and I
hear the sound of the nearby glacier waterfall and smell
the pines swaying in the gentle breeze whenever I think
of Switzerland.

The main hot meal of the day in ordinary Swiss life is
eaten in the middle of the day, and even in our industrialized age most offices and factories still have two-hour
lunch periods to allow the employees to go home for their
dinner. Even the women who have jobs cook midday
dinner for their husbands and children. I once asked the
personnel manager of the Tobler Chocolate factory if a

II   (*About the Swiss and Their Food*)

work-through day would not be more convenient, especially for the women, allowing the employees to get
home much earlier at night. He answered that they
preferred the long midday break, because they had to be
home for the schoolchildren, who also have a long
midday break. The picture, however, is changing in
favor of "English working time"—that is, our own kind
of working day with a short lunch hour and earlier
closing. And more factories and offices are installing
their own inexpensive eating places. In the countryside,
where the men don't get home from the fields at noon,
the women or children carry a hot dinner out to them in
aluminum containers consisting of several dishes stacked
one on top of another and held together by a handle.

Only recently have people begun to eat out at noon, at
least in the cities. I am talking not of wealthy businessmen who can afford the restaurants, but of lower-income
employees such as secretaries, accountants, etc., who live
in furnished rooms and don't earn a lot. Formerly there
were no places for them to get an inexpensive hot meal,
except the temperance and vegetarian restaurants. But
now many of the cafés serve sandwiches, and in the main
cities the man who transformed Swiss eating habits, Uli
Prager, has introduced quick eating places similar to New
York's Chock Full o' Nuts which serve good, cheap
food in surroundings copied from their American coun-
terparts.

A Swiss family midday meal is a cooked meal. It is not
a complicated one, and it does not necessarily include
meat more than twice or three times a week. The representative menus I quote here come from the excellent
standard German Swiss cookbook by Elisabeth Fülscher,
and they are typical of middle- to upper-class family
living—even the very rich Swiss live very simply. In
French or Italian Switzerland the meal leans toward

French or Italian cooking, but is on the simple side. A "simple dinner," without meat, might be bread soup, potatoes *à l' Anglaise* and various salads; or tomato soup or juice, dumplings with onion sauce, cucumbers and lettuce. A "simple dinner" with meat might consist of fruit or oatmeal soup, bread soufflé with bacon and cheese, field salad; or meat balls, carrots, vanilla pudding and fruit; or vegetable soup, potato pie with ground meat, tomato salad and fruit. Bread is served, but no butter. The grown-ups drink a little wine or water; the children, water more commonly than milk.

Suppers are even simpler, and they may be warm or cold. Gone are the days when in rural households the whole family sat around the table and, after listening to the head of the household saying grace, dipped their spoons into the communal porridge or potato dish in the center of the table; the meal was ended when the father stopped eating. Now, to quote from Elisabeth Fülscher again, a warm vegetarian supper might be a cheese tart with salad; or boiled potatoes, cottage and other cheese, and radishes; or fried cornmeal mush with cucumber salad. A supper with meat could include hash, with potatoes and salad; or spaghetti with meat sauce and salad; or minced liver and salad. All of these suppers would be served for old and young with tea or herb teas, or with the Swiss national drink, *café au lait*. And it would not be unusual to find families who make their supper of bread, butter, jam, a bit of cheese or sausage, with *café au lait* or herb tea, or a glass of beer for the men.

An institution of the German-speaking parts of Switzerland is the sweet supper, which is especially popular in the rural districts. Here the main dish would be one of the delicious open fruit tarts, called *Wähen*, which are made with a yeast or cake dough that is thickly covered with sweetened apples, pears, cherries, plums, blueberries or any seasonable fruit, with perhaps some cottage cheese on the side and the ubiquitous *café au lait* or tea. Or there might be a dish of rice pudding with stewed fruit, or a semolina soufflé with a compote of dried fruit.

The Swiss passion for pancakes expresses itself especially at suppertime. In the rural districts *Omeletten*, as the pancakes are called, are a favorite dish. The women bake them by the dozen because they have to satisfy hardy outdoor workers. These pancakes, as well as the sweet suppers, have caused ructions between the farmers and the imported Italian or Spanish laborers without whom they could not survive. Latins are not used to this kind of sweet diet, and they don't understand or like it, just as the Swiss farmers' wives don't like to have their food questioned.

In-between snacks, such as the *Z'nueni* (the 9:00 a.m.) snack, evening snacks and so on, rely heavily on the innumerable and invariably excellent Swiss sausages, eaten with bread and *café au lait* or beer. Sausages are what one would order for a non-sweet in-between meal in one of the beer restaurants that are incredibly popular, and very good they are, too. Children get sausage and bread, or a piece of chocolate and bread, or fruit for in-between meals; they don't drink nearly as much milk as American children, but far more cocoa and, of course, *café au lait.*

FESTIVE MEALS

The Swiss are not given to inviting people to pot-luck meals. An invitation is an invitation, and guests, however inconvenient, are honored with a festive spread. Since the Swiss take their entertaining seriously, an invitation to a good restaurant is considered equally as elegant as a home-cooked meal, and perhaps more so.

Here, quoting Elisabeth Fülscher again, are some home menus for special occasions or for guests (restaurant ones would be more elaborate). The occasions might include a confirmation dinner, an engagement dinner, an anniversary, etc. A summer dinner can be: clear broth with tiny marrow dumplings, asparagus soufflé, roast duckling, new potatoes, watercress-and-lettuce salad, banana boats. A winter dinner: rich spinach soup, molded whipped eggs, beef stew with spaghetti and salad, apple charlotte with sweet cream sauce. To quote a formal family dinner: small hors d'oeuvre, consommé Royal, *champignon* patties, fillet of beef with vegetables and potatoes, *pêche* Melba, cheese and fruit.

III

Swiss Regional Specialties

ALL PARTS of Switzerland are rich in regional food specialties, and even a hurried tourist can find time to sample some of them. After all, he has to eat. Any of the Swiss National Tourist Office branches, or the local tourist offices, or the concierge of his hotel, or the waiters in a restaurant, or the local shopkeepers or, for that matter, any native of a place will be happy to inform the traveler about the local fish, the sausages, the meat dishes, the cakes, the wines and all the hundred and one specialties that he should not miss, and where to find them. Here are a few suggestions.

In Geneva the lake yields one of the most delicious fish, the *omble chevalier,* a kind of salmon trout, which is cooked in the French manner. Equally excellent are the different kinds of mushroom that go into hot sandwiches or are cooked with chicken. The little cheese tarts— *ramequins*—and the local sausage called *Longeole* are not to be neglected.

The canton of Vaud, famous for Lausanne, offers great fresh and smoked pork specialties, such as hams, the *Cayerne* sausage, pigs' trotters cooked with Madeira, and any number of cheese dishes like fondues, sandwiches, etc.; all these foods are perfect mates for the local dry white wines.

The idyllic lake of Neuchâtel gives us the *bondelle*, a small, very delicate fish, perch and pike. A dish of duck cooked in red wine should be tried, and for lovers of tripe there is an especially tasty way of cooking it. In the Jura Mountains the roast chamois, when in season, the *escargots* and the mushrooms are not to be missed.

Fribourg, too, has excellent game, wild strawberries served with fresh cream, and aniseed cookies. A gentian and a nut liqueur, distilled by the pious town's monks and nuns, are very pleasant indeed.

The canton of Valais is the country's kitchen garden and orchard. The asparagus, grown in the sandy soil and served with rosy home-smoked (but not cooked) ham, is superlative. So are the apricots, strawberries, plums, apples, pears and grapes; no wonder that Hero, Switzerland's famous jam-maker, has its plants in the Valais. Not to be forgotten are the beef of Herens, a local breed of cattle; the roast baby mountain lamb and kid; and the *raclette*, made with the special cheese from Conches or Bagnes.

On the other side of the Simplon and the Gotthard, in the Ticino, the food is Northern Italian but with local variations. This is the country of laurel, fennel and rosemary, olive oil, *risotto* with mushrooms, *osso buco*, *minestrone*, *busecca* (a tripe soup), lake perch, trout, grayling and the mild Piora cheese. Polenta—cornmeal cooked to a solid consistency—serves as a base for sauces and excellent game stews, and *grappa*, the local spirit distilled from grapes, is the worthy finish of a Ticinese meal, together with *espresso* coffee.

In central German-speaking Switzerland the three original cantons of the Confederacy, Uri, Schwyz and

Unterwalden (they correspond to our thirteen original states), and nearby cities, such as Lucerne and Zug, were among the first to know foods other than the milk and cheese dishes prompted by their pastoral economy. The ambassadors of the foreign courts brought with them their cooks, and their formal food trickled down to the local people; one of these Baroque specialties still. exists in the form of the *Luzerner Pastete,* a decorative pastry shell filled with spiced meats and herbed mushrooms. Another reason for the early refinement of the food was the tourist industry, which started in these parts. The rich English, first of the demanding tourists, and the aristocracy of old Russia and other European countries were made to feel at home in the prototypes of the luxury hotels we associate with Switzerland, and they knew and wanted the best of food.

Today the local cooking of central Switzerland is savory and hearty, given to substantial casseroles of lamb or pork, cabbage or potatoes. The old town of Zug is famous for superb food, including two exquisite specialties. One is a local fish, the *Rötel;* one of the special ways of serving this fish is to fillet them (small fish remain whole), poach them with a mixture of herbs and white wine and serve them with a sauce made with the poaching liquid, or with a Béchamel or a *hollandaise* sauce, accompanied by lemon wedges and boiled potatoes. The other specialty of Zug is the magnificent *Zuger Kirschtorte,* or Cherry Cake (see page 316), a gateau made not with cherries as the name might indicate, but with Zug's superlative Kirsch brandy—Switzerland's best, I think, and may all the other Kirsch-producing districts of Switzerland shoot me at dawn.

In this part of Switzerland very good cookies which date back for many centuries are made by specialty bakers, not at home, with recipes that have been in the bakers' families for generations. Among them are the *Chneublätz* of Lucerne and the *Schafböcke* of the Abbey of Einsiedeln, world famous as a pilgrimage site and for the beauty of its Baroque buildings. As their names indicate, they all come in the shape of lambs or feature lambs, since the lamb is the symbol of Our Lord. The pilgrims bought these cookies centuries ago, and today we still buy them in the time-honored shapes.

Branching out farther in German-speaking Switzerland, we find in Zurich the grand meat casserole *Zürcher Topf*, the *Gschnetzeltes*, which is minced veal, and the *Leberspiessli*, skewered liver. Zurich's baked goodies are memorable, especially the strange, century-old *Tirgelli*, molded cookies with elaborate images that remind one of picture books; the *Springerle*, another picture cookie (made by professional bakers only); and the delicious fried Carnival cookies called *Fastnachtsküchli*. In Bern, on the monumental *Berner Platte*, smoked pork, ham, sausage and even tongue rest on a bed of sauerkraut or green beans. *Gnagi*, a piece of lightly salted pork, is the afternoon snack that delights the strong Bernese men. The ladies love the roast *Mistkratzerli*—chicken with a salad. Neither men nor women can resist the big and bold meringues.

Basle, that cosmopolitan town on the Rhine, excels in salmon, and some of the best cervelat sausages in the world, called *Chlöpfer*. The hazelnut cookies, *Basler Leckerli*, are popular far beyond Switzerland's borders.

In eastern Switzerland you can tell where you are by the rich odors wafting from the soup pots. Soup is a much more important part of the daily diet here, and, accordingly, it is prepared with greater substance and thoroughness.

Here, the Rhine and Lake Constance are an inexhaustible reservoir of superb specialty fish, such as the *Blaufel-*

chen, the *Äschen* and the Rhine salmon. In Schaffhausen, Arbon, Stein am Rhein and Ermatingen, all charming and picturesque, the art of fish cookery has been practiced for generations; you never ate fresher, more delicious fried, sautéed, steamed or sauced-up fish.

Going farther east, in the cantons of St. Gall, Appenzell and Glarus we come to the regions of Switzerland's outstanding sausages and cakes. The St. Gall *Schübling*, *Bratwurst*, *Knackerlie*, the Appenzell *Mostmöckli*, the Glarus *Kalbswurst* enjoy a reputation throughout Switzerland that can only be described as massive. Equally famous are the cakes and sweets; these regions are the home of the country's original and best pastry cooks, who for centuries have gone out into the world to make people happy. The *Biber* of St. Gall and Appenzell, spiced and decorated honey cakes, and the puff-pastry creations of Glarus, such as the Glarner Pastete, a baroque, swirled puff-paste pie filled with prune preserves on one side and almond paste on the other, are glorious eating. Most of these goodies are beyond the capacity of the home baker. The tourist need not despair, for any number of irresistible pastry shops sell them.

The Grisons is a canton of 150 valleys, where German, Italian and the fourth national Swiss language, Romansh, are spoken. The food is accordingly varied and substantial; people get hungry at these altitudes. There is a stress on substantial soups; old-fashioned gruels of cornmeal, barley or oatmeal are still eaten, with milk or a sauce of stewed game. The roast kid, *Gitzi*, is excellent, and so are the salami, liver and other sausages, as well as the *Engadiner* nut cakes. But the great glory of the Grisons is the *Bündnerfleisch*, air-dried beef cut into wafer-thin slices and eaten as hors d'oeuvres or a snack with a hunk of fresh whole-meal bread and a glass of the local Veltliner wine. *Bündnerfleisch* is unexcelled among the world's preserved meats, and now the demand exceeds the supply even in Switzerland, so that some *Bündner-fleisch* is artifically dried rather than being exposed to the thin mountain air. This *faute-de-mieux Bündnerfleisch* is very good, but the original sun-and-wind-kissed variety remains a unique gastronomical experience.

Throughout Switzerland this bonanza of food is washed down with wine, beer or spirits. Of these, more on pages 109–121.

IV

Oh, to Be in the Emmental!

CERTAIN PARTS of Switzerland are more Swiss than others. Among the Swissest of them all is the Emmental, a pastoral mountain region northeast of Berne, with meadows, forests and clear brooks full of dancing trout, famous for magnificent old farmhouses, the Swiss cheese to which the region gave its name, voluptuous yodeling, a wrestling game called *Schwingen* (which I've never seen, but which I understand takes muscular strength, athletic skill and mental cunning) and another antique, weird and difficult game named *Hornussen*, in which a saucer-like disk is walloped with a flexible seven-foot bat and intercepted by the opposing team with gigantic flyswatter-like flails on a field three hundred yards long.

The Emmental is also famous for the food of its country inns; these rank high among the nation's temples of gastronomy known as *Fressbeizli*, or stuffing spas. Besides their food, the Emmental country inns are admired for "*Gute, sorgfältige und vor allen Dingen reichliche Bewirtung, freundliche Bedienung and genügendes Nachservice*," meaning "Good, careful and, above all, ample amounts of food, pleasant service and enough second and third helpings." This is how one of the Emmental inns puts it, and forsooth, that's what you get in every single one of them.

The Emmental country inns are the favorites of such hard-core connoisseurs of good food and wine as the Swiss federal councilors (equivalents of our cabinet members) because they are near these worthies' place of work in Berne and also refreshingly free of tourists. My father, friend of a number of the portly, deliberate and sometimes mustachioed federal dignitaries, used to repair with them to the Emmental several times a year to comfort himself with menus such as the following:

Flaedlisuppe (consommé with crêpes)
Brook trout en Bleu or Meunière
Roast or fried chicken garni with fresh cauliflower,
peas, mushrooms, beans and vegetables in season
French-fried potatoes
Vacherin Coupe Glacée or Meringue Glacée with
Nidel (whipped cream fresh from the dairy)
Coffee with Kirsch
Dôle du Valais
Emmentaler Eierzöpfe (braided breads rich with eggs)

The Emmental landscape is soothing rather than dramatic, a Vermont with a backdrop of snowy Alps. Side valleys branch out from the main one, where the River Emme flows under covered bridges, and forests and pastures climb up the hills between the neat, homey little towns with unobtrusive textile, brewing, ceramic and tobacco industries. The glory of the Emmental is the enormous wooden farmhouses, perhaps the most imposing in all of Switzerland, which sit in splendid arrogance on the hillsides, with deep roofs and gables, balconies running the width of the house, carved and decorated, red geraniums lining every window—they are magnificent examples of eighteenth-century rural architecture. There are the *Stöckli* where the farmers' retired old parents live; orderly outbuildings surround the main house, the gravel paths are raked, wood piles are stacked high and geometrically, orchards are planted in strict order, and the compost heap, a goldmine to its owner even in this age of chemical fertilizers, squats fragrantly behind the vegetable patch. Cheese is made up and down the Emmental valleys in small modern cheese factories that produce it from the milk of speckled brown-and-white cows which look very pleased with their diet of tender Alpine grasses and fragrant flowers. Watching them, I have often thought that it would be lovely to be a cow in the Emmental, leading a pleasant and simple life with a single purpose.

The faithfulness of the Emmentaler to their land is proverbial; many farmsteads have been in the same family for many centuries. The old local law of inheritance has helped this steadiness. It awards the farm to the youngest son at a low price, and he has to indemnify his older brothers and sisters. They may leave or stay to work for the brother who owns the land, and the old people go on living near their lifetime home, in the *Stöckli*, the dower house, in a way that promotes peace between the generations.

I spent some time in the Emmental and came away with splendid memories of magnificent food, superb yodeling and very up-to-date cheese-making. My headquarters was Langnau, a little town which offers that very Swiss mixture of rural and citified living. I was there in the spring, and the first roses were blooming against the big, whitewashed, gabled old houses. During the day, when the people were working in the linen factories, the tannery, the machine plant or the bell foundry, all located amid the fields at the town's outskirts, the only sounds to be heard were the chirping of the sparrows, the swishing of the postman's bicycle and the clop-clop-clop of the big horses dragging tire-wheeled wooden wagons filled with wood and hay through the cobbled streets, and an occasional *Grüezi*. In the morning I used to buy the Paris edition of *The New York Times* and *Time* and *Life* at the railroad station and fortify myself in the second-class buffet with a cup of coffee or a glass of wine, alongside the peasants and workers who were coming and going on the local trains. Langnau's air of isolation is misleading; it is a cheese-buying center. Groups of Swiss and French, German and Belgian cheese-buyers sat every day in the dining room of the venerable Hirschen Inn, where I stayed. Snowy starched napkins tucked under the chin covered vast expanses of watch-chain-adorned vests, eager eyes watched closely the boning of armies of blue trout and the dishing up of *tournedos* as big and tender as young love, served with french-fries so light that they wouldn't stay put on their plates. Critical glances scrutinized the labels of vintage Moselles and Burgundies from the Hirschen's exemplary cellar.

Ah, those meals I ate up and down the Emmental in country inns called Ilfisbrücke, Bären, Löwen, Rössli, Hirschen, Wilden Mann and the like. Consommé strong enough to float a little child. Trout that had been wriggling in their tanks a few moments before they sat in front of me. Wild mushrooms on toast in thick cream. *Spiessli*—little butter-bathed nothings of fillets of veal, pork and beef threaded on a skewer, with a few slivers of white chicken meat and smoked ham in between, served with a watercress salad. Crisp little puff-paste *vol-au-vents*, without gravity, filled with cream and truffled sweetbreads. Medallions of veal in a garden of grilled tomatoes, asparagus tips, infant string beans and baby peas amid snowy mounds of creamy mashed potatoes. The *coupes*—pristine whipped cream frozen with fresh-fruit purées, topped with more fruit and spread with a snowfield of whipped cream. Among the desserts, the undisputed crown went to the *meringues glacées;* now I knew what my father had meant when, with misty eyes, he spoke of these buxom beauties. Invariably, one portion consisted of three of them, made from the freshest of eggs. White, crisp and round as a goddess' breast, they hid a treasure of vanilla ice cream, and they were covered with extravagant swirls of whipped cream in baroque patterns that would have done credit to Bernini. These meringues lit up the room as the sun lights up the Mont Blanc massif and beckoned irresistibly to the diner, no matter how replete. Then *espresso,* as strong and devilish as the meringues were angelic, sipped with the standard double portion of white plum brandy or Kirsch or the heavenly Williamine pear brandy.

When faintness overcame me on my afternoon walks, I stopped somewhere for a *Zvieri,* a four-o'clock snack of *Bureschinke*—rosy smoked peasant ham—pickles, homemade bread and a glass of fiery Dôle or local hard cider.

And the loving service of the waitresses, the *Serviertöchter!* These matter-of-fact maidens whom no Swiss man in his right mind would kid around with wore the traditional black dresses, with tiny figleaf-like lace aprons underneath which they hid their change purses. With great deftness, and wishing me the traditional *"Guten Appetit,"* they heaped my plate from the serving dishes kept on the electrically heated *rechauds,* the hot-plates no self-respecting Swiss restaurant would be without. As they poured my wine or Kirsch, their *"Zum*

Wohle" rang sweetly in my ears since it was so obviously sincere.

Among the many walks I took for my spiritual and gastronomical edification in the Emmental hills, a few emerge as especially lustrous. I had reread the books of Jeremias Gotthelf, the nineteenth-century Emmental minister-writer, and I thought it impious not to visit the house and grave of a favorite author in Lützelflüh.

What was once a quiet village is now industrialized, but, as so often in Switzerland, you wouldn't know that in the utter quiet of those bucolic surroundings, flourishing plants manufacture furniture, hats, parquet floors, and other items. The parsonage was closed to the public on the day I was in Lützelflüh, and no pleading would move the current minister to let me see the writer's sanctum; I had to be content to visit his grave. The tombstone is very plain; what remains in my memory is the extraordinary neatness of the cemetery. All the graves were exactly the same size and shape, bordered by yew straight as parading soldiers; it seemed unbelievable that any outdoors could be that orderly.

At the inn, the Ochsen, I was the only guest on that spring day. The *Wirtin* herself waited on me; the scarcity of help was as evident in this corner of the country as in the big international resorts. Her children were away—a daughter was studying to be a lab technician; a son, who always had wanted to go overseas, cooked in one of the big hotels in Montreal. She herself was interested in modern nutrition and Chinese cooking. While she went to prepare my meal, I looked around and again wondered at the worldliness of these out-of-the-way Swiss corners. All the major Swiss, German and French newspapers hung on racks, under large beribboned laurel wreaths, trophies of the local gun club. Yet I had seen women drawing household water at the tree-shaded fountain in the quiet village square.

The meal was excellent, but the vastness of the helpings exceeded anything I had ever encountered, even in
the Emmental. In the silver soup bowl from which the
Wirtin ladled pea soup into my plate there was enough
to feed four good eaters. The veal cutlet, so delicate and
tender I cut it with my fork, weighed one pound; this
amount was expected by her customers, the *Wirtin* said
to my comments. With it came roast potatoes, and Brus-
sels sprouts the size of a fingernail, and it was garnished
with strips of red and yellow peppers wound around
bundles of tiny green beans. To top it off, I was served
the only dessert in the house, a coffee *crème* in a bowl
almost the size of a basin, rich with whipped cream
within and without, in a handsome design of swirls.
With all of this, I drank the local cider and a Kirsch or
two with my coffee. There wasn't any question of my
walking home; I took the neat local train back to Langnau
and the Hirschen.

On my way up to my room, I saw a charming sight.
The first four grades of the local schoolchildren, all
dressed in their neat clean school aprons, were assembled
in two of the dining rooms for the annual display of their
talents to the local school board. The gentlemen were
ensconced behind bottles of excellent wine, the children
grouped around them. One grade after another sang
their songs, and then all the children sang in unison.
Several little boys and girls recited both serious and
humorous pieces—the first in German, the other in the
local dialect—while the school board nodded amiably at
children and hovering teachers.

The night before, over what the Hirschen menu called
an "ample *Berner Platte*" composed of at least three slices
of each of five different kinds of meat, red beets, green
beans and boiled potatoes, the whole appetizingly

garnished with pickles and radishes and dished up with various mustards, I had been studying the local papers. However small a Swiss community, there are always several newspapers belonging to the different political parties, and they make illuminating reading. Among the pages and pages of want ads for every kind of hotel, industrial and home help, the announcements of lectures on the Common Market and the future of Red China, mission bazaars, end-of-the-school-year parties, visiting baby-nurse hours, the army inspection of horses and mules due for military service, home-economics courses and the drafting of men for the local fire brigades, not to mention the official notification that several gentlemen, by order of the judge, were barred from visiting an inn for periods from six months to a year, I found one that enchanted me. It was for a concert and play by the Yodel Club in Trübschachen, and it seemed too good to miss, since the Emmental Yodler groups are famous throughout Switzerland. Combining food, art and a nature walk seemed an ideal way of spending a Sunday, and indeed it was.

I arrived in Trübschachen with a delightful appetite. The village rambles around the River Ilfis; its only claim to fame is that in 1772 the first Swiss cheese exports were sent from here. For this meal I had resolved to stick to two things: blue trout and meringues, the specialties of the Bären, and I was not disappointed, though the host shook his head at my small order, wondering if I was not feeling well. The trout were superb. Snatched from their tanks only seconds before being plunged into the *court-bouillon*, they curled in a trusting manner amid the parsley on a napkin-lined dish. Their flesh was white, firm and nutty, needing only a trickle of sweet mountain butter and a squeeze of lemon for utter perfection.

The show was to take place in a large attic that had a

small stage at one end. This being Sunday afternoon, it was children's day. The place was packed, and I noticed that the Emmentaler are a dark-haired race, but with wonderfully white-and-pink cheeks. There was nothing citified about the children, and I imagine that the majority of them had seldom, if ever, seen a movie. The girls' hair was in long braids, the boys' in short, home-made haircuts. They wore hand-knitted long woolen stockings and homemade sweaters, and though fright-fully excited, they were extremely quiet, as their mothers had told them to be. The few unruly children were told by the grown-ups to behave or else, and this they did.

The Jodlerklub Trübschachen opened the show with six songs, sung in the local dialect. The men, portly parties all, wore the local *Sennen* costume, with short red jackets over white shirt sleeves, and small round skull-caps. They sang like large, sweet angels, though I was disappointed that they omitted the Emmental theme song *"Niene geit's so schön und lustig, wie daheim im Emme-tal,"* which translates roughly into "no place swings like home in the Emmental." Contrary to what one usually thinks, true yodeling has a melancholy, mournful quality which either affects one with delicious sadness and thoughts of the sunset over the Alpine snows, or else with pure irritation and unflattering comparisons to tunes the old cow died to. The harmonies are difficult and complicated, and, as anyone knows who's tried, it isn't easy to yodel. One number especially had us mushy; it was called *"Emmentaler Alpauffahrt"*—that is, the cattle's spring trek to the Alpine pastures—and it melted in our ears.

As for the play, I can't report much of it because I simply could not follow most of the thick local dialect. It was a comedy about the 1914 war mobilization, with a mountain farmer, his wife and sons and assorted figures such as a peddler, a baker, the village half-wit, the mayor, and innkeeper's wife, a lieutenant and soldiers. All I can say is that the audience followed with bated breath, laughing riotously at the jokes and moaning at what must have been deplorable happenings.

When you walk on a Sunday morning through the winding hillside lanes, bordered with a riot of daisies, black-eyed susans, camomile, yarrow, sorrel and dandelions, past the houses where the old folks are sunning themselves against the wall of their *Stöckli*, the women knitting and the men whittling, it is hard to believe that the faithful you meet on their way to church are the descendants of religious fanatics.

The men wear old-fashioned black over snowy shirts, and many of the women a modified version of the splendid traditional local costume, with a sprig of fresh rosemary tucked into the bosom. As you exchange the *Gruezis* it seems strange that the placid Emmental was once the center of religious strife and the home of Jacob Amman, the spiritual father of the fundamentalist sect that as "Amish" still bears his name. The Amish came to America to escape persecution, and today there are many more of them here than in their original German and Swiss homelands. If you want to see what eighteenth-century rural life in Switzerland was like, you'll do far better in a strict Pennsylvania or Indiana Amish settlement than in present-day Switzerland or Germany.

Many of the brawny descendants of the early Emmental mystics work in factories today, deserting the farms' long and hard hours of work. Three quarters of the income of the ones who work the land comes from dairying, and the milk money is the most important part of it. And milk, in the Emmental as in the other parts of Switzerland, means cheese.

Some two thousand years ago the Romans imported *"Caseus Helveticus"* from what is now called Switzerland, and Julius Caesar included in his menus a special type of cheese made in the country around Lake Lucerne. Cheese is probably the most palatable, nutritious and convenient traveling food, and five hundred years ago Switzerland started to export cheese on a regular basis, after her mercenaries had acquainted Europe with its virtues. Today, there are some 2,500 cheese-making establishments in Switzerland, small, independent and decentralized. About half of them belong to family dynasties in which the profession has passed from father to son for generations, though the son now attends special dairy schools and takes courses in chemistry, bacteriology, botany and hygiene—it takes about ten years of study and apprenticeship and a week or so of state exams to become an approved cheese-maker. The other cheese factories are dairymen's cooperatives.

For centuries Emmentaler cheese was made on the Alps only, in wheels much smaller than the ones we buy marked in a red-star pattern with the word Switzerland which testifies to its authenticity. The original cheeses had to be small enough to fit into the special baskets in which they were transported on muleback from Alp to valley. Only when Swiss agriculture changed to more organized dairy farming and when the farmers banded together in dairy associations at the beginning of the nineteenth century did cheese-making in the valleys become a practical reality which alone made production and export on a large scale possible.

Emmentaler and Gruyère are the two best-known Swiss cheeses. The first is made in the German parts of Switzerland, the second in the French ones. The two cheeses are brothers, and are constantly mistaken for each other, especially in Europe. There is a historic reason for this confusion. Until cheese was made in the valleys, Switzerland mostly exported Gruyère to western Europe from the high Alps where it was made. During the last century Emmentaler topped Gruyère in manufacture and export. However, a good many people outside Switzerland stuck to the old name, saying Gruyère when they meant Emmentaler or any Swiss cheese. Details about the cheeses are found on pages 122–133, but here they are in a nutshell.

Emmentaler cheese comes in bigger loaves, weighing from about 155 to 200 pounds. Gruyère loaves weigh an average of 100 pounds. Emmentaler is a moister, softer cheese, and better known to Americans, which is why I describe it at greater length than Gruyère. Emmentaler has a golden rind, Gruyère one that is brownish-yellow and moist. The eyes of Emmentaler are large and numerous, those of Gruyère small and scanty. Gruyère is more piquant than Emmentaler. Both cheeses are made in a similar manner, but their care and ripening in the fermenting cellar is different. Gruyère is ripened in a cool and humid room, and its surface is constantly washed. Emmentaler remains for several months in dry and tempered cellars, and it is subjected to a second fermentation; this is responsible for the famous hole-forming process. Its rind is regularly rubbed off and dried. Gruyère gets its flavor from outside, whereas the taste of Emmentaler is formed from inside to outside. The Swiss think the best fondue is made by using equal parts of each cheese.

Finally, for anyone who wonders what the Emmentaler dairy farmers and cheese-makers eat in their homes every day: For breakfast, *café au lait*, bread and maybe *Berner Rösti* potatoes. For the *Z'nueni*, the second breakfast: tea, coffee or cider with bread and possibly some sausage or cheese. For midday dinner: soup, vegetables and potatoes, meat on Sundays and perhaps once or twice during the week, or spinach with fried eggs, or open-faced cheese or fruit tarts with *café au lait*. For the *Z'vieri*, the mid-afternoon snack: *café au lait*, bread and cheese or sausage, and on Sundays cake or white braided egg bread with the coffee. For supper: soup and bouillon potatoes with cheese, or noodles or rice and a green salad, or rice pudding or pancakes with a fruit compote, washed down with cider or *café au lait*. On Sundays, special occasions, wine and *Bätziwasser*, clear white fruit brandies, are commonly drunk, especially in the country inns.

AN OLD-TIME CHRISTENING MEAL IN THE EMMENTAL

Few writers have ever described their surroundings as acutely as Jeremias Gotthelf (1797–1854), the pastor of Lützelflüh in the Emmental near Berne. As a writer, he ranks with Mark Twain; from his books we get a complete picture of a rural society that was anything but simple. His character insights are marvelous. The complicated relationships between the rich and the poor peasants, between property owners and hired help, attitudes toward teachers, pastors and city people, are great literature, and as fascinating to read today as when Gotthelf's books were written.

From the excerpt that follows, taken from the tale *Die Schwarze Spinne* (The Black Spider) and translated by myself, we see how one of the great events of rural life was celebrated in the eighteenth century.

It had been announced that a christening would be celebrated in the house, and the midwife, as clever a cook as a deliverer of babies, had to hurry to cook everything custom demanded, seeing that the stove was a simple one.

A well-built man came out of the cellar with an immense piece of cheese in his hand. From the shiny dresser he took the first handy plate, put the cheese on it and was about to carry it into the parlor and put it on the walnut table. "But Benz, but Benz," called his beautiful and still pale wife, "how people would laugh if we didn't use a better plate at a christening!" She went to the cupboard made from shiny cherry wood, called a buffet, where the house's treasures shone behind glass doors. From here she took a beautiful blue-edged plate. In the middle it sported a large painted bunch of flowers and, surrounding the flowers, a number of reflections [rhymed in German] such as:

Mankind, consider this: Butter costs three bits.

God gives grace to mankind, but I live in the Maad.

It is hot in hell, and the ostler works hard.

The cow eats grass; man, he must go to the grave.

Next to the cheese the woman put the gigantic *Zöpfe*, that strange Bernese bread, braided like women's hair, with a beautiful brown and golden crust, made from the finest flour, eggs and butter, as big as a year-old child and almost as heavy. Next to the bread she planted two more plates. On them, piled up as high as towers, were the appetizing fritters, *Halbküchlein* on one and *Eierküchlein* on the other. Thick, hot cream, in a beautiful flowered bowl, stood well covered in a corner of the stove, and coffee was brewing in the shiny, three-legged coffee pot, the one with the yellow top. This breakfast was waiting for the godparents, a breakfast enjoyed by few princes and by no other peasants than those from Berne.

With polite manners the midwife placed the godmother at her seat behind the table, and the young mother came with the coffee pot. The godmother fussed and refused the coffee, claiming that she already had had some. Her father's sister would not let her leave the house without eating first, because this would be a very bad thing for young girls, so she said. But she was rather old, and the maids had not yet gotten up, that's why she was so late; if it had depended on her alone, she would have arrived a long time ago. But the coffee was poured, and some of the thick cream went into it and—much as the godmother protested, saying that she did not care for it—the young mother insisted on adding a piece of sugar to the cup. For a long time the godmother would not allow that the bread be cut—it wasn't worthwhile—but nevertheless she got a big piece and had to eat it. For a long time she refused the cheese—it wasn't necessary to give her some, she said. The young mother answered that she did not appreciate the cheese because she thought it was made of semi-skimmed milk, and the godmother had to give in. She absolutely refused the fritters—she didn't know where to put them, said the godmother. The answer to that remark was that she probably thought they were not clean, and that she was used to better ones. What else could she do but eat fritters?

During all this urging she had drunk her coffee in small, deliberate sips, and now the two women began to quarrel. The godmother turned her cup upside down, showing that she could not swallow any more of any of the goodies, and said to leave her alone, for goodness' sake. The young mother replied that she was sorry the godmother found the coffee so poor, she had asked the midwife to make it as strong as possible, and she couldn't bear that it should have turned out so bad that nobody could drink it, and there was no reason to spare the cream, it was fresh today, whereas it might have been a few days old. What else could the poor godmother do but drink another cup?

The two male godparents sat in the other room, refusing the coffee they could drink every day, enjoying the steaming *Weinwarm,* that old-fashioned but excellent potion consisting of wine, toasted bread, eggs, sugar, cinnamon and saffron, that old-fashioned spice which must be included in the soup, some of the meats and the sweet tea of a christening meal.

The Christening Meal

Finally, they all sat down and the soup was put on the table. It was a beautiful soup, a meat broth flavored and colored with saffron, and so thick with the fine white bread, cut generously by the grand-mother, that the broth could hardly be seen. Now all the heads were bared, hands folded, and long and devoutly did each guest pray silently for the giver of such bounty. Only then did the people reach for their tin spoons, wiping them on the beautiful table-cloth before digging into the soup. Many expressed the wish to have such a soup every day, declaring that then they would not want anything else to eat. When the guests had finished with the soup, they again wiped their spoons on the tablecloth. The braided loaves were passed around, each person cut off his own piece and looked at the meats of the first course, in their saffron broth, that were being brought in: brains, lamb and sour liver. When the company had eaten their way through these with deliberation, there came dishes high with fresh and smoked beef, to suit all tastes, together with beans and dried pears, both cooked with wide slices of bacon, as well as splendid cuts of loin of pork, so beautifully pink and white and juicy. All these courses followed one another in a stately manner, and when a new guest appeared, everything, beginning with the soup, was served again, and everybody had to start all over; none was spared a single course. In between, Benz, the newborn's father, kept on pouring wine out of the big white bottles which were richly decorated with coats of arms and traditional sayings.

Thus, amid much laughter and joking, the guests ate a great deal of meat, and neither did they neglect the dried pears. Finally the older godfather spoke up, saying that he thought that for the time being everybody had had enough to eat, and that it would be a good thing to leave the table for a spell, his legs under the table were getting very stiff and, furthermore, a pipe never tasted better than after eating meat. This advice met with general support, although the young parents protested against it, saying that once people had left the table there was almost no getting them back to it. "Don't be worried, cousin," said one of the men, "when you put something good on the table you'll have little trouble getting us to come back, and if we stretch our legs a little we'll be far better able to do justice to the food."

V

------◄◆►------

------◄◆►------

Of Cakes, Cow Pictures and Tibetans

------◄◆►------

I ONCE CHASED the recipes of two honey cakes called *Biber* and *Chlausebickli* and of a puff-paste tart by the name of *Glarner Pastete* over three cantons, to find out if they could be made at home. They can't, in a satisfactory manner, but it was a great trip. In the process I ate a spaghetti dinner with a Tibetan prince, as well as loads and loads of splendid sausages and superlative cakes, and improved my cultural standing by discovering the most amusing of folk arts, the *Appenzeller Bauernmalerei.* These were only the highlights of the trip, but then, you can't put everything into a cookbook.

The honey cakes went back to my childhood in Switzerland. My godparents, who were Swiss, used to hand out the dark, glossy *Biber*, rich with honey, spices and an almond filling. On top the cakes were stamped with a bear, and they were made in St. Gall. The *Chlausebickli*, too, came from the same kind people at Christmas. Made from a *Biber* dough, they sported on top colorful pictures painted on a round or square of white sugar.

This was real folk art, with cows going up and coming down Alps, nativity scenes and so on; I remember especially one where a distraught peasant father sought to quiet howling triplets, and another of a maiden pondering whether to marry for love or for money. One splendid Christmas my godfather, the *Götti*, who came from Appenzell, brought me a *Chlausezüüg*, the traditional Christmas decoration of his canton, a sort of pyramid several feet tall. Its base was a large wooden bowl, the kind that was used in butteries to let the cream rise from the milk. The edge of the bowl was festooned with shiny red apples. In the middle, flat and dry cakes made from milk and flour, called *Philebrot*, were mounded into a pyramid-shaped container, which was filled with cookies, walnuts and dried apples and pears. On the outside, *Chlausebickli* were mounded closely on the pyramid, all the same size and marching around, with more apples between the rows. On the top stood a tiny tinseled Christmas tree. This was the magic of Christmas; I can still see the gay, childish color of the decorated cakes, and smell the fragrance of the honey, the spices and the dried fruit of the *Chlausezüüg*.

The *Glarner Pastete* I had never even seen. But an aura of mystery and romance surrounded it. When I had asked Swiss friends for traditional specialties to put into this book, they always mentioned the *Glarner Pastete* as something unbelievably good and beautiful. But they were hazy about details. Finally, since I couldn't buy it in Zurich to get acquainted, I decided to track it down in its home in Glarus, in northeastern Switzerland, and to go after the honey cakes at the same time, in the nearby cantons of St. Gall and Appenzell.

Glarus, one of the smaller cantons, is almost entirely cut off from the neighboring cantons by chains of high mountains that enclose it like a stockade. It is like a passage with two entries. One, from the north, with train service, is open all the year round. The other, to the southwest, leads over the highly picturesque Klausen Pass, getting narrower and narrower as you near the pass, and because of the snow it is closed in the winter. Glarus is a thoroughly Alpine place. The mountains are not in a class with the Jungfrau, but they do fine for height, picturesqueness and cows. Some of the most ravishing Alpine lakes are to be found among them. If you wander around the Glarus towns, villages and Alps, you will see Swiss life *au naturel*.

I got to Glarus, the capital city, on a Sunday by train. What charmed me as we entered the canton was that the citizens of the small towns were taking Sunday-afternoon walks for relaxation. Whole families were wandering on the paths that cut through the fields, the men in their muscle-bound Sunday black, the hatted women in citified clothes and the children in hand-knitted outfits. The smaller children held their parents' hands. The little towns were not particularly picturesque by Swiss standards. As in all of Switzerland, land is scarce and expensive, and there were apartment buildings in what looks to a foreigner like a village. Each apartment had its airing balcony, with clothes strung out on the line to air in the spring sun. In the tilled fields of some villages there were factories standing peacefully beside large, clean-looking heaps of manure; I remembered that cotton-spinning is a trade many centuries old in the canton. A pretty young girl, a social worker, told me more about it. The labor shortage is extremely acute, and the factories rely on foreign workers, notably Italians and their wives. To make it possible for the women to work, the factories have excellent modern nurseries, where the babies are deposited before the working day and picked up after it. I asked this girl, from another part of Swit-

zerland, what she did on her day off. "I walk," she said,
and she had taken the train to the starting point of a
particularly scenic walk. For relaxation during the working week she had joined a local glee club.

The town of Glarus is an anachronism in this pastoral
canton. The south wind or *Föhn*, which sweeps down
the main valley with a vengeance, caused a fire in
1861 which burned down the whole town. It was completely rebuilt, and, fortunately, not in a fake quaint
style, but with quiet dignity reminiscent of a small
French provincial town. It was all the more touching
when the schoolchildren and housewives with their
string bags wished me the traditional *Gruezi*.

There are all sorts of things in Glarus you wouldn't
expect. Ulrich Zwingli, the father of Swiss Protestant-
ism, was parish priest here. The locals, sturdy lovers of
liberty, got their independence from the Hapsburgs in
1388 and have remained free ever after. The Tschudis,
one of the most famous names in Switzerland, came from
Glarus and for centuries filled all the government posts,
and the most famous one of them wrote the history of
the Swiss Confederacy. Tschudis still fill the government
offices of Glarus. The last witch trial in Europe took
place in Glarus in 1782, when a serving girl had her head
cut off. The town's church serves for both Catholic and
Protestant services, and the bookstore is simply magnificent. Furthermore, Glarus is one of only three cantons
in Switzerland (Appenzell and Unterwalden are the
others) that have retained the ancient custom of the
Landesgemeinde, a sort of town meeting—or, rather,
canton meeting—held in the open air in the spring of
every year. This meeting is one of the last existing forms
of direct democracy, as opposed to the representative
form of democracy. All the male citizens of the canton
assemble around the administrators and say directly

"yes" or "no" to the budget, tax and all other govern-
mental proposals. Women are excluded—in Switzerland
they don't have the vote. The male citizens become eligi-
ble at the age of twenty, and to prove this they carry a
short sword in their hand. These swords are inherited,
but, obviously, somewhere in Switzerland there must be
a sword factory that makes them for the new voters. The
pride in the sword goes with pride in the Swiss army.
The *Glarmer Heimatbuch*, a compendium of everything
relating to the canton, sums it up in a way any Swiss
would subscribe to: "Military service is more than a
duty. It is an honor. For a Swiss, there is nothing more
degrading than to have a dishonorable military dis-
charge."

The people of Glarus are quiet and matter-of-fact, but
they are said to harbor strong emotions. These have been
compared to the local cheese, the Glarner Ziger, sold in
America as Sabego, which is powerful, to put it mildly.
The cheese is made from fermented whey, which is
combined with salt and with the powdered leaves of the
Klee, a plant that resembles alfalfa. As early as 1588,
Ziger, ground to a powder, was sold as far away as Milan
and praised for its pungency on the local macaroni as
well as for its tonic effect on upset stomachs. The cheese
can also be mixed with butter and used as a spread or, by
exceptionally brave and strong people, eaten undiluted.
As for me, I admit that it is bigger than myself and not
worth the struggle.

The home of the *Pastete* is a pastry shop that has been
in the Aebli family for over a hundred years. I saw it
enthroned among an encouraging display of elaborate
cakes, cookies and sweets called *Damentorte, March-
torte, Nidelmandeltorte, Nalagatorte, Zehnerbonbons,
Mailänderli, Schneeballen, Öpfelbeggeli* and so on. It
indeed was a queen among cakes, and quite different

from what I anticipated. Here was a large wheel of puff paste looking like a rococo rose, with scalloped shell borders that lifted and sank in a perfect circle as if the *Pastete* were sighing gently. Its color was golden brown, and the top had decorative dents such as you make in fancy pies. And the *Pastete's* secret: two fillings under one roof, like the love for two women in one heart. One filling consisted of fragrant almond paste mixed with butter, eggs and flavoring, the other of a velvety, spicy prune mixture. Over the whole lay a light dust of powdered sugar, reminiscent of the snow flurries on the Glärnish, which towers over the city.

The *Pastete* tastes good, in an interesting, dry manner, as contrasted to the sloshiness of a Napoleon. The taste and the ornate, eighteenth-century look of the thing reminded one, like a work of art in a museum, of the time long past when ample cooks in the sumptuous palaces of the canton (you can still see the palaces) prepared enormous meals for the big merchants, the governors, the military and their staffs—meals that had been inspired by the court cooking of Europe. The *Pastete* ended their meals on a noble note, since it is to be savored rather than wolfed down. It added elegance to the feasts of the rich in far distant London and Vienna, big as a wheel or a mere twelve-inch size, for then, as now, it was sent all over the world by the family which is still the keeper of this treasure of the peruked age. Its making was explained to me, and it is very clear that this is not a cake for the home kitchen, and one whose successful makings you must feel in your blood. But the Aebli family, whose weekly recreation from sweets-making is walking up and down their mountains, will mail one—and other specialties, too—for a reasonable price to anybody who writes them: Gebruder P. and D. Aebli, Burgstrasse 36, Glarus, Switzerland.

V (Of Cakes, Cow Pictures and Tibetans)

The habitat of the *Chlausebickli* is the canton of Appenzell, and to get there you have to go to the canton of St. Gall first, since it completely surrounds Appenzell. St. Gall, the capital, is an extremely interesting and educational city from every point of view. It has the most beautiful rococo library in the world, part of the abbey that was the center of Christendom in the Middle Ages, with some of the most ancient manuscripts in existence, including one of the *Nibelungenlied*. St. Gall has been a town of fancy lace-makers and weavers from the thirteenth century on, and it invented the colored handkerchief after women started painting their lips in the 1920's. St. Gall is equally famous throughout Switzerland for its traditional *Bratwurst*, a sausage made from veal, bacon and milk flavored with salt, pepper and nutmeg and cooked in a skillet, as well as for the *Biber*, glossy, dark-brown honey cakes stamped with effigies of animals and angels, scrolls, etc. The *Biber* are very highly regarded, especially as Christmas goodies, but it is the *St. Galler Bratwurst* that brings out the tenderest sentiments in any Swiss heart. I've seen tears welling up in the eyes of ruthless bankers and tough hydroelectric dam contractors at the sight of a hefty length of the sausage, pan-fried to a healthy tan, adorned with fried onions and nestling on a bed of *Rösti* potatoes. With a catch in the throat, and in the tender tone of voice a king reserves for the birth of the firstborn son who ensures the succession, these men murmured: "How beautiful, how beautiful!" Similar sentiments are expressed over the *Schübli*, a hard, dry sausage made from beef and bacon, to be eaten out of the hand for snacks.

St. Gall is a very self-sufficient town, with a pace all its own. The considerable textile industries are on the outskirts of the town; the center is dominated by the buildings of the cathedral and former abbey. I admired the way very modern buildings had been fitted harmoniously into the old town. The shops were both fashionable and substantial. Lots of large, substantial dogs were leading little old ladies along the streets, and equally substantial cats were sunning themselves on substantial windowsills and balconies, where substantial clothes had been put out to air. Many women, of all ages, were indulging energetically in the national pastime of window-polishing. The food department of the local dime store would have passed as a gourmet shop in New York, and the menu featured all sorts of soup, fancy cold cuts, wine and apéritifs. The museum contained lovely old painted furniture, including "house organs," all rococo scrolls and paintings, which were played standing up.

The St. Gall lace museum is a monument to the industries that are indigenous to the region. Lace, to my mind, is the most exquisite accomplishment of human hands. Looking at the exhibits, I thought it incredible that anything as heavy and probably as uncared-for as a peasant woman's hands could have produced such an enormous variety of gossamer textures and patterns in the centuries before decent lamps, let alone electric light. All in all, I could think only of the thousands of women who must have gone blind to make such ephemeral beauty for a few.

The crowning glory of the city of St. Gall is the *Stiftsbibliothek*, the library of the former abbey. In the rather austere town, its interior, hidden behind chaste walls, glows like a rose in winter, so beautiful that it makes one weep. It is an airy, light, perfectly proportioned room, all white and gold and pastel, all rococo graceful curves and cascades of flittering woods, marble columns, plaster medallions, painted ceilings and intricate floor patterns made with inlaid rare woods. One exchanges one's shoes at the entrance for soft, floor-massaging slippers. The best of the library is that it is not a museum, but a 100,000-book working library that houses miracles of medieval calligraphy and incredible thousand-year-old manuscripts that are still living literature.

To come back to the *Chlausebickli:* When I started asking about them, St. Gall friends steered me off the subject and said that I shouldn't waste time on such foreign knickknacks, but concentrate on the *St. Galler Biber* instead, especially since without *Biber* there would be no *Chlausebickli*, as the *Chlausebickli* dough is a *Biber* kind of dough. To persuade me, they produced the most beautiful almond-filled, spiced honey cakes, the color of the noble wood paneling of the houses in which they'd been eaten for centuries, stamped with a wealth of breathtaking designs. They showed me the stamps that produced the designs; these were intricate works of art, some three hundred or more years old, and of museum caliber. "Search no farther," my friends said, "here is the noblest expression of the *patissier's* art." However, when it came to asking for the recipes, a curtain fell. "They are deep, dark secrets, cozened in the breasts of our *patissiers*. Sure, honey and spices go into the *Biber*, but we cannot tell you in what proportions. Neither can we reveal the subtleties of the almond-paste filling. Anyway, you couldn't possibly make such exquisite *Biber* at home. Desist from prying and enjoy eating." Which I did.

You wouldn't think that a six-mile ride on a streetcar through rolling green countryside dotted with toylike villages under the distant wall of snow-capped mountains would bring one into another world. But it does, and the world is Appenzell, a tiny canton that comes in two parts, one Catholic and one Protestant. It was divided in this sensible way when the two religions couldn't get on with each other. Beneath its bucolic exterior this canton is perhaps the most original in Switzerland, and the Swissest of them all. The people are a race apart. They are small and dark and quick, and their women have delicate features and limbs. Their costumes are magnificent and of splendid colors, with an enormous coxcomb-like pleated black headdress, velvet skirt, silk apron and much jewelry, worth a fortune. The men's costumes are the prototype of the *Senner,* the Alpine herdsmen and dairymen, with white shirts, yellow breeches, embroidered red vests with silver buttons and embroidered skullcaps or round flat hats adorned with a bunch of Alpine flowers. The women's costumes are worn on high Catholic holidays, the men's when the cows go up or come down from the Alps with the largest, fanciest and heaviest cowbells in existence. In the villages you still see men with one golden earring, which is said to be good for the hearing. The Appenzeller love music and play strange, primitive clarinets, zither-xylophones and other loud instruments. Their yodeling is beyond belief, brisker in style than the melting Bernese way of yodeling. Alone in Switzerland, they permit healing in other ways than by orthodox medicine, and the Appenzeller wonder doctors are famous throughout Switzerland. All the other Swiss say they don't believe in these nature cures, but they still come to crowd the offices and sanitaria of the healers. The Appenzeller are fond of unusual forms of wrestling and hurling. Many of their houses have curly gables, painted façades that are almost all window, woodwork carved within an inch of its life, with a gay, fairy-tale effect that would make Disneyland blanch with envy. Appenzell, the capital, an overgrown village, is all that way, and enchanting beyond belief. Photographers go mad, not knowing what to photograph first. The local Alp is the Säntis, with one of Switzerland's widest views, where you get a well-served, handsome dinner with wine for around two dollars at a height of 8,215 feet. Apart from *Chlausebickli* and a dazzling number of other pastries, the locals make much cheese and the *Appenzeller Alpenbitter*, a powerful tonic composed of scores of Alpine herbs, which does wonders for the digestion after meals in the fairy-tale country inns, or so the Swiss say.

The other Swiss come to the cozy little Appenzell resorts for vacations, and to replenish their stocks of Appenzeller jokes, which can be compared to Down East jokes and are returned with far greater wit by the Appenzeller. They also send their children to Appenzell's internationally famous private schools. International orphans are educated at the Pestalozzi Children's Village in Trogen, one of Europe's great humanitarian institutions. On Trogen's elegant eighteenth-century square the *Landesgemeinde*, similar to that of Glarus, takes place yearly.

In the Appenzell, man proposes and God disposes. Werner Breu, who runs a superb restaurant near the station in Teufen, had been recommended to me as the fountainhead of wisdom when it came to honey cakes; he bakes them in profusion at Christmastime. In a general way he told me how he made them: "Five pounds honey, two pounds sugar and one quart of water are boiled together and let cool to lukewarm. Ten and a half pounds of flour are mixed with grated lemon rind and four ounces of mixed ground coriander, cinnamon, cloves and nutmeg and kneaded into the honey mixture. The dough then rests for two days. During that time an almond paste is made with about two and a half pounds of ground blanched almonds, sugar, water, Kirsch, lemon rind and nutmeg. The dough is then rolled out, cut into rounds, spread with the almond paste, covered and left to repose for one hour before being painted with gum Arabic for gloss and baked in a hot oven for about ten to fifteen minutes." All this was very well, but what determines the flavor of these honey cakes is the proportion of the spices. And on this subject Herr Breu remained cagey during an excellent luncheon of trout and grilled meats from a supermodern grill.

We dropped the subject and turned to his other specialty, the collecting of the *Appenzeller Bauernmalerei,* the nineteenth-century Grandma Moses folk art of the Appenzell peasants. Though peasants have gone in for vivid painting of their furniture, household and work utensils in many parts of the world, such as Norway and Pennsylvania, the *Appenzeller Bauernmalerei* is quite different, being concerned only with motifs relating to the dairymen's lives. These Alpine scenes are found on the outsides of houses, on furniture, and on the bottoms of the milk pails that are part of the cowherd's costume when he takes his animals up to their pastures or down from them. (Alas, nowadays, due to the shortage of rural labor and to excellent roads, cows often travel in trucks, and their milk comes down from their pastures in pipes, just as oil comes from an oilfield.) Most of the pictures are painted on wood, often in the shape of long narrow strips.

The paintings are extraordinarily vivid, and done with an astonishing amount of detail. A wealth of colorful decoration is in each, and they are executed in a most literal and orderly manner, far more so than Grandma Moses'. The painters were peasants, tenant farmers, artisans and hired hands with no education or training except their ordinary schooling. Some gave up their jobs and turned full-time painters, others painted after the day's chores. Of course, some are better than others. But they all fetch a fortune, and museums and collectors are

wild for the pictures. What is fascinating about the
Appenzeller Bauernmalerei is that it sprang up sponta-
neously, and died down in the same manner when the
peasants' art was supplanted by photographs and prints
from the cities. After 1900 there were only isolated
instances of good peasant painting, and there are none at
all in our day.

Everybody I met in the Appenzell seemed to be deter-
mined to feed me the world's most luscious cakes, such as
*Mandel Torten, Haselnuss Torten, Gianduja Torten,
Mocca Torten, Schokolade Torten, Silvana Torten,
Moulatine Torten, Engadiner Torten, Haselnuss Creme
Torten, Bündner Nuss Torten, Schwarzwälder Torten,
Sacher Torten, Finnische Torten* and so on, as well as
delicious desserts called *Schwedische Punschtorte, Charlotte Russe, Réligieuse, Italienne, St. Honoré, Vacherin
Glacé, Cassata Siciliana, Ananas Dessert, Profiteroles,
Vermicelles, Savarin, Holländische Mille Feuille,* etc.
This was done, so my friends explained, to uphold the
fame of the Appenzeller *patissiers,* who've been at their
art for centuries. I hasten to say that few, if any, of these
goodies can be made or are made at home, and why
should they be, when a choice of them can be bought in
any town? Swiss women have to have many virtues
along many lines, but they are not expected to be professional pastry cooks.

However, there is a point when the human frame can
take no more, and after all of these sweet orgies I took
myself on a walking tour, for obvious reasons. And this
was when I ran into the Tibetans.

I'd heard of a Swiss program sponsored by the Swiss
Red Cross to settle Tibetan refugees in the parts of
Switzerland which resembled the homeland they had had
to flee when the Chinese took over their country, and
that there was such a settlement in the Appenzell. I

found it in a bare new house in Waldtstatt, a simple little mountain village of eight hundred souls on the slopes of the Säntis massif.

Three families, five bachelors and five orphaned boys and girls had been settled there. The Dalai Lama himself, in the Indian refugee camp from which the refugees came straight to Switzerland, had chosen two lamas to look after their spiritual welfare and a Tibetan prince to serve as their interpreter. The Red Cross had allocated them *Schwester* Erika Schybrig, who deserves to be written up for the *Reader's Digest* as a Most Unforgettable Person. A blonde, energetic soul in her thirties, she looked after her charges as you look after children, and served as a bridge between East and West for people who had walked over the Himalayas from the Tibetan Middle Ages into modern Switzerland.

The idea behind the Tibetan settlements is to make the people self-sufficient by teaching them local trades. All the men were working at apprentice wages for local farmers, lumbermen and carpenters. The women were keeping house, and some kept on with their weaving. When I met her, Sister Erika, as mother, guide, vocational counselor, housekeeper, cook, accountant and everything else for the group, was sewing a layette for one of the women who was about to give birth. She also had made most of the orphans' clothes from her own things. Among her tasks was acquainting the women with such amenities as indoor toilets, baths, brassières and the clothes worn by Western women, and how to live with and in them, which did not come easily to her charges. Her workday began at six and ended at midnight.

The Swiss have always been most generous to refugees, and I think that special praise should go to the peasants of Waldstatt, no cosmopolitans themselves, who took the Tibetans to their hearts from the first. Before the Tibetans built their own house, the villagers housed and fed the group, and the women washed the newcomers' clothes. The schoolchildren looked after them in school, with none of the cruelties children so often reserve for outsiders.

I was invited to stay for supper. The house was of the plainest, with built-in bunks of light wood and the simplest of furniture; it is one of the tenets of the Red Cross that the settlements should be as self-sufficient as possible.

We all sat in the dining room, at several tables. My conversation was limited to the younger of the two lamas and the Tibetan prince, who spoke faultless Oxford English. With the men I spoke in German, which they understood somewhat after having worked with the Swiss. The women could not speak anything but their own language. The children were best off; they chatted in the local Waldstatt dialect as if they had been native-born.

Our meal was spaghetti with tomato sauce, bread and tea. Not the buttered tea of the Tibetans, but regular tea, to which they finally had become used. I've never seen people eat as much spaghetti, not even at spaghetti festivals in Italy. It was awe-inspiring. What fascinated me most was that, without talking to them, you could recognize the group's social composition. The families were obviously peasant families with a simple background. The young men were, so to speak, classless— emancipated from their background and not yet settled in the new one. The older lama, who spoke no English (and I beg forgiveness for the cliché, but no other words fit), exuded a spiritual light that enveloped even me. The younger one, who did speak some English, wanted to give up being a lama and study engineering instead, and

I've heard that since then he has done so. The Tibetan
prince, an extremely handsome tall man in his late twen-
ties, wore rough work clothes like the rest, and even
dressed like this he would have looked at home in the
Savoy in London. There was just no question that he
was a leader, from a class of traditional leaders. I think
this was one of the merriest suppers I've ever had. The
Tibetans are gay and vivacious by nature, and there was
a lot of laughter and banter as they told of the day's
happenings. They were happy in Switzerland, the prince
said, and they believed that one day they would go back
home to Tibet. The children were enchanting, all smiles
and shy caresses when I took them in my arms.

Since then the settlement has moved to a larger house
and new members have come, including nubile maidens
for marriage, Swiss style. I had asked Sister Erika about
that and she said that so far she had not succeeded in
explaining why polygamy and polyandry are not practiced in the Swiss Alps, much as they resemble Tibet.
The settlement has prospered, and I no longer send them
clothing and other parcels. But I have a charming
memento, a page of Tibetan manuscript (whose meaning
is unknown to me) that they sent me one Christmas with
love and kisses, which hangs over my desk as I write this.

VI

Life in a Swiss Chocolate Factory

LIKE ANYBODY ELSE who has been brought up in Switzerland, I grew up looking upon chocolate as food—something you ate with bread after school, or took along mountain-climbing. I took chocolate for granted until recently when I went to a party in Berne and overheard a remark that struck me. "A Swiss chocolate factory is not at all what you'd think," said a Paris-dressed Swiss lady. "It's much more like the *haute couture*. Twice a year our *chocolatiers* have to create brand-new lines to keep their customers interested, just as the Paris dressmakers do. Then they sit back with the same kind of bated breath to see if the new collections catch on."

The speaker turned out to be the wife of a man who supplies much of the Swiss chocolate industry with wrapping materials. She urged me to see for myself if she wasn't right and offered to arrange for me to visit a big chocolate factory right in the city.

No traveler in Switzerland can have helped noticing the *confiseries*, the chocolate shops that line the streets the way bars line an Irish neighborhood. In them you find not only scores of chocolate bars with all the famous names—Tobler, Lindt, Villars, the Nestlé combine, and so on—but dozens and dozens and dozens of house chocolate specialties filled with fruits, creams, liqueurs and anything that can be put into a chocolate shell and taste good. These goodies also look like little *objets d'art,* though their beauty has never prevented anybody from wolfing them down. *Confiseries* are beloved by the Swiss, and when you go to another town, people will tell you to be sure not to miss a certain *confiserie.* The sight of a sedate Swiss paterfamilias hastening home with a pretty little *confiserie* parcel dangling from his capable hands is a common and heartwarming one. Then there are the chocolate displays in the supermarkets—I once counted eighty-seven famous-brand chocolate bars and thirty-seven different kinds of boxed chocolate candy. Sales were brisk; the housewives, with pointing children, were choosing their chocolate with all the deliberateness of wine connoisseurs choosing their wine.

All Swiss chocolate is excellent, and, apart from a few house secrets, it is all made more or less the same way. Thus my visit to Chocolats Tobler in Berne can be described as quite typical. But it was such an astonishing experience that I will relate it in some detail, since it sheds a light on a part of Swiss life that few Americans know.

Chocolate-making is an extremely competitive business which accounts for fifteen million dollars' worth of Swiss exports every year and is considered a showcase of Swiss quality. But the Swiss are chocolate's own best customers. Tobler (and the figures for the other manufacturers are not very different) makes around 350 standard varieties for the Swiss alone, who eat it for food and for pleasure. It is a staple food for children, soldiers and mountaineers, and Tobler chocolate sustained the last

Himalayan expedition. Chocolate candy, put up in ravishing boxes, is the present par excellence for Christmas, Easter and whenever people want to impress; some boxes cost a small fortune.

On the appointed day I found myself in the Länggass-Strasse, a broad middle-class residential street with nothing to show that here was a plant employing more than 1,200 people. Young schoolchildren holding each other by the hand were crossing the street, housewives with baskets or string shopping bags were strolling in and out of the neighborhood stores, and the two or three lone men you always see sitting in Swiss cafés were sitting in the Länggasse cafés. Red geraniums lined all windows, as they do everywhere in Berne, even in office buildings, banks and the Diocese, giving the town an incredibly festive air.

The windows of the Tobler factory, a block-long four-story building, were also lined with geraniums. The place looked like a pre-World War I prosperous office building, and only at the factory entrance, in a side street, do you get an impression that this is an industry—and a slight smell of the product.

I presented myself at the showroom, where a slight, grandmotherly figure with a twinkle in her eye took me in charge. She was Fräulein Imhof, the showroom manager. She asked me to look around while she ministered to a customer, a matronly local lady with a string shopping bag who owns a newsstand that sells chocolate. Usually, Tobler salesmen call on customers, but you can come to the showroom and order three boxes, as this lady did, or a thousand. The showroom is also one of the leading local attractions. There are ladies' gymnastic and other clubs, male glee clubs and schoolchildren who come every year for a conducted tour of the factory and depart laden with free sweet gifts.

The showroom was the size of a small ballroom. The walls were lined with big showcases and the center was filled with tables. The number and variety of chocolates displayed was staggering. The boxes ranged from three-inch midgets to thirteen-by-seventeen-inch giants. All were exquisitely printed in color and swathed in ribbons. There were boxes with Swiss landscapes of every kind on them—Alps, lakes, chalets and Swiss herdsmen swinging Swiss flags and going up onto the Alps or coming down from the Alps, boxes with Swiss cities and villages, with Alpine flowers or antique roses or modern carnations, boxes in the shape of antique books, treasure chests, jewel cases, picnic baskets, boxes with sixteen different kinds of dog and five different breeds of pussycat, and boxes with built-in action, where you pull a tab and out comes a herdsman blowing an Alpenhorn while two cable cars move overhead. For children there were special toy boxes that also move, with bears, racing cars and Disney figures.

All of these boxes were filled with *néapolitains*, little chocolate bars in a number of flavors; or with chocolates in all sorts of shapes containing orange, lemon, apricot, pineapple and nut fillings; or with the chocolate creams called truffles; or with chocolates holding coffee or liqueurs of every kind. The finest cognacs, Kirsch, Bene-ictine, etc., go into these liqueur chocolates, which are a Tobler specialty. They are called *grisettes*, and their sisters are the *griottes*—cherries put up in fine spirits and encased in a chocolate shell. Alas, American federal law forbids their import, since in this country no chocolate with real spirits may be sold.

The glossy, beribboned and beflowered boxes were only the beginning. The showcases were lined with chocolate bars numerous beyond description, called Marietta, Teresina, Nimrod and the like. They were plain or filled with nuts, raisins, creams, caramels and combinations thereof and such exotica as a coffee filling that feels chilly to the taste, and one made from honest-to-goodness gin and lemon called Gin Fizz. There was also plenty of chocolate sculpture—bas-reliefs with the traditional Berne bears and figures of witches' houses, more bears and chocolate Santas weighing up to twenty-five pounds. The spirit of Christmas was running riot in the middle of the showroom, with endless boxes sporting Christmas motifs, chocolate Christmas-tree decorations and favors. Among them I spotted the delight of every Swiss child: cream-filled chocolate mice wrapped in colored foil, with a mouse face and a string tail. The latter has to be attached by hand, which makes the mice expensive to produce. Then there were a lot of chocolate trifles, such as bananas, walking canes and chocolate money, including enormous chocolate coins that Tobler makes for charities which sell them at a profit, or for promotional gimmicks. One of these big coins touched me. It had been made for a hotel, to be put at the guest's bedside, and it said "Pleasant Dreams" in four languages.

I had been joined by Tobler's chief of production, Herr Hertig, a dapper gentleman who has been with the firm thirty years. He took my awe at the displays with calm. "All this is for the Swiss," he said, "We don't export nearly as many varieties." He continued to say that the chocolate rationing during the Second World War was one of the greatest hardships on the Swiss, who were suddenly deprived of one of their regular foods.

As Alice in this chocolate wonderland, I was curious to know who decided on what was to go into a new collection, and if it was possible to predict a best-seller. The first is decided by the Novelty Commission, factory brass who meet twice a month to look at the competition and at new packaging, to taste new products and to make decisions—such as whether a chocolate bar is to be called Dragetta rather than Hazetta, and that girls' heads should not be put on German export packages because the Germans don't like girlies on their food the way the Americans do. I had the impression that meetings of the Novelty Commission resembled somewhat those Vatican meetings that decide on new saints, insisting on all-round impeccability. As to the second, Mr. Hertig told me, you play your hunches based upon past experience, and forget the flops, or change their packaging, which may do the trick. He added that I would learn more about various chocolate preferences later. As for the best-seller of all time, he said reverently, it was the Toblerone bar, which comes in various sizes. Its formula is a deep dark secret, and it is mixed behind a wire-netted basement window in the factory, which I had noticed because hundreds of bees hovered around it, attracted by the honey and almond nougat that go into this illustrious candy bar. Toblerone, invented in 1908, took the world by storm and has been imitated by dozens of countries, including Japan. All imitations, however, have sunk into ignoble oblivion. Herr Hertig then took me to Herr Moser, the firm's chief buyer, to get a little briefing on chocolate-making itself so that I should truly profit from the factory grand tour later.

In all Swiss offices everybody sits behind closed doors and you knock before going in. Herr Moser turned out to be a good-looking man in his late thirties who was sipping peppermint tea in an office lined with maps of the world. "The best cocoas come from Ecuador, Ceylon, Java, Trinidad and, especially, Venezuela. These top grades, which are called *criollo* types, are rich in the desirable flavors needed for fine chocolate. Ordinary or 'forester' cocoa, which is commonly classified as *amelonado*, is particularly grown in West Africa and Brazil.

Also, good cocoa is perfectly fermented." I asked what that meant. It seems that cocoa beans, which resemble dried-out almonds and are whitish, have no flavor when they are raw—which is also true of coffee beans. To ferment them—and this is done on the plantation—they are put into large boxes with pierced bottoms for four to six days, during which they are frequently shuffled. They are fermented when they turn a dark reddish brown. Then they are dried and finally weighed and packed in sacks. The more skillfully the beans are fermented, the better their taste. Improperly fermented ones can't be used for fine chocolate. The top-quality beans, Mr. Moser went on, are used for the dark chocolates, because that's where the flavor shows, since there is no milk or other ingredient to hide the beans' taste. I asked him what cocoas he bought, but that he would not tell me, since it is a trade secret. Every cocoa has a flavor of its own, and every chocolate is a blend of these flavors. The manufacturers guard the blend formulas with their lives, since the flavor and character of their brands depend on them.

The beans are roasted in the Tobler factory after they have been cleaned of the inevitable debris that accompanies them in their sacks. I saw the process later, in sheds stacked ceiling high with cocoa sacks. The roasting, just as with coffee, is another tricky process that affects flavor. It is done in enormous drums. Subsequently the beans are peeled, roasted once more, broken into pieces and cleaned again before being ground into a powder. The powder is then degreased to make the white cocoa butter. Later, cocoa butter and cocoa are again combined, and the proportions of these two ingredients determine the flavor and texture of the chocolate.

Then Mr. Moser told me about the other ingredients that go into the firm's chocolate. Almonds come in a dozen different shapes, but the Swiss don't like them nearly as well as hazelnuts, of which the best come from Piemonte, in Italy. The honey which goes into the Toblerone together with ground almonds comes from, of all places, the highlands of Yucatán in Mexico, since, apparently, nowhere else in the world could Tobler find honey that always has the right flavor, color and consistency and the proportions of sugar, acid and ash that make for a uniform product. As for the milk powder that is as much a basic ingredient in milk chocolate as cocoa, Tobler makes its own in a little town in the Bernese Alps, buying the milk directly from the local dairy farmers. This is a rather unique approach, since most chocolate-makers buy their milk powder where they find it. But Mr. Moser assured me that it made all the difference to the taste of the chocolate—"the intangible flavor of true Alpine milk that makes Swiss cheese so infinitely better than all its imitations. Milk varies with the seasons; the summer milk, when the cows are grazing high up in the Alps, is quite different from the barn-fed milk." I guess he was right, since the Tobler milk chocolates are especially tasty and melting.

At this stage I wanted to go through the factory, but my education had not yet been completed. The next call was on Dr. Buser, Tobler's chief chemist, a blond, white-coated scientist among other white-coated scientists, and quite as gallant as all the other Tobler men I'd met. His lab was large and full of complicated equipment. The lab not only keeps up quality control of the chocolates, but also looks after the quality of everything connected with chocolate—wrappings and the like (Tobler's and the competition's), since the keeping qualities of the candies depend largely on these. I brought up a question that had puzzled me all along: the formulas—could anybody steal them? Not so, said Dr.

Buser. It seems that there is a master cookbook of formulas which exists in only a few copies, one of them on microfilm in a bank vault and the others in the hands of the firm's president, Mr. Sandoz; Mr. Hertig; the controller; and Dr. Buser. I asked him how they guarded the formulas against spying, since chocolate is made in public by a large number of workers. "Very simple," said Dr. Buser. "No one worker knows more than a tiny fraction of the formula, the one that affects his work. This little piece is transmitted, often in code, to the Chocolate Master, the foreman of a group of workers engaged in this particular process. If one of the Chocolate Masters, trusted employees all, should want to piece the whole formula together, it would be both difficult and conspicuous." Even if the formula were stolen, it would neither ruin Tobler nor benefit the thieves, since chocolate can be analyzed and reproduced with the same ingredients. What defies analysis is the industrial know-how of the firm: the treatment of the beans, the length of time the chocolate is heated and cooled, kneaded by machine and so on. "Besides," Dr. Buser continued, "people associate certain kinds of chocolate with certain firms that have made them for years and advertised them heavily."

He then fascinated me by talking about chocolate tastes. The Swiss prefer a very tender, melting milk chocolate, but the Germans, Europe's number-two chocolate-fanciers, go more for the bittersweet dark chocolate, along with the Danes and the French. Italians, Swedes and Finns prefer sweet chocolate. The taste of chocolate depends not only on flavoring and texture but also on consistency. Milk chocolate tastes best when thick, bittersweet when very thin. Also important is the way one bites into a piece of chocolate. He attributed part of Toblerone's fabulous success to the shape, size and thickness of the triangular bite-sized pieces into which the chocolate is shaped: each is just a mouthful. The amount of fat—that is, of cocoa butter—also affects a chocolate's taste; too little makes for a coarse, dry kind. Tobler both makes chocolate in other countries and exports it in enormous quantities, always mindful of national likes and dislikes, which also affect the labeling and the colors of chocolate wrappings. Chocolate in a blue wrapper won't sell in Shanghai or Hong Kong because the Chinese associate blue with death. Neither Swiss nor Germans like girl pictures on their chocolate packages, but want a realistic reproduction of the contents. And under no circumstances is the Tobler logo to be printed across the lovely illustrations on the box covers (some are real works of art) because it would spoil the pictures for the many customers who frame them.

The factory tour turned out to be a visit to the assembly line on Rock Candy Mountain. Everything that moved carried chocolate—including the workers, who propelled it on in buckets and bags, on carts and trays. I would have thought that the people working there would be hardened to all this sweetness, but no. My guide ripped into trays of chocolate pieces, popping them into his mouth with glee and looking askance when I protested that my capacity had been dulled. Tobler allows what is called the *Mundraub*. That is, a worker can eat as much as he likes on the spot, but must not carry away any chocolate. What he likes, he can buy at a discount in the company store.

Among all the endless conveyor belts, drums and overhead pipes pouring the raw materials into big kettles I was impressed by the machines where the chocolate, after having been mixed, is heated, cooled and heated once more to be cooled again. This tempering changes the large crystals into tiny ones and gives chocolate the fine, soft and melting quality, the *Schmelz,* which is so important; the Swiss especially like it, in chocolate as well as in yodeling. The lengths of time these processes take are another trade secret that can make a considerable difference in the taste. They vary according to the use the chocolate will be put to.

Chocolate-makers in Switzerland claim that one of the main reasons their chocolate is superior lies in the "conching" process. What conching boils down to is the kneading and pounding of the chocolate, which is done in special machines consisting of kettles with a gigantic, pounding roller. The conching machine was invented in 1879 by Rodolphe Lindt of the famous Lindt chocolates, and it produces a perfect melting smoothness, since the minute edges of the sugar and cocoa crystals are fined down and coated with a thin film of cocoa butter. The best chocolates in Switzerland are conched for seventy-two hours, a costly process, but one that tells in the end product. Foreign chocolate-makers, especially the American ones, begrudge the long conching; my guide told me, with utter disgust, that some conch their chocolate in a few hours.

Some other sights stuck in my mind. There was a kitchen with big copper kettles and a fairyland assortment of fruits, nuts, brandies, liqueurs, mounds of fresh butter and gallons of fresh cream plus an Arabia of spices and essences. Here a small elderly man mixed some of the chocolate fillings in small batches, to preserve flavor and quality, going about his work with the same speed and ease as an old farmwife mixing pie dough. Another sight was rows and rows of women sitting at long tables, encased in white coats, hair hidden completely by white nets. They were filling the candies by hand. Chocolate bars are molded by machine, and it takes about half an hour to make a chocolate bar like Toblerone, but it takes four to five hours to make pralines. Other women were wrapping the candies in foil, packing them into boxes, wrapping the boxes in cellophane and tying them with billowing ribbons. To make them fully into the things of beauty the Swiss expect their chocolate boxes to be, they even tucked artificial flowers and favors into the bows. What with all that handwork, I am no longer surprised that American chocolate-makers stick to plain boxes.

Thinking back, one remark keeps on popping up. Everybody I spoke with made it at one time or the other, quite unself-consciously. It ran along these lines: "Let's give our modern machines their due. But if you want to make the best chocolate, you must give it time. And with us, it is the quality that counts most."

VII

The Pleasure of Swiss Trains

A NYONE who likes to combine the best elements of faultless transportation, nature worship and excellent food should ride the Swiss trains. It is a delectable experience to sit by the extra-large window of a Wagon Restaurant Car zooming along the terraced vineyards of Lake Geneva in the company of a delicate Truite Meunière and with a glass of sparkling Côte wine. The majesty of the Gotthard massif is all the more impressive when viewed between mouthfuls of a Croûte de Gourmet, Tournedos Romanoff with tiny potatoes and a tender little salad, followed by assorted cheeses and fresh fruit. If any of the dishes on the menu doesn't make you happy, the waiters will exchange it for roast beef, scaloppine or a schnitzel, with a smile.

If I had to pin my admiration for Swiss things down to one, I would vote for the Swiss transportation system, which includes the lake steamers, postal buses and any number of funiculars, cog railways, ski lifts and all the other conveyances that lift one up to fabulous heights. The Swiss railway system, government-owned and run, is the best in the world, a marvel of cleanliness and efficiency. The smaller stations are bowers of flowers, the large ones a miracle of organization, with large arrival and departure tables for every local and international train. The Swiss railroad system is linked up with all the exciting trains that go to Copenhagen or Istanbul. Trains are always on time; when an Act of God decrees even a few moments' lateness, this is announced with shamed, stifled sobs.

Swiss trains are almost a hundred percent electrified, so that you can ride through the endless Gotthard and Simplon tunnels with the windows open and still emerge bandbox clean. To make sure of the railroad's cleanliness—and cleanliness is the prevailing Swiss obsession—the trains are constantly swept, hosed down and polished by neat blue-smocked railroad employees. All schedules for all transportation are correlated so that it is possible to reach even remote Alpine resorts within half a day from the nearest air terminal; and there is no part of the country, however remote or high up, that cannot be reached by public transportation. In addition, the Swiss railroads and all their side enterprises are cheap. As one of the world's most promotion-minded businesses, they offer a range of reduced-price combinations that is positively staggering and makes a Swiss holiday really ridiculously low-priced. Tickets cover not only train travel, but also the lake steamers and the yellow postal buses which go where trains don't go. The sound of a bus's melodious three-tone horn wafting around a hairpin curve on a steep Alp brings nostalgia to my heart that is too deep for tears.

The Swiss have a thing about their railroads. The country's timetable is as universally read by the adult population as the Bible was by our forefathers. There is a short version of it which every self-respecting Swiss male (and all Swiss males are super-self-respecting) carries on his person at all times.

The Swiss use their trains the way New Yorkers use the subway, and on a train you see a lot of local life you would otherwise miss. There is a terrific business in shipping bicycles by the hundreds. Complaining baby calves travel in special little calf cages. Neatly pigtailed little girls with starched aprons and apple-cheeked little boys in short pants, all carrying their schoolbags rucksack-like on their backs, take the train to the next stop to go to school. Ample matrons, also incredibly neatly dressed, look like friendly maternal hens as they travel with their straw baskets, and the old farmers, puffing on pipes or rolling themselves a cigarette, wear spotless dark suits and black felts, tilted at a slightly raffish angle to show that the old devil isn't quite dead. Whoever gets on or off says the inevitable "*Gruezi*" or "*Adieu miteinand.*" All this is in Second Class, more simply furnished than the First, which is upholstered in an embracing manner and decorated with heavily framed, gorgeous photographs of the country. In the First you find those well-dressed, substantial, polite Swiss businessmen, the kind of men who restore a woman's faith in the male sex, going to their high-powered meetings in Basle, Zurich or Geneva. All these possessors of Mercedes, Bentleys and Cadillacs take the train on their year-round commuters' tickets to save time, Swiss traffic being what it is. In the winter the skiers, in and out of casts, and in the summer the heavily laden mountaineers crowd the trains. In between, innumerable male and female clubs and associations (and the Swiss are joiners indeed) take themselves to see the mimosa in the Ticino when there is nothing but snow in their northern cantons, or to rejoice in the autumnal grape harvest in western Switzerland, or simply to admire their nation's charming capital. All are watched over by fatherly conductors with romantic caps and the shiniest, reddest and largest collection bags, which they wear like shoulder-strap pocketbooks, way below the hips, so that the bags won't push against the passengers as they collect the tickets.

But the Swiss railroads know that man wants more than cold efficiency. He wants food, and good food, and this they give him. The Schweizerische Speisewagen Gesellschaft, to give the company its resounding German name, is a reassuring one. To quote from its brochure, and these are not words only, but facts: "It is run for the convenience of passengers, especially those from other countries. Travelers by international trains, which may be delayed, do not have to worry as to whether there will be sufficient time at the frontier station for breakfast, lunch or dinner; they will find that an excellent service awaits them on their connecting train," and so on. The company even has a special timetable listing the trains with Wagon Restaurants. And they let you have the works.

Breakfast, with fresh crisp rolls, comes continental style or English style (with bacon and egg). Lunch, dinner, afternoon tea, snacks, hot and cold beverages, wines, spirits, and even herbal teas—all can be had on the Swiss trains. I have in front of me an admirable catalogue which, with Swiss accuracy, tells you exactly what you are getting for your money. A luncheon or dinner might be: Potage Parisienne, Bouchées à la Reine, Entrecôte Grillé à la Provençale, Haricots Verts au Beurre, Pomme Château, Salad, Fruit or Cheese. This costs a little more than $3.00 and even less if you omit the soup or Bouchées. Afternoon tea, consisting of tea, two slices of toast, two pats of butter and one slice of pound cake, costs you about 60 cents. You can choose from twenty-five superior Swiss wines, all under $4.00 a bottle, six French vintages, two Italian ones, three champagnes, seventeen non-alcoholic beverages such as mineral waters, fruit juices and colas, six Swiss and imported beers, thirteen apéritifs, with or without soda, and twenty-one of the best brandies and spirits, Cointreau, Grand Marnier and cherry brandy, all unbelievably reasonably priced. Gentlemen may indulge in a choice of seventeen excellent imported and Swiss cigars, plus a choice of American and European cigarettes. And so that travelers may keep up their strength between the *table d'hôte* meals, the *à la carte* menu lists eighteen dishes, plus a choice of six egg dishes, including two three-egg omelets. Fifteen cold meats, sandwiches and cheese plates, and thirteen breads, cakes, cookies and fruits, etc., round out the assortment—all for eating between regular meals. Maybe not all the Wagon Restaurants carry every single item all the time, but they do carry the great majority, if only in self-protection, for the Swiss are literal-minded.

Each Wagon Restaurant has its own kitchen, and the sight of a benevolent Swiss chef hanging out of his window at the station is as familiar as that of the Alps. So is the sight of him eating his own dinner in the reserved space at the end of the dining car, flanked by his assistants. These friends of the public cook almost everything on their menus from scratch, on the train, though they do not bake the *vol-au-vent* patties or the cakes, or make the *pâtés* when on wheels. I once rode in one of the train kitchens to observe the action. The kitchen had an electric range with ovens and plate-warmers, a broiler, a stainless-steel sink and drainboard, a garbage-disposal unit, a hot-water tank in the ceiling, automatic refrigerators and food lockers. Ingeniously placed hooks and shelves held about every kind of kitchen equipment you would find in a restaurant kitchen, and the eggs were kept in a drawer. Next to the kitchen was a pantry, where the linen, flatware, bottles, sugar, salt, spices and similar things were kept. The chefs have their regular runs, their regular helpers and their regular customers, whom they oblige as any good restaurant chef would.

At the beginning of the run the chef arrives with the day's luncheon and dinner menus. The large foods, such as roasts, are staggered to be freshly cooked. Short orders from the three-language menu—broiled chicken, paprika game steaks with mushrooms and cream sauce, pork chops and potatoes—are cooked as ordered. The chef I was with, Charles Rauch, a professionally trained cook, started by telling his menials to peel the potatoes and to make the *crêpe* batter; but he himself made the stuffing of sherried sweetbreads. He cut all the fat off the roast beef and salted and peppered it. He also readied the fish dish, a sole stuffed with shrimp before being rolled up and gratinéed. The chef also made the tartar sauce for the Russian eggs *hors d'oeuvre* and prepared a few skewers with assorted meats in case there should be a call for them. Meanwhile the helpers were fixing fresh fennel, cauliflower and mushrooms as if their lives depended on it, and fiddling with kickshaws like radish curls and tomato roses to make the *à la carte* dishes of *pâté*, sausages, cold cuts and the like look pretty. It was a heart-warming sight. And God forbid that there should be a shortage of desserts on a Swiss train. On that day the menu listed *vacherin* with pineapple, chocolate cream with whipped cream and pear Hélène.

Old-time practitioners as they are, each Wagon Restaurant chef is totally responsible for his kitchens, just as in a restaurant, and he signs the menu with his name. These chefs can foresee the number of customers with remarkable accuracy, so as not to waste food. I asked Chef Rauch if the food preferences were different on the various runs. Indeed they are. Between Zurich and Geneva the travelers prefer *entrecôtes* and pork, but on the Gotthard trains they like veal schnitzels better than pork. The traveling English go for pork chops, beans and potatoes. As for being finicky, the Swiss themselves are far the hardest to please, followed by the Italians; almost all the complaints come from the nationals of these two countries. The Germans count every penny, and the Americans are delighted with the available booze.

The Swiss Dining Car Company, however, does more for travelers. Lest they should starve on Wagon Restaurant-less trains, snack bars with hot and cold drinks are wheeled around by uniformed stewardesses. Or else they will make up a box lunch with anything your heart desires and leave it on your seat. If your group likes greater formality, they will serve you a grandiose dinner, according to your own menu, with as much floss as a grand hotel. Or you can rent a whole dining car and staff for as long as you like, with a deposit of a thousand Swiss francs. Furthermore, should you be an anxious type, you can buy fruit, cookies, sandwiches and whole box lunches, complete with wine, at any fair-sized station.

And now I ask you. Is there any better way of enjoying nature than from the window of a Swiss Wagon Restaurant?

VIII

Hospitality Par Excellence

I F A POOR HOTEL or a bad meal is rare in Switzerland, this is due not only to the Swiss will to please the customers, but also to the fact that they are professionally trained to know how to do this. Hotel- and innkeeping is as proud a tradition in Switzerland as banking is in America, and nobody, however small his establishment, would consider practicing it without adequate training. A rural innkeeper's son who is to take over the family place, or the director of a luxury hotel who will earn better than $30,000 a year, thinks nothing of putting in time as dishwasher, bellhop, busboy, graduating to room clerk or waiter, and going on from there either to the paternal *Gasthof* or to the higher echelons of international hotelkeeping. In other words, they take part in the apprentice system common to all Swiss trades and professions, before they can graduate as master. Besides, café, restaurant and hotel people must have official permission to carry on their business, and they must prove to the authorities that they know it.

Swiss professionals go to the hotel schools, which are to the business what M.I.T is to engineering. There are a number of them, and they are attended by both Swiss and foreigners; the best known is in Lausanne. "The hotel school of Cornell is great for accounting," say those in the know, "and many Swiss hoteliers take courses there. But for food and service, there is nothing to beat the training of a Swiss hotel school."

As I was curious to see how these fountainheads of knowledge operate, I investigated the school at Bellevoir, in Zurich. One of the smaller schools, it specializes in individual training, to assure, as the catalogue says, "the training of a professionally competent and morally impeccable younger generation of hoteliers."

The background of the director, Walter Hammer, is typical of the men in Switzerland's hotel and restaurant industry. His parents owned a small hotel and restaurant near Lucerne, where he helped from childhood on. After graduating from a scholastically tough high school in Basle, his parents let him take a cooking course in Zurich. From there he went to the hotel school in Neuchâtel, and after graduation he worked in the kitchens, dining rooms and front offices of leading hotels in Switzerland, England, Scotland and Egypt. Then, after his father's death, he took over the paternal hotel, to which he added a cooking school for girls which soon became so well known that the Hotel, Restaurant and Café Owners Association of Switzerland asked him to run one of their professional training schools in Zurich. In between, he acts as a consultant for many big hotels in Europe and in the United States.

There is an excellent reason why the Association is so concerned about the younger generation of innkeepers. The acute labor shortage in Switzerland has made itself felt greatly in the hotel business. Young country men and women who once would have automatically become waiters or chambermaids, busboys or bellhops, now prefer to go to work in the factories, where they get more money for far shorter and more regular hours—and the hours matter perhaps even more than the money. All Swiss hoteliers are forced to employ foreigners, and even if their German chambermaids or Spanish kitchen help show all the goodwill in the world, they don't have the same ingrained, inherited knowledge of the business that the Swiss have. It isn't only that the pride of the hotel men suffers when the service is no longer as perfect as before the Second World War; their business sense is more than chagrined, for the service of Swiss hotels has always been legendary. If you point out to them that it still is incomparably superior to that of other countries, they are not cheered, but describe to you the finesse that was possible in other days when the help outnumbered the guests. Any Swiss restaurateur is doleful at being forced to accept at least partially the "Teller Service"—that is, the food being put in the kitchen on the plate from which it will be eaten, rather than being properly served at the table from a serving dish which is kept warm on a hot-plate. This kind of service—lowest of the low in all respectable Swiss eyes, though in America even many of the astronomically priced restaurants do not flinch at subjecting their diners to it—is avoided whenever possible. And the fair-minded Swiss charge less for this vulgarity (in their eyes) than for a properly served dish.

To come back to where I started, the Bellevoir School is located in a charming mansion deep in a park on Lake Zurich. An excellent restaurant is attached to it, to give the students firsthand experience. The students are male and female, of all ages, because many seasoned innkeepers come back for refresher courses. A number of specialized courses are taught at the school, and by the time the students are through, they know how to cook a simple lunch or a banquet, make menus, wait on table, carve meats before the guests, select, chill, decant and serve vintages, mix cocktails, buy food and calculate food costs, prepare bills, do bookkeeping, conduct hotel business and greet guests in three languages, look after the silver, linen and furnishings, and handle beer, and they understand food laws, nutrition and food hygiene. Throughout all this instruction there is constant and strong stress on being clean, hard-working, cooperative and, above all, pleasant.

I went to a number of classes. In one, the teacher showed the pupils who were sitting at desks in a most orderly manner, each with a slide-rule, how to make up yearly balance sheets and calculate the profits and losses in the various food categories. All the students got up and said "*Guten morgen*" when Director Hammer and I entered the room, and they did not sit down again until he said: "Sit down." In another class, a number of girls training to be waitresses (and about ninety percent of waiting on table is done by women in Switzerland) were learning the care of table linens and how to darn holes invisibly. In another, the students, one of them an American boy from Georgia who had gone to the Bordentown Military Academy, were instructed in the art of sauce-making. They clustered around a stove and cooked while their teacher fired basic questions at them, not mincing words if they were slow to answer. The pupils wore professional uniforms of white coat for the cooks, black pants and white shirt and jacket for the men waiters, black dress with a little white apron for the waitresses. All were as intent on the courses as if their lives depended on them.

What made the greatest impression on me was the books. Each student is requested to keep a scrapbook with his notes. This book is considered part of the curriculum because the student keeps it for life, referring to it continually in his profession. These books are miracles of neatness that have to be seen to be believed, and some of them are decorated with colorful drawings. One of the books I studied featured on the first page a reproduction of a Vermeer painting. The first sentence, written in decorative script, said: "For cooking, you need love for the job, and besides that, the food, tools and necessary equipment." The book began with instructions for the care of the kitchen equipment, and the admonition that everything made of wood had to be scrubbed twice daily, though the meat block was to be scraped after each use. I read in it how to staff a medium-size restaurant with the appropriate personnel: one CHEF DE CUISINE; one SAUCIER, who does all the meats and fish served with sauces; two GARDE-MANGER, for all the cold dishes and salads, and kitchen supervision; one ENTREMÉTIER for the soups, vegetables, eggs, pastas and potatoes; one ROTISSIER, who roasts, broils and prepares the foods for frying and sautéeing; one PATISSIER for cake and desserts; one TOURNANT, who substitutes for each of the others on his day off; and one COMMUNARD, who cooks for the help. Apart from definitions and recipes, the book contained a sample breakdown of the costs of barley soup, with each component, however small, listed for profit and losses, a complete wine book; and a dissertation on the theory and practice of every type of room and single- and multiple-table service. I quote from the book:

What is expected of service personnel
1. Cleanliness of body and spirit
2. Politeness and attention
3. Honesty and faithfulness
4. Punctuality and reliability
5. Exemplary love of order
6. Faultless professional knowledge
7. Hard work and stick-to-itiveness
8. Good memory and quickness in taking orders

9. Languages

10. Team spirit

The duties of the waiter and waitress

How to receive guests: (1) Friendliness. (2) Call by name. (3) Never be temperamental because people won't come back. (4) Be nice to children, they are tomorrow's customers. (5) Serve invalids as quickly and pleasantly as possible because they may be shy. (6) Don't stand around and talk. (7) Give guests, if possible, a clean table. (8) Crumb not only the table, but also the chairs. (9) Don't lean on tables and chairs.

Your own inner attitude: (a) Be sure to be quiet and dignified with difficult guests. (b) Keep calm in the rush hour. (c) Be helpful to guests and other help.

Outer attitudes: (a) Don't talk with guests, you waste time. (b) Don't talk during working hours. (c) Be ready to serve. (d) Be clean and neat. (e) Be comradely with the people who work with you during and after service. (f) Don't look after departing guests or mimic them.

Important: Write orders so kitchen and buffet can read them.

Included in the book were a treatise on banquets of the most diverse kinds, including suitable flower decorations; a résumé of the Swiss food and drink laws; samples of business correspondence, such as an apology to a complaining guest for the mistakes of a foreign waiter who was rude and overcharged; and an outline of cost accounting. And all of these notes, I repeat, were in the neatest possible handwriting, and as clear to me as to their compiler.

IX

---◆▶

---◆▶

Festivals

---◆▶

IN SWITZERLAND there used to be an almost unbelievable number of folk customs and festivals, as diverse
as the scenery of the country and as the history, traditions and dialects of the various villages, towns and
cantons. Many of these customs, which are still alive,
came down from pagan times, when men still lived in
close contact with nature and were dependent on propitiating it. These festivals relate to the winter solstice and
the coming of spring, as in the *Chalandamarz* of the
Engadine, when the children chase winter away with
cowbells and rattles. To celebrate the *Alpaufzug,* the
moving of the herds to their high Alpine summer
pastures, in the Rhône Valley a fight between cows with
filed-down horns takes place to determine the queen of a
herd; she then walks decorated with a bunch of flowers
fastened to her head and an enormous fancy cowbell.
The grape harvest is celebrated in Neuchâtel with a
parade with very fancy floats, followed by a paper-
confetti fight, dancing and other rejoicing. Religious
celebrations of great pomp and display include the

Corpus Christi events in the Catholic cantons, such as the magnificently costumed ones in Appenzell.

The Swiss are also given to monumental glee-club singing contests and sporting events which they combine with a patriotic mood. Among them there are sharpshooters' conventions, which are popular, and a spectacular Alpine variety of wrestling, which is called *Schwingen*. Another strange and traditional game is the *Hornussen*, a batting game played by two teams with a small disk, which requires considerable skill. All of these bring out the kind of group-muscular mysticism which is part of the Swiss soul and quite alien to the American soul.

Of the purely patriotic events, the greatest is the celebration of the pact of the three original cantons in 1291, which was the beginning of Switzerland. This Swiss equivalent of the Fourth of July happens on August 1, and its main feature, apart from the many parades and assemblies, is lighting huge bonfires on hills and mountaintops, making a fiery chain throughout the country. What's interesting about it is that until the eighteenth century the Alpine landscape was considered fearful and desolate and to be avoided. Its beauty and its consequent role in Swiss affairs were literally invented by a Bernese called Albrecht von Haller, who wrote a poem glorifying the Alps and the moral virtues they gave to their inhabitants, as contrasted to the iniquitous goings-on in his native city. I often have wondered what these were, since there is nothing in the current Bernese character to make one suspect such a piquant inheritance.

Most of these festivals involve ancient costumes and masks, and many are obsolete, in spite of official efforts to keep them alive. But what is surprising is how many festivals survive as part and parcel of Swiss life, with their distinctive food, drinks and attire.

I wish it were possible in this book to describe these festivals in detail. But it isn't, and therefore I have chosen

to write about the two that struck me as the most
unusual.

A very ancient custom followed in many parts of the
country is the burning of a straw puppet in the spring to
celebrate the death of winter. In Zurich the festival takes
place in April and involves the whole of the city—with
bells on, too. This is the one time when the naturally
reserved Zürcher let go, including the children, for the
festival includes a children's parade and children's balls.

The name of the festival is *Sechseläuten*, "Six O'Clock
Bells," and it is closely connected with the town guilds
that ruled Zurich for centuries in the manner of professional associations with a social mission. They still have
their houses on the Limmatquai, with fabulous restaurants. What's more, they still exist in the way of clubs,
but with great pride and jealousy of their own traditions
and with various degrees of social status.

The name *Sechseläuten* originated in a public ordi-
nance of the burghers in the golden age of the town's
guilds. On the first Monday following the vernal equi-
nox, the bells of the great cathedral were rung, announc-
ing the beginning of festival time for masters and jour-
neymen. In those days the greater part of the feasting
and merrymaking transpired in evening and night hours.
In the afternoon the various guilds gathered in their
respective halls. When the bells began to ring out six
o'clock, they arose from their chairs and the guild
master, in a short speech, wished health and prosperity to
the governing body, city and country. In the meantime
the remaining townspeople gathered in front of the guild
halls, sitting on high places and on the bridges, waiting to
celebrate the great moment with shooting and drumming. Piles of wood were ready for the spark that would
set them ablaze to burn a straw dummy representing
winter.

Since that time the spring festival has developed into

an annual demonstration of the splendor of Zurich's guilds. Zealous festival poets and stage managers were on hand each year to help with the arrangements; the pageants became more artistic in appearance, and their themes—from history, the arts and local events—varied from year to year. Meanwhile Zurich's guilds made some elaborate displays of the signs of their trade. Various chroniclers of the times report that the butchers once paraded with a sausage eighteen yards long, the bakers with a loaf of bread weighing 250 pounds, and the fishermen with gigantic fishes.

The *Sechseläuten* is a two-day affair, and it is reported in every single detail in the newspapers, including the august *Neue Zürcher Zeitung*, which is infinitely more formal than *The New York Times*. It begins with the children's parade on Sunday, and this begins with the weather report. I listened to the telephone company's report, which said: "Because of unstable weather conditions warm underwear is recommended for the paraders." Very often, till the last minute, there is no knowing if the parade will take place, and its starting point is full of parents keeping down the excited kids.

With thousands of watching citizens, I stood in the streets to watch the parade. What got me was the politeness of the people; grown-ups made way for small children and for fathers carrying them on their backs, old ladies were let stand in front and nobody was trampled down for a good view—quite the contrary. Meanwhile people were refreshing themselves with the street vendors' cookies and sweets that are typical of the occasion. I did, too, and I can only report that they were very sweet and rather stodgy and obviously historical foods that you don't want to reproduce at home.

The kids marched in admirable order. They were costumed in every possible way, from rococo ladies with white wigs to cowboys and Indians, Chinese, nobles on horseback with their ladies and knee-high medieval warriors with flower-hung halberds pulling display wagons filled with poultry or vegetables. In the evening the kids went costumed to special children's balls, advertised in the papers. They polkaed and even twisted under the benevolent gaze of their elders, lined on chairs around the ballroom. Some were too timid to pair up with a member of the opposite sex and danced alone. They sang children's songs, admired professional child ballerinas and a movie, and ate lots and lots of sausages, fried cookies and chocolate. At no time were they anything but extremely well behaved. All this was a prelude to Monday's great bash. Throughout the night I could hear the staid citizens of Zurich shedding their reserve with wine and song, women having no part in the *Sechseläuten*. It was quite a shaking experience, seeing that usually the town closes tight as a clam every midnight.

The weather was hideous when the afternoon grand march began down the main street of Zurich, across the Quai Bridge and over to the huge green square called Alter Tonhalle Platz. Bunting and flags did their best under the frequent April downpours. But the streets were jammed with raincoated and umbrellaed spectators standing or sitting on benches and camp chairs. All were in the sunniest and most patient of moods. Twenty-four guilds marched by, fortified by the ceremonial pre-march dinner in their clubhouses. Some were on horseback; all had music. They wore historical costumes dating back to the Middle Ages, the Renaissance, the Rococo and so on, a splendid sight indeed. I remember especially the white horses of a baker's guild, the red dragoons of the St. Nicholas guild, the Renaissance mercenaries guarding the coffers of the carriage of the merchants' guild and the enormous top hat of the hatters' guild. Many of the marchers carried flowers, and so did the horses and floats. And some had wrapped plastic raincoats over themselves. The marchers waved and exchanged pleasantries with their friends on the sidewalks, children were lifted up to see Daddy marching, girls threw flowers at their sweethearts.

They were still marching when the *Böögg* was put on his fifteen-foot pyre on the big square. The life-sized Old Man Winter puppet was dressed in white with a black top hat, and he was fastened to a pole and a broom. The crowd was thick and quiet. At the stroke of six all of Zurich's bells burst out pealing, and a few minutes after, a little smoke started to escape from the bottom of the pyre. Then flames began shooting up, and soon the *Böögg* was ablaze. The fireworks concealed in the various parts of his body started going off with loud bangs, and the crowds cheered wildly as guild horsemen galloped madly in a great circle around the fire. Once more the *Böögg* had died according to tradition. For the guild members, more was to come. It is traditional for the members of each guild to have a large meal in their own house prior to the traditional formal visits to the other guild houses; women are strictly excluded from all of this. Throughout the night I saw little groups of costumed men walking through the city with their lanterns, banners and bands, to lift many a glass and speak many a word in praise of friendship and civil-mindedness.

You wouldn't believe it, but the Swiss are given to Carnival celebrating as much as the people of Rio. They celebrate it at two different times. The Catholics have theirs first, just before Lent, and the Protestants, because of ancient calendars, a week later. To give you an idea: One year (of course the dates change yearly) among

Switzerland's Catholic areas the Carnival spirit got in an "advance" in Baden on the 27th of February with a grotesque Carnival procession, and in Olten on the 28th of February with this town's famous "Fool's Pot." After this "build-up," Carnival time reached its real zenith in Lucerne on the 1st and 5th of March. In Solothurn the time from the 1st to the 6th of March was devoted to a Carnival celebration known locally as *Chesslete*. In Biel, people were celebrating Carnival on the 3rd and 4th of March, and Baden, Olten and Kreuzlingen all staged Carnival processions on the 4th of March.

Murten's procession came one week later on the 11th of March. In the Italian-speaking part of Switzerland, townspeople went in for a really "nourishing" kind of Carnival celebration: in Ascona, Bellinzona and Lugano the famous rice dish known as *risotto* was cooked outdoors in city squares and served to all who came to enjoy it. In Zurich two big artists' masquerade balls were held in the Congress House on the 10th and 12th of March, when the Carnival spirit engulfs Switzerland's biggest city.

All these festivities involve costumes, masks and prizes. The newspapers are full of ads for various restaurants, promising everything from a "cozy family evening" to a "*postillon d'amour* night" to a "devil's dream in heaven and earth."

Over the years I've danced at many a Swiss Carnival. But the one that shook me as nothing has shaken me since adolescence was the Carnival of Basle. It is like nothing else in the world; as a writer put it, "it is not a folk festival nor a tourist attraction, but a cataclysm of nature," at which the people of Basle want no outsiders.

Basle is the most uppity and reserved of all Swiss cities, disdaining to lure the tourists. It is ancient, very cultured and equally rich. The city is mad for art and music. It has the most beautiful cathedrals and museums, a great university, an outstanding zoo, a big international port on the Rhine, big chemical plants, lots of international banking and a famous international trade fair. The people talk in a witty, indirect way all their own, and they prefer to talk to other Basle people only. At their Carnival, which, being Protestant, is a late Carnival, the citizens for once allow their artistic imaginations free rein and act in public what they would like to be but do not dare to.

The Basle Carnival is more than the usual parades and masked balls. It is a living broadsheet lampooning all and sundry events of local significance and incidents of the city and federal governments' faults and blunders in very frank pictures and language. Furthermore, anybody safely disguised in costume and mask can walk up to any acquaintance, no matter how highly placed, and tell him in a disguised high-pitched voice what he thinks or knows about him. This is best taken with a large dose of humor.

This ancient tribal rite, which goes back to the thirteenth century when the people had to have a final blast before the very real rigors of Lent, is planned by the "cliques," secret and loosely organized associations of kindred souls, including the town's most elevated citizens. They exist solely for Carnival purposes, and stew about it for the whole year, debating which specific events they want to lampoon. Another function of the cliques is drumming in an intricate fashion that is an integral part of the Carnival and unique in the world. In Basle there are about thirty drumming academies that teach boys from eight years up as well as grown-ups, all the year round. Only four weeks before the Carnival do the police permit practicing on live drums in the houses;

the rest of the year, drumming is done on felt pads
mounted on wooden racks at an angle corresponding to
the drum carried in walking.

The Carnival in Basle comes in bits and pieces, all most
intensive and on its own time schedule, since Protestant
and Catholic beginnings of Lent vary in Switzerland. It
begins on the Monday after Ash Wednesday, at the
stroke of 4:00 a.m., no less. I had come with one of the
special trains from Zurich, and I stood on the sidewalks
with thousands of bleary-eyed people. The usual night
lights had been on in the beautiful old town, and restaurants and cafés had kept open. But at four o'clock sharp
every single light in the town went out, leaving a
pitch-black night. To make the effect even eerier, the air,
on all sides, became full of the sound of drums and fifes.
The cliques had left their headquarters, all drumming the
"Morgenstreich," a morning reveille. All the members of
each group wore similar costumes, topped with enormous, fantastic masks in the shape of birds, beasts and
anything the imagination could conjure in the way of
bizarreness. Preceding the group of drummers and fifers,
each group carried a large transparent lantern, resting
upon the shoulders of four men, illuminated from within
by candles, acetylene or electric lights. The lanterns
represented supremely satirical scenes, caricatures and
written words about a particular event. Almost all of
them were true artistic creations (and, indeed, they are
done by leading artists), very clever color compositions,
with special attention to the effect created by the
lantern's inner light. There were hundreds and hundreds
of mummers in big and small groups, marching through
the city by the light from their transparencies, and all
were drumming, drumming, drumming and marching,
marching. The rhythms of the various drummers
differed, and the effect was atavistic, unlike any I've ever

heard. All the spectators were very quiet, and I was scared. The whole scene had a feeling of underlying violence, the violence of the Middle Ages. I was reminded of the great processions of the penitentes, and the wild fantasy of the masks added to the terror.

I was standing next to an old working-class woman who was minding her two costumed grandchildren. She was weeping silently, and I asked her what I could do to help. She said that the kids were tired but that she did not know how to bed them down. The parents had pawned all the household furniture to be able to take part in a clique and buy masks. Admittedly this is an exceptional case, but it does show how the people feel about their Carnival.

As the hours went on, marchers and spectators, including myself, repaired to restaurants and cafés which had been open since before dawn. We strengthened ourselves with the clove-flavored Basle Brown Soup, with onion-and-cheese tarts and with wine. Even here there was comparatively little noise. Then, around six or seven, the marchers went home to change for their business day, which lasts only until two p.m. I spent the morning in a cultural manner, looking at churches and museums.

At two the Carnival began in earnest. This time the cliques went all out with even more incredible costumes, masks and floats that related to their chosen satirical theme. Each was a self-contained entity, marching where they wanted through the town, drumming, fifing and playing the *Guggenmusik*, a monstrous instrument made from unrelated parts such as stovepipes, faucets, horns and loudspeakers.

The parades go on until evening, with handbills distributed to the watchers by the various cliques, telling in local dialect verse about the subject of their satires. At night, throughout the town, there are masked balls with prizes for the most original masks. The idea of these balls is not that ladies be pretty and elegant; if they come at all, and they do, they too must disguise themselves as completely and wittily as possible. I was taken to one of these balls, disguised in Arab robes with the papier-mâché head of a sphinx. There was an air of determined abandon in the dancing, and no fooling about this. Close to unmasking time, when every mask must fall, a hooded lady sat on my lap whispering sweet nothings to my grunts. I'll never forget her face when she saw me, another woman, unmasked.

Tuesday is a working day, though a somewhat tired one. On this day the Carnival lanterns and all the Carnival equipment of the cliques are on display, and very well worth seeing.

On Wednesday there is no early-morning Carnival. But in the afternoon, between two and seven, the cliques again parade around town in full plumage. As on Monday night, during the evening many of the groups make their rounds of the restaurants with their *Schnitzelbank*, artistically executed satiric posters to which they sing a corresponding text in verse. Awards are handed out for the most original ones. At night there are more masked balls until the early hours of Thursday, when Basle becomes a staid albeit tired city, hoping and planning for the next *Fasnacht*.

True or not, I will pass on a fact that I read somewhere: the annual increase in Basle's births does not take place in the usual time after Carnival, but after the national holiday of *Bus und Bettag*, when the nation officially prays and does penitence.

It seems odd that the Swiss do not celebrate Christmas with any special foods, except for traditional cookies and cakes. In German-speaking Switzerland, Christmas Eve brings the candlelit tree and the presents. On Christmas

Day the families entertain each other, and the day after, they entertain their friends. In French- and Italian-speaking Switzerland the holiday is celebrated as in France and Italy, generally speaking. In any case, each family eats whatever they consider particularly festive, be it chicken, roast beef or veal.

Santa Claus, as we know him, does not exist in Switzerland, but St. Nicholas comes on December 6, to bring the good children fruit and candy and small gifts, and the bad ones a switch.

At Eastertime there are colored eggs, chocolate bunnies and bunny cakes, and also some other ritualistic bakings which go back to antiquity, celebrating the coming of spring and propitiating the gods who could grant a good harvest.

X

━━━◄◆►━━━

━━━◄◆►━━━

Swiss Wines

━━━◄◆►━━━

A̲s IN France and Italy, wine is part and parcel of
Swiss life, both food and pleasure. It is the drink
of the people, and not limited to mealtimes. You see
families on their Sunday excursions enjoying a glass of
wine with their sausage in the garden of a country inn, or
workers refreshing themselves in the second-class station
restaurant before taking the train to work, or peasants
sitting down with a convivial glass after Sunday church.
Grapes are grown in practically all the cantons, and some
of the Swiss vineyard landscapes are unforgettable. I am
thinking of the pocket-sized terraced vineyards of the
Rhône Valley, which cling to rocky slopes at absurd
angles and are joined together by steps hewn into the
rock; when the rains wash down the topsoil, it has to be
carried back up in baskets, literally. The best Swiss red
wine, the Dôle du Valais, comes from here, and so does
the splendid dry white Fendant du Valais. Around the
bucolic shores of Lake Neuchâtel the grapes grow in an
air as luminous as that of the French Impressionist
painters. The wines here, too, are luminous, pale and
fruity. The northern shores of Lake Geneva, home of the

superior La Côte, Lavaux and Chablais wines, are a vast expanse of vineyards open to the sun like avid sunbathers; the vineyards have swallowed practically all the trees and gardens around the stone farmhouses and villages. The tiny enclosed vineyards near the cathedral of Chur, in the Grisons, and their delicious, light red wine remind one of the Middle Ages, when they were planted to provide the holy wine for the clerics' Mass and the drink that brightened their tables.

In the Ticino, the Italian-speaking part of Switzerland, the grapes are trained to grow on gray stone pillars around Lake Maggiore and Lake Lugano and in the mountain villages above the lakes. The red Merlot and the Nostrano should be drunk in the old-fashioned cups, sitting in a *pergolato* where the ripe grapes hang overhead, and where you see the lake water sparkling behind the thick green clusters of grape leaves. The sight that moves me most is a vineyard in the earliest spring, when the first sunshine has warmed the bare wooden trunks of the vines and their poles so that they throw off enough heat to melt the snow around them. I can still see the snow bursting into funnel-shaped holes, from which tiny rivulets streamed downhill. A few small and humble spring weeds, which had survived under the snow, now enjoyed a short bloom before the vintner's hoe touched them; their very insignificance spoke far more hopefully of nature's new life than all the glorious flowers of the proper spring.

The ancient Romans, on the way to their northern conquests, brought the grapevine to Switzerland, transforming so many of the wild slopes of the country into civilized land. When Rome's influence declined, the monasteries became the custodians of the vintner's art, and many remain that to this day. From the earliest, grapes and wine were protected by the law. In a document dated A.D. 515, we read that grape thieves, when caught during the day, would be heavily fined if they were freemen, or given three hundred lashes if slaves. And by night both kinds of thief would be killed without further ado. Grape-growing, wine-making, and the serving of wine, like all other trades and professions, stood under heavy legislation throughout the centuries. They still do today, with stringent federal and cantonal rules that safeguard the honesty of the operations.

The overwhelming majority of Swiss wine is drunk open, served from carafes that range from one deziliter (a little more than half a standard American cup), through a quarter, a half, and a whole liter (about one quart). When ordering, one simply asks for the desired amount; one or two dezi, as they are called, is what I drink with my Swiss meals. The most beautiful carafes are the old (or the modern copies) pewter *channes* or *Kannen*, heavy, decorative lidded jugs straight out of the Renaissance.

Swiss wine is very good most of the time, and carefully made. The Swiss drink practically all of it themselves, and are self-sufficient in the matter of white wines; but they import large quantities of red *vin ordinaire* from France and Italy. Alas, the best Swiss wine has to be drunk in Switzerland, since very little of it gets exported; some of the very best wine does not get exported or even bottled at all. The quantities are so limited that it has to be drunk locally; it does not even reach the larger Swiss cities regularly. To find it, one should ask the waiters or the innkeepers for the best local wines, and whether they have their own house stock. It should also be made clear that the wine does not have to be bottled wine! Many Swiss innkeepers seem to think that Americans will drink nothing but bottled wine, and they urge them to since it is much more expensive.

In spite of outstanding vineyards and splendid soil and climatic conditions, Switzerland does not produce great vintages, as France and Germany do. Why this is so is a moot question. One of the several plausible answers is that the conservative Swiss like the wine they make, and since it is they themselves who drink it anyway, they see no reason to change it. Another reason given is the choice of grapes planted. By far the largest is the white Chasselas grape, whose sturdiness, yield and taste seem to please the citizen of the Confederation as no other.

Most of the wine grown in Switzerland is white, light and fresh and not of a high alcoholic content. It resembles the wines of nearby Alsace, Germany and Austria, and it is made from the white Chasselas, which, interestingly, has never taken hold in California. In the Valais, wine made from the Chasselas is known as *fendant*, and *fendant* has become almost a generic name for many white Swiss wines, which are almost always known by their origin rather than by the name of the grape that produces them.

Though wine is made in practically every canton, very often by small peasant producers, only the cantons of western Switzerland make it in commercial quantities and export it. To describe them, I quote from *The Bright and Fragrant Wines of Switzerland*, a pamphlet published by the Swiss Wine Growers Association in Lausanne, which I think an interesting and accurate description of the local products.

GENEVA   The Canton, whose capital is the city of the same name, is situated at the southwest corner of Lake Geneva. It is the smallest canton in the Swiss Confederation, having an area of 109 square miles, of which 11½ are lake. Voltaire (who lived there) said that when he shook his wig, he powdered the whole Genevese Republic.

The canton is well cultivated, but its fertility is almost entirely due to the unremitting industry of the local people. Sunlight plays on the vineyards, market gardens and orchards which occupy the slopes running down to the river Rhône. Here and there a clump of trees casts a dark shadow on a mosaic of soft yellow, browns and greens.

On the slopes are old houses which for centuries have been closely associated with the wine-growing district. Some of them date back for many centuries. Such a house is the old priory of Satigny which, according to a deed gift dated 912, gained possession of the vineyards of MANDEMENT. The wines produced there are named after the charming little villages of the district—PEISSY, RUSSIN and SATIGNY itself, which is actually the biggest wine-growing parish of Switzerland.

Geneva wines are light and dry, with a trace of hazelnut in their bouquet. They are wines for the long summer evenings, refreshing and pleasing to the palate.

LA CÔTE is a delightful, unspoilt place which follows the coastline on the west side of Lake Geneva. There is nothing meretricious about the scenery, which owes its charm primarily to the vineyards, fields and orchards that play hide-and-seek on the hills and in the valleys.

The vineyards are to be found mostly on the upper slopes, the lower ones being devoted mainly to farming. La Côte is the largest wine-producing district of the Canton of Vaud. It is studded with pretty villages such as FECHY, MONTSUR-ROLLE, VINZEL, LUINS, which skirts the famous *road of the Vaudois wines,* leading from MORGES to NYON. Two old castles, Vufflens and Nyon, stand guard over the vineyards.

The wine of the region has been described as "robust" and, like the industrious local people, "unsophisticated."

LAVAUX AND CHABLAIS *Coteaux Vaudois* Traveling eastward along the north coast of Lake Geneva, just beyond Lausanne, one comes across the charming village of Lutry where the Lavaux—at one time spelt "La Vaux" (The Valley)—district begins. It is believed that wines were made there in the time of the Romans. It was not, however, until 1137 that the cultivation of the vine was taken very seriously, thanks mainly to the Bishop of Lausanne. In that year the Bishop called in the friars of the order of Citaux to cultivate the land and they became the first important wine-growers of the region.

There are several old castles in Lavaux, including Glerolles and Chillon, made famous in verse by Lord Byron.

On this wonderful "Swiss riviera," between Lausanne and Montreux, many small terraced vineyards cover the mountainside in a series of steps that climb up from the lake. The soil is very fertile and the climate is ideal for wine-growing. The district has, as the poet Ramuz said, "two suns: one from above and the other from below"—the latter being the reflection of the sun in Lake Geneva. Vines grow in every fold of the mountainside. They must be tended with great care and this is more laborious than in any of the other districts, because the wine-grower here can use no machinery to help him.

When spring comes, earth washed away by rain and storms must be carefully replaced. At harvest time hoppers laden with freshly picked grapes must be carried up very steep paths to a vat on a wagon waiting by the roadside.

The villages on the slopes of Lavaux—LUTRY, CULLY, GRANDVAUX, RIEX, EPESSES, LE DEZALEY, RIVAZ, SAINT-SAPHORIN—all produce the most delightful wines. Swiss wine-growers are fond of giving their wines a personality of their own, and they describe the Lavaux wines as "bright and elegant."

Further east, where the lake ends, is VILLENEUVE and, in the Rhône Valley, YVORNE and AIGLE. It is said that the best white wines of Switzerland come from this region and from the DEZALEY.

NEUCHÂTEL The Republic and Canton of Neuchâtel is situated in the northernmost part of the wine districts of French-speaking Switzerland. The capital bears the same name as the Canton and lies near the northeast corner of the Lake of Neuchâtel. From the hills overlooking the city one looks down at the austere sixteenth-century castle and the thirteenth-century collegiate church of Notre Dame, the two most prominent features of Neuchâtel.

The city is surrounded by vineyards which date back to ancient times. Vines grew there in the tenth century when the Abbey of Bevaix was founded.

The soil of the district is chalky and the wines receive special treatment to give them a delightful and distinctive flavor. They have more sparkle to them than other Swiss wines. They are dry, light and delicate and very suitable for festive occasions, and they are the ones most frequently found in the United States.

The labels of Neuchâtel wines bear also the names of AUVERNIER, CORMONDRÈCHE, SAINT-BLAISE and CRESSIER, wine-producing villages of the region.

VALAIS—sometimes called "Vieux Pays" (Old Country)—is situated in the southernmost part of the French-speaking region, bordering on Italy in the south and on France in the west. The canton is the source of the river Rhône which rises in the eastern extremity of the Valais. Sheltered by the Alps, Valais has a very warm and sunny climate. Vines were first cultivated in the time of the Romans. The people have many quaint customs which originated centuries ago; they have a particular pride in their past and are very conscientious in keeping up old traditions. At certain times of the year the people of Anniviers, who work in the lower valley, march down from their homes in the mountain villages playing fifes and drums to give them heart for the long daily labors in the vineyards. In October, when the harvest is over, they carry eight-gallon barrels of Glacier wine up to their villages and the wine is then left to mature for ten or fifteen years in casks made of larchwood staves.

Vineyards climb right up the mountainside, and high up on the slopes one sees row upon row of terraces. As the soil is for the most part arid, aqueducts—miles of them—span the mountains. Water in these parts is very precious indeed.

The best-known of the wines of the region is FENDANT, which was first grown by a mercenary returning from France. He brought back the original chasselas vine with him—and this was the progenitor of a rich variety of wines. JOHANNISBERG, *not* to be confused with the superior German wine, is another well-known wine made from the Sylvaner grape. It is light with a lot of character. Other wines of the region—all full-

bodied and with a velvety texture—are MALVOISIE,
ARVINE, ERMITAGE, AMIGNE. There is also the red
wine DÔLE, distinguished by its "gun flint" flavor.

Like many others, I feel that the Swiss Wine Growers
do not do sufficient justice to the deep red Dôle wine of
the Valais. The best Dôle is made from the pure *pinot
noir* grape, the grape of Burgundy, or it may be blended
with the *gamay* grape. A good Dôle is far better than
many a second-string Burgundy; it is full-bodied, with a
fairly high alcoholic content and a long life in the bottle.
To my mind, it is one of the most agreeable table wines
above the *vin ordinaire* level. The Dôle of the Caves de
Provins, an outstanding vintners' cooperative, is excellent, as are all their wines.

There are far too many superior local wines in Switzerland to be able to mention all of them here, and I can
only urge my traveling readers to sample them wherever
they find themselves in Switzerland. But I would like to
mention a few. The wines of the Bieler See, in the canton
of Berne, are as arcadian as the lake and its lovely shores.
Both the white TWANNER and the SCHAFFISER are light
and flowery, ideal companions for the delicate local lake
fish. There is also a very good red TWANNER, which the
local people regard so highly that they like to keep it to
themselves. This proprietary attitude is one found
throughout Switzerland: in the white-wine districts, like
Neuchâtel, there is always some red wine that is splendid, but of which there is not enough to distribute
largely. The only way to find out is to ask, and the same
applies to the white wines of the red-wine districts, as in
the Ticino.

This part of Switzerland is known for two red wines.
One is the MERLOT, made with the grape used so much in
the Bordeaux country, and the other the fiery NOSTRANO.

The Merlot is an agreeable fruity wine with a pleasant bouquet, and greatly superior to the Nostrano, a rather ordinary *vin du pays,* the kind you find in all of northern Italy.

The Swiss wines that I prefer to all others are, alas, never exported, and even in a town like Zurich you have to search for them. These are the outstanding light red wines from the Grisons, made from the *pinot gris* grape. The wines of MALANS, ZIZERS, MASANS and CHUR, to mention a few of the places that have named them, have a verve and gaiety of their own, and they are utterly delightful morning, noon and night.

Also extremely pleasant are some of the rather positive red wines of the canton of St. Gall. SARGANS, WALENSTADT and PORTASER are among the names to look out for.

Around Lake Constance grow a number of pleasant wines, both white and red. The white wines, such as BERLINGEN, ERMATINGEN and SCHLOSSGUT BACHTOBEL are fresh and flowery, and good to drink with the superlative lake fish. The red wines from OTTENBERG, NEUNFORM and other places in the Thur Valley are smooth, with a pronounced bouquet.

BEER AND SPIRITS

The Swiss don't drink only wine; they also drink a good deal of very good beer in the cafés and in the *Bierstuben,* the beer restaurants, which also serve excellent sausages, cheese and cheese dishes which go well with beer. The beer of the lager kind is made locally. Among the best-known brands are Berne's Gurtenbier, Zurich's Hürlimannbier and the Cardinal of Fribourg. Much as the Swiss like their beer, they don't venerate it as the Germans do theirs, and you certainly don't see in

Switzerland the beer monsters you see in Munich.

One of the glories of Switzerland is the white brandies that are distilled from fruit; they have nothing in common with sweet liqueurs, but are crystal-clear, fragrant and strong pure spirits and truly ambrosial. A great many connoisseurs prefer the Swiss white fruit brandies to the same kinds made in France or Germany, which are not so pure and often have sugar and alcohol added to them.

Distilling fruit brandies is a centuries-old Swiss country practice. The peasants indulged in it during the winter, when there was little field work, for their own edification and also to make a little extra income. Many still do, though the government frowns upon such practices.

The most famous of these brandies is Kirsch, made from cherries, and by far the best Kirsch there ever was, to my mind, is distilled by the firm of Paul Etter Söhne, in Zug, home of fine Kirsch, though Basle also prides itself on its Kirsch. The Etter family has made Kirsch since the 1700's, when they still were farmers, and commercially since 1846. The Kirsch is made from a specially grown cherry, the *Lauerzerkirsche*, which is small, very sweet and thin-skinned. The cherries are stemmed, but used whole, with the stones, which give the spirit the necessary amount of bitterness. The cherries used for Kirsch are not for eating, just as the grapes used for wine are not table grapes. Kirsch ought to be aged for at least three years in glass or tanks, but not in wood, since it must remain crystal clear. Its ideal age is from three to ten years; after that it becomes milder with aging, and reaches its limit at about thirty.

When I think of the lovely qualities of Kirsch, my heart runneth over. The Swiss think so, too, drinking it at the end of meals, or as *café Kirsch*, when you can drink it alongside your black coffee or pleasingly pour it into the coffee. Kirsch is good with fruit, sprinkled on cake and dribbled over puddings and ice cream.

Like all strong potions, Kirsch, in the past far more so than at present, used to be considered a man's drink. This did not stop Swiss womanhood from liking it as well, which gave rise to a charming custom called a *canard*, or a duck. It consists of dunking a piece of sugar in a glass of Kirsch, which the lady then takes with her coffee. Husbands give a *canard* to their wives, boy friends to girl friends, and there are even special little receptacles for the ritual.

If there is anything I like even better than Kirsch, it is Williamine, an equally pure white firewater distilled from fragrant Williams pears. The Etter people make this, too, though an equally good variety, called Williams Pear Brandy, is made in the Valais, where the soil and climate produce pears more fragrant than any other. * Williamine has a pronounced smell and taste of pears, but sublimated pears. It reminds one of an orchard basking in the hot summer sun with the bees and wasps buzzing around, and of oneself lying in the grass under a pear tree, looking up at the dappled light and the blue sky above.

Very good too, though not quite as blissful, are the Pflümliwasser, also a strong white brandy distilled from plums, and the Bätziwasser. This is an applejack which is good when mellow, and the logical development of the cider which, both soft and hard, is a traditional rural Swiss drink.

Other Swiss spirits include those distilled from grape pressings—that is, the mass of skins and seeds left on the press after the juice has been extracted. In the Ticino, as

* The Etter Kirsch and the Williams Pear Brandy are imported to the United States by Dreyfus, Ashby & Co.

in northern Italy, it is called *grappa;* in the French-speaking cantons, as in France, *eau de vie de marc,* or simply *marc.* Unaged, it is on the rough side.

Today, both in town and country, the consumption of spirits and wine is no longer as great as in the last century. At one time drunkenness was sufficiently prevalent to have given rise to a temperance movement which is still active and which maintains good, inexpensive restaurants in all major Swiss cities. Nowadays life, even rural life, offers other stimulants than alcohol. Besides, people are better fed, so instinctively don't rely on drink as they once did. There is also the competition of soft drinks, including some very good grape juice and the usual carbonated soft drinks.

There is a category of spirits in Switzerland to which you have to be born to like them. These are strong herb-flavored liqueurs that are taken as an *apéritif* or after a meal because they are good at stimulating the appetite, help the digestion and promote radiant health in general. They are usually made from Alpine herbs and flowers, and strong-flavored ones at that, with a liberal dash of bitters thrown in for good measure. The best known are the Enzian, which is not distilled from the lovely blue Alpine gentians but from the roots of another variety, and the Appenzeller Alpenbitter, which manages to be sweet as well as bitter. Some brands boast that they are made from a hundred herbs; true or not, they certainly taste herbal like mad. The Swiss have an innocent, childlike faith in the salubrious properties of these potions. I happen to like them, perhaps because I met up with them in early youth. The reaction of most people is that the Swiss are welcome to them.

XI

———◄◆►———

———◄◆►———

Swiss Cheese

———◄◆►———

HOW SWISS CHEESE (EMMENTALER) IS MADE

WHEN YOU first see a Swiss cheese factory you are surprised by the smallness of the plant and the fact that the daily production of the big cheese wheels averages only from one to four cheeses. As it seemed odd to me that so efficient a country as Switzerland has not streamlined its cheese production, I asked Willi Bühlmann, an executive of the Swiss Cheese Union in Berne, to explain cheese to me. He did, as expounded in this chapter. Incidentally, the Cheese Union is not a labor union, but a manufacturers' association which, with government backing, keeps a strict eye on the strict execution of the strict laws that govern the making of Swiss cheese. The Cheese Union is largely responsible for the unfailing and continuous high quality of Switzerland's cheeses.

The excellence of Swiss cheese made in Switzerland does not depend only on the care with which it is made by experts trained for years in schools and in the trade. It depends also largely on the quality of the milk. The cows eat the good Alpine grasses fresh in the summer and as hay in the winter; the law prohibits feeding silage to cattle whose milk is used for cheese, since silage might affect the milk's flavor. Furthermore, the utter freshness of the milk is equally important for the taste of the cheese. This, in Switzerland, means that the milk destined for cheese must be put to the purpose at once, when its bacterial count is perfect, rather than being accumulated in large storage tanks, a necessity when the cheese factories are as large as in the United States. Unlike America, in Switzerland the distance from farm to cheese factory is small. This makes it possible to have the milk brought directly from farm to cheese plant twice daily, after milking in the evening and the early morning. There are no big milk trucks zooming about the countryside. In the Emmental you can see the charming sight of shiny milk cans sitting on little wagons that are pulled by huge, woolly, amiable St. Bernard dogs under the supervision of the dairy farmer's apple-cheeked children, after school at night and before school in the morning. This charming, archaic transportation makes quite a contrast to the supermodern equipment in the cheese factories, all shiny copper and stainless steel, with oceans of scalding-hot water to keep the plants spotless and free from any bacteria except those which belong in the cheese, or, rather, are necessary for making this or any cheese.

At the cheese plant the evening milk is poured into aluminum containers and left in a cool room overnight. The fresh morning milk plus the milk left overnight are poured into big copper vats, each of which holds about 350 to 400 gallons. The yield of a vat is between 200 to 250 pounds of cheese. It takes 12.5 parts of milk to produce 1 part of cheese—in other words, *1.6 gallons of milk to produce 1 pound of cheese.* By means of hot steam or hot water the contents of the vats are warmed to about 86 to 93°F. At this stage a certain amount of leavening ferment and a powder made of calf's rennet are added to the warm milk. The ferment completes the lactic-acid fermentation, while the rennet brings the milk to coagulate. After thirty minutes the milk has reached the right degree of coagulation. The cheese-maker tests it with a wooden ladle and then cuts the jellied mass crisscross with a tool called a cheese harp. The jellied pieces are then broken up with two wooden ladles, whereupon the cheese harp goes into action again until the pieces are of the size of a wheat kernel. After the cheese grains are of the desired size, the stirring is done automatically. Simultaneously with this automatic stirring, the contents of the vat are heated for approximately thirty minutes and brought to a temperature of about 120 to 130°F. This heating is necessary to make the grains more solid and compact and to extract as much water as possible. After another forty to sixty minutes the grains are dry enought to be pulled out.

At this point a cheesecloth is tied to a special instrument looking very much like a crossbow. The skill of the cheese-maker lies in the art of sliding the cheesecloth under the mass of young cheese to capture it in a first attempt. Then the four corners of the cloth are knotted together very solidly to prevent the grains from spilling. The young cheese is lifted up by a pulley and swung across the room to a wheel-like form.

In this wooden form the mass is pressed in order to eliminate a lot more liquid (whey) and to permit the cheese grains to grow together gradually. At this stage the fermentation by the lactic acid is completed. In the course of the day the young cheese is turned a couple of times, marked with the date of birth and transported to the salting cellar. The whey is used to feed pigs.

In the salting cellar the cheese is left in its wooden frame for another twenty-four hours, during which time it is continuously sprinkled with salt. The next day it is put into a saturated salt solution for about another forty-eight hours. The adding of salt is necessary for rind formation. The young cheese remains in the cool salting cellar for about fourteen days.

The next step is the fermentation cellar, where the temperature is kept between 72 and 79°F. The loaves stay in this room for six to ten weeks. Here another fermentation takes place—namely, the fermentation by propionic acid. Due to this ripening process some CO_2 gas becomes free within the cheese and collects and expands between the cheese grains, producing the famous holes or eyes within the cheese. This hole-forming process is over after about nine weeks, and the loaves are taken to a cooler cellar again, where they remain until they are ready for sale. A cheese is edible after about four months. Young cheese, in general, tastes rather flat, while six- to eight-month-old cheese is more flavorful than young cheese.

Those of my readers who have had the patience to read through the technicalities of cheese-making on the preceding pages, and on pages 126–133, will notice that no coloring matter is added to the cheese as annatto, a yellow vegetable dye, is added to Cheddar to make it golden. And those of my readers who have eaten their way through Switzerland Swiss cheese will have noticed that its color is not always uniform, being sometimes paler and sometimes more golden. As with farm-fresh butter, the color of Emmentaler depends on the milk, and this, again, on the cows' feed. When those belled beauties graze on Alpine grasses and flowers in the summer months, their milk will give a far yellower cheese than when they eat their winter hay.

For readers with orderly minds who may wonder why it would not be more practical to make square cheeses that would be so much easier to store: square cheeses do not ripen as well as round ones, the hole formation goes off balance and they don't taste as good.

What makes Switzerland Swiss cheese infinitely better and more expensive than similar varieties produced elsewhere is not only the inimitable milk of the Swiss Alps, but the custom-made way it is processed and the amount of handwork involved in this, such as in the salting and turning of the cheeses, and in their proper aging. This takes up expensive warehouse space and also requires a good deal of labor.

A SURVEY OF SWISS VARIETIES OF CHEESE

Original Swiss Cheeses Which Are Exported

EMMENTALER (*usually known as Swiss cheese in the U.S.*)

Emmentaler cheese derives its name from the Emmental Valley in the canton of Berne (pages 39). The name is known to have been in common use as early as the sixteenth century, but the character of the cheese has undergone many changes in the course of time. The cheese is now produced in every canton in German Switzerland. It is also the most copied cheese. As long ago as 1820 Swiss cheese-makers had established their craft abroad, particularly in such countries as France, Germany, Italy, Austria, Finland, Russia and the United States.

Emmentaler cheeses for export must weigh not less

than 145 pounds, but their weight is usually between 155 and 175 pounds and sometimes even more. The diameter of the wheels varies according to weight between 27 and 31 inches, and the height between 5 and 10 inches. The rind of the Emmentaler is dry and hard and ranges in color from golden yellow to brown. The cheese's flavor is reminiscent of walnuts or hazelnuts. The size of the holes or eyes varies between that of a cherry and a walnut. According to the regulations, the fat content in the solids must not be below 45 percent and is usually about 47 percent. The water content is 34 to 37 percent and is thus lower than in foreign imitations.

Emmentaler must be made from cow's milk free from any non-lactic additives. Only calf's rennet is used to coagulate the milk, which has already undergone preliminary treatment. Emmentaler is left to mature 3 to 4 months, but the maturing period can be extended to 8 to 10 months at the customer's request; older cheese is tastier.

GRUYÈRE

Gruyère cheese is called after the valley of the same name in the canton of Fribourg, but is also made in the cantons of Vaud, Neuchâtel and in the Bernese Jura as well as in the French Jura and the Savoy outside Switzerland. The manufacture and treatment are somewhat similar to those of Emmentaler. The following are the most important differences.

Gruyère is made in Alpine and in valley dairies, Emmentaler only in valley dairies.

Gruyère cheese wheels are smaller than Emmentaler, weighing between 45 and 110 pounds, but usually between 77 and 88 pounds.

The diameter of the cheese wheel varies between 16 and 25 inches, the height between 3.5 and 5 inches.

The curd is cut up into larger pieces, usually about the size of a hazelnut.

The whey is heated to approximately 135°F., but for a shorter time than with Emmentaler.

The cheese is subjected to more considerable pressing and cooling and is more liberally salted.

In the curing cellar the temperature is cooler—between 53 and 64°F.—which produces smaller eyes.

The rind is not dry, but slightly greasy, which brings about an additional maturing from the outside inward.

The flavor is similar, but is distinguished by a special smell.

The curing period is longer—about 8 months or even a year.

The prescribed fat content is also 45 percent, but usually varies between 47 and 49 percent; the water content is, however, somewhat lower than in Emmentaler.

The eyes are smaller and vary in size between a pea and a hazelnut. There are fewer of them.

Gruyère is known to have existed as early as the twelfth century, but has undergone various changes in the course of the centuries, although these have not been so great as in Emmentaler.

SBRINZ

The name Sbrinz probably relates to the place Brienz in the Bernese Oberland. It may well be that Sbrinz is the oldest Swiss hard cheese, for the Caseus Helveticus mentioned by the Roman writer Columella was probably a Sbrinz or one of its predecessors. The cheese from Argentina which is sold in the United States under this name is not a Sbrinz at all, but a variety of Parmesan.

Sbrinz somewhat resembles Gruyère, but differs in the following points:

The cheeses are much smaller, with a weight of only 45 to 100 pounds, a diameter of 20 to 27 inches and a height of 4 to 6 inches.

The curing period is 2 to 3 years. Consequently the cheese is very hard and therefore suitable for grating. The rind is dry but darker in color than Gruyère.

Eyes are entirely absent or are only the size of a pinhead.

The fat content is higher, varying between 47 and 50 percent.

The dealer stores the cheese vertically, not horizontally. After a year the rind is rubbed with linseed oil to prevent further evaporation and loss of weight. Young cheeses not yet suitable for grating must be sold not as Sbrinz but as Apalen cheese.

SCHABZIEGER OR GREEN CHEESE

Schabzieger or Glarus green cheese comes from the canton of Glarus in eastern Switzerland. In its present form the cheese has remained unchanged for five hundred years.

Schabzieger is made of skimmed cow's milk to which buttermilk may be added. The albumin is precipitated by heating to 92°C. (approximately 198°F.) and then left to a natural fermenting process, dried, milled and mixed with pulverized blue melilot (*Melilotus coerulea,* a plant) and then shaped into *Stöckli*—i.e., flat-topped cones. The blue melilot gives the cheese, which has no eyes or rind, its characteristic pungent flavor. Schabzieger is also marketed in powder form to be mixed with butter and used as a sandwich filling.

PROCESSED CHEESE

The processing of cheese was discovered in 1910 by Walter Gerber and Fritz Stettler after years of experiments, and for a long time remained the monopoly of Gerber & Co. in Thun (Berne). The inventors aimed at finding a form of cheese which would keep longer than Emmentaler; in this they were successful, and, gradually, processed cheese was imitated in most cheese-producing countries. In Switzerland the most usual base material for processed cheese is Emmentaler, but occasionally also Gruyère, Sbrinz, Tilsiter, Schabzieger and other cheeses are used. The triangular shape in which the portions are marketed and the addition of ham, spices and wine were first introduced in Switzerland.

Original Swiss Cheeses
Which Are Not Usually Exported
(Do not miss eating them when in Switzerland)

APPENZELL FULL-FAT CHEESE

Appenzell full-fat cheese derives its name from the canton of Appenzell in eastern Switzerland (page 37), but today it is manufactured also in increasing amounts in the cantons of St. Gall, Thurgau and Zurich. Probably the cheese was being made as early as in the days of Charlemagne.

Appenzell full-fat cheese is made only of whole cow's milk by a process similar to that for Tilsiter. The cheese is put into a solution of cider or white wine with spices added, but only for a few days or at the most a week. The cheese weighs from 15 to 22 pounds, and in all cases the fat content in solids is in excess of fifty percent. The rind and cheese are golden yellow, with few eyes and none larger than a pea. The flavor is very delicate.

APPENZELL RÄSS CHEESE

This variant form of Appenzell full-fat is distinguished by the fact that skim milk is used in the manufacture.

The cheese is put in spiced cider or spiced white wine for several weeks or even months. The fat content must not be below 20 percent. The cheeses weigh from 11 to 17 pounds, are from 10 to 18 inches in diameter and from 4.5 to 6 inches high. The color is gray, with numerous eyes the size of a pinhead. The flavor is extremely pungent.

VALAIS RACLETTE CHEESE

Raclette cheese is made only in the canton of Valais, and apart from its table use, it is employed principally for preparing *raclette,* a local dish made of melted cheese. It is also used in the Valais fondue. The cheeses weigh from 15 to 26 pounds. The fat content in all cases is in excess of 50 percent. In the curing cellar the temperature does not exceed 12 to 15°C. (53 to 59°F.). Three months are required to complete the curing.

FRIBOURG VACHERIN

This is a variant of Gruyère and is produced only in the canton of Fribourg. The cheeses weigh from approximately 15 to 25 pounds, are from 8 to 12 inches in diameter and from 3 to 4.5 inches in height. The manufacturing and cellaring processes differ somewhat from those for Gruyère. The fat content is in excess of 50 percent. The curd is not yellow but whitish. The cheese is used alone or mixed with Gruyère for making Fribourg fondue.

Vacherin is not to be confused with a meringue dessert of the same name.

BELLELAY CHEESE

Bellelay cheese or Tête de Moine was originally made only in the Abbey of Bellelay near Moutiers in the Bernese Jura, but today it is also manufactured in other local dairies. The cheeses usually weigh from 10 to 13 pounds, and more rarely up to 22 pounds, the diameter being between 6 and 8 inches. The rind is somewhat greasy. The cheeses take from 10 to 12 months to cure in a cold cellar. The fat content is over 50 percent. The cheese is exceptionally delicate in flavor.

SAANEN CHEESE

This variety of Gruyère is produced chiefly in the Saanen Valley in the Bernese Oberland. It is also known as Hobelkäse (plane cheese) because in the district of its origin a special cheese plane or else a ham-slicer is used to cut this very hard cheese. The cheese acquires this very hard texture during the curing period, which lasts at least 5 to 6 years. The cheese will subsequently keep for as long as 100 years. The cheeses are similar to Gruyère in weight and size.

VACHERIN DU MONT D'OR

This cheese is the only original soft cheese made in Switzerland. Vacherin du Mont d'Or is made exclusively in some twelve mountain dairies in Joux Valley (Vaud) from whole milk, but only in autumn. The cheeses weigh 9 to 11 pounds, are 8 to 12 inches in diameter and 2 to 3 inches in height. As the cheese tends to run after complete maturing, which takes 2.5 to 3 months, it is packed in a wooden box which withstands the cheese's moisture. The cheese exterior develops a red grease; the taste is mild and creamy. The commercial center is Lausanne. The marketing period ends with the beginning of the warmer weather. The fat content is in excess of 50 percent.

PIORA

Piora is exclusive to the canton of Ticino in Italian-speaking Switzerland, where three varieties are produced. Vero Piora is made exclusively from whole cow's milk on the Alp Piora in the north of the canton; Tipo Piora likewise of cow's milk on other Alps in the canton; and Uso Piora from a mixture of cow's and goat's milk. The manufacturing and cellaring processes are the same for all three varieties. Vero Piora fetches the highest prices. The cheeses weigh 22 to 44 pounds, but usually 26 pounds. The fat content is in excess of 50 percent. The curing period is 4 to 6 months. The cheese is soft to cut, like Tilsiter, and delicate in flavor.

TOGGENBURGER CHEESE

Toggenburger of Blöder cheese is made exclusively on the Alps of the St. Gall Toggenburg, and in the Werdenberg district, and in the principality of Liechtenstein. It is the only Swiss sour-milk cheese. The skim milk used is allowed to set for from 48 to 72 hours so as to curdle of its own accord. The curd is placed in square or round molds. The curing period in a cold cellar takes 6 to 9 months. The fat content varies greatly, the albumin content from 40 to 42 percent and the water content from 46 to 50 percent. The curd is white and granular. The cheese does not develop a true rind, but what is called a *Speckschicht*, or layer of fat. Toggenburger is eaten only where it is produced, chiefly by the makers, whose principal income from dairy farming is provided by the butter they make.

Imitations of Foreign-Type Cheeses

Besides the original Swiss cheeses, exported or not, Switzerland produces a certain number of Reblochon, Gervais, Limburger, Romadour and Bel Paese cheeses, and especially Tilsiter, introduced as early as 1896 by the Swiss cheese-maker Wegmüller from East Prussia.

Note

All recipes in the following pages will make four to six servings unless otherwise specified.

XII

Appetizers

THE KIND of tidbits Americans call appetizers and hors d'oeuvres and serve with drinks are not part of Swiss living, for the simple reason that the Swiss are not a cocktail-drinking nation. Aside from the few who try to live like Americans, the Swiss will serve an apéritif or a simple gin cocktail before a meal, with the simplest of accompaniments. These might be nuts or a canapé or a cheese thing or potato chips. But a great many Swiss, especially outside the big cities, will sit down to their meal without any preliminaries.

Hors d'oeuvres served as a meal's first course resemble French, Italian and all the known varieties, and they are part of restaurant rather than home eating. At home the meal most likely begins with soup, or a salad of tossed fresh greens, or fruit in a coupe, though this is an imported American habit that the Swiss are taking up because it is healthful.

Elaborate cooked or open-faced sandwiches are eaten as snacks, or they are served for an evening party. They are frequently glazed with a meat aspic, bought in gelatin form and beautifully decorated with vegetable cut-outs.

HEIDI'S CHEESE APPETIZERS

Mash together equal quantities of sweet butter and Roquefort or Danish blue cheese. Sandwich a little of the mixture between 2 walnut halves. Chill before serving.

FRIED CHEESE BALLS

Käsekugeln

A good hot hors d'oeuvre or appetizer.

2¾ cups grated Swiss cheese	1 teaspoon salt
½ cup all-purpose flour	¼ teaspoon pepper
2 eggs, well beaten	⅛ teaspoon nutmeg
1 egg yolk	fat for deep frying
	parsley

Combine the grated cheese, flour, eggs, egg yolk, salt, pepper and nutmeg. Work into a stiff paste; if necessary, add a little more flour, one tablespoon at a time. With a melon cutter or a teaspoon, shape into balls. Fry in deep fat at 380° (on thermometer) for 6 minutes or until golden brown. Drain well on paper towels. Garnish with parsley. As a main dish, serve with a favorite sauce. Serves 4 as a main dish.

CHEESE MEDALLIONS

Käse Medaillon

Serve as an appetizer or with a tossed salad.

¾ cup finely grated Swiss cheese	12 3-inch rounds of Tilsiter cheese
¼ cup heavy cream, whipped	6 ¼-inch slices of tomato
1 tablespoon horseradish	salad greens or spears of Belgian endive
¼ teaspoon paprika	

Combine the cheese, whipped cream, horseradish and paprika. Spread the mixture on 6 rounds of Tilsiter cheese. Top with the remaining Tilsiter cheese rounds. Then top each medallion with a slice of tomato. Place on salad greens or endive spears. Makes 6 medallions.

CHEESE SPREAD

Beurre au Fromage

1 cup grated Swiss cheese   *salt*
¼ cup heavy cream   *pepper*
½ cup butter   *dash of nutmeg*
2 tablespoons Kirsch,
*   brandy or dry white*
*   wine*

Combine the cheese and the cream and beat them until the mixture is smooth and fluffy. Cream the butter with the Kirsch. Combine the two mixtures and add salt and pepper to taste and the nutmeg. Beat until very smooth. Chill before using. Makes about 1¼ cups.

Variations: Finely chopped chives, or crushed aniseed to taste, may be added to the spread.

CHEESE TARTLETS

Ramequins

Traditional. Excellent as appetizers or snacks. Serve the tartlets with a well-chilled Côte or Neuchâtel wine.

pie dough or puff pastry   *¼ teaspoon salt*
*   for 16 tartlet pans*   *¼ teaspoon dry mustard*
2 cups grated Swiss cheese   *⅛ teaspoon cayenne*
1 cup heavy cream   *   pepper*
2 eggs

Line 2-inch tartlet pans with pie dough or puff pastry. Beat together the cheese, cream, eggs, salt, mustard and cayenne pepper. Spoon the mixture into the lined tartlet pans; each should be about half full. Bake in a preheated hot oven (400°) for 15 minutes, or until golden brown. Makes about 16 tartlets.

HEIDI'S DEVIL'S DIP

Heidi's Teufel Dip

½ cup mayonnaise
   (preferably homemade)
½ cup heavy cream,
   whipped
¼ cup minced prosciutto

2 tablespoons minced
   parsley
½ teaspoon Dijon
   mustard, or more to
   taste
½ teaspoon lemon juice

Combine all the ingredients and mix well. Serve as a dip or spread on dark pumpernickel slices. Makes about ⅔ cup.

POTATO BALLS WITH CHEESE

Kartoffelkugeln mit Käse

Traditional.

1¾ pounds potatoes,
   peeled and cubed
boiling salted water
4 egg yolks, well beaten
6 tablespoons all-purpose
   flour

2 cups grated Swiss cheese
1 teaspoon salt
⅛ teaspoon nutmeg
fat or oil for deep frying

Cover the potatoes with boiling salted water and cook until they are tender. Drain, and press them through a sieve or a food mill. Cool the potatoes. Beat in the eggs, flour, grated cheese, salt and nutmeg. In a frying kettle heat the fat to 380°. With two spoons, shape the potato mixture into balls the size of a walnut and drop directly into the hot fat. Wet the spoons occasionally to prevent sticking. Fry the potato balls 2 to 3 minutes or until golden brown. Drain on paper towels. Spear on toothpicks and serve hot as an appetizer. Makes 50 to 60 potato balls.

HEIDI'S STUFFED RAW MUSHROOM CAPS

Heidi's Champignons

6 anchovies, drained and mashed

1 3-ounce package cream cheese

1 cup finely diced prosciutto

2 tablespoons minced parsley

about 30 1-inch mushroom caps

capers

Mix the anchovies and cream cheese. Blend in the prosciutto and parsley. Wash the mushroom caps very briefly under running cold water. Pat them dry immediately with a towel. Stuff the caps with the cheese mixture. Garnish each cap with a few capers. Serve as an appetizer. Makes about 2½ dozen stuffed mushroom caps.

PATTY SHELLS WITH CHEESE

Feuilleté Jurassien

Traditional.

2 tablespoons butter	*½ teaspoon Dijon mustard*
2 tablespoons flour	*1 cup shredded or grated*
1 cup light cream, heated	*Gruyère cheese*
salt	*6 baked puff-paste patty*
pepper	*shells, not frozen*

Melt the butter, then stir in the flour. Cook, stirring constantly, until smooth. Stir in the cream, salt, pepper and Dijon mustard. Cook until the sauce is smooth and thickened. Keep the sauce hot. Remove from heat and stir in the cheese. Heat the baked patty shells in a preheated hot oven (400°) for 3 minutes. Spoon a little of the cheese sauce into each shell. Return to the hot oven for a few minutes or until the tops are golden brown. Serve as appetizers, or as a luncheon dish with a salad of green beans. Serves 6.

SAUSAGE ROLLS

Schüblingwecken

Traditional, served primarily on Sylvester (New Year's Eve).

2 cups all-purpose flour	*¼ cup ice water*
½ teaspoon salt	*(approximately)*
½ cup butter	*24 cocktail frankfurters*

Sift the flour and salt together. Cut in the butter until the particles are the size of small peas. Add ice water gradually, stirring with a fork until the dough cleans the bowl. Knead lightly. Roll out on a lightly floured board to ⅛-inch thickness. Cut into squares large enough to roll around the cocktail frankfurters. Wrap the frankfurters in the dough. Pinch the ends together. Prick with a fork. Bake in a preheated hot oven (400°) for 10 to 15 minutes. Serve hot. Makes 24 servings.

XIII

Salads

O NE OF the most pleasing sights in a good Swiss restaurant is the salad cart, with its assortment of
tender, crisp and extremely fresh salad greens. These
include all kinds of lettuce, including some we don't
know in America, watercress, and any vegetable that can
be eaten raw. From these promising ingredients, each
diner constructs his own salad.

Fresh uncooked salads have always been a basic part of
Swiss eating, in town and country alike, and long before
vitamins were called that. And they still are basic, more
so than ever.

A diet that includes so much starch—in the form of
Hörnli, potatoes, and pancakes—needs other dishes to
pep up the carbohydrates. Hence not only the raw salads, but the cooked ones made from vegetables, meats
and anything that tastes good with a piquant sauce, or
with herbs, and so on.

Each of the following recipes will make 4 to 6 servings.

GREEN BEAN SALAD

Grüner Bohnensalat

Traditional and very popular in all of Switzerland.

1½ pounds green beans
boiling salted water
½ cup olive oil
2 to 3 tablespoons vinegar,
*   or more to taste*
salt
pepper
1 teaspoon prepared
*   mustard*

1 medium onion, minced
*   or thinly sliced*
2 tablespoons parsley
1 teaspoon dried tarragon
*   and/or chervil, or 1*
*   tablespoon fresh*
*   tarragon and/or chervil*
*   (optional)*

Cook the beans in boiling salted water until they are tender but still crisp. Make a dressing with the oil, vinegar, salt, pepper, mustard, onion and parsley. Drain the cooked beans and put them in a bowl. While they are still hot, toss with the dressing. (If the beans are allowed to cool, the salad will not be as flavorful.) Add the herbs, if desired. Let stand at room temperature for 2 hours. Do not chill.

MOTHER'S CHEESE SALAD

Käsesalat nach Hausmütterchen Art

2 cups cubed Swiss cheese
2 cups cubed cooked
*   potatoes*
2 cups diced celery
1 cup mayonnaise
1 tablespoon prepared
*   mustard*

1 tablespoon
*   Worcestershire sauce*
salad greens
½ cup coarsely chopped
*   blanched almonds or*
*   walnuts*

Combine the cheese, potatoes and celery. Blend the mayonnaise with the mustard and Worcestershire sauce. Add to the cheese mixture and blend well. Line a flat dish with salad greens. Pile the cheese salad on it in a mound. Sprinkle with the nuts.

HEIDI'S POTATO SALAD

Heidi's Kartoffelsalat

This salad must not be chilled, but served at room temperature.

12 medium potatoes
beef or chicken broth to cover
⅓ cup dry white wine
1 to 2 tablespoons wine vinegar, or more to taste
⅓ cup olive oil
1 teaspoon salt

½ teaspoon freshly ground pepper
1 to 2 tablespoons capers, drained and chopped (optional)
⅓ cup finely chopped parsley

Scrub the potatoes with a stiff brush under running water. Put them into a deep kettle, and cover with beef or chicken broth. Bring to a boil. Reduce heat and simmer about 15 to 25 minutes (depending on the kind of potatoes) or until tender. Drain and peel. While still warm (this is very important), slice the potatoes into a bowl and sprinkle them with the wine. Cool to room temperature. Combine the vinegar, olive oil, salt and pepper. Sprinkle this mixture over the potatoes, and toss carefully with a fork. Do not break the slices. Before serving, sprinkle with the capers and parsley.

HOT ONION SALAD FROM ZURICH

Heisser Zwiebelsalat

Traditional.

4 large onions	*ground pepper*
½ cup bacon fat or beef	*1 tablespoon all-purpose*
drippings	*flour*
1 ½ teaspoons salt	*2 tablespoons wine*
½ teaspoon freshly	*vinegar, or more to taste*

Peel the onions and cut them horizontally into ¼-inch slices. Over medium heat, cook the onions in the melted fat until they are soft and golden, but not brown. The onions must cook, *not* fry. Drain off the fat. Season the onions with salt and pepper. Sprinkle with the flour and vinegar. Toss with a fork. Cook, stirring constantly with a fork, for 2 to 3 minutes. Do not break the onion rings. Serve hot with roasted or broiled meats.

ONIONS IN VINAIGRETTE SAUCE

Oignons Vinaigrette

boiling water	*1 inch beef consommé*
30 small white onions	*vinaigrette sauce*

Pour boiling water over the unpeeled onions and let stand 5 minutes. Drain. Peel the onions and cook them in the consommé—there should be 1 inch of it in the saucepan. (If consommé is not available, dissolve 1 bouillon cube in 1 cup boiling water and add.) Bring to the boiling point and cook uncovered for 5 minutes. Cover, and continue cooking for 15 minutes or until the onions are crisp in texture but tender when pierced with a fork. Drain, and add vinaigrette sauce.

VINAIGRETTE SAUCE

2 tablespoons fresh lemon
   juice
2 tablespoons cider vinegar
1 clove garlic, chopped
¾ teaspoon salt
⅛ teaspoon ground black
   pepper
1 tablespoon sugar
¾ cup salad oil

1 tablespoon chopped
   green pepper
1 tablespoon chopped
   parsley
1 tablespoon chopped
   cucumber pickles
2 tablespoons chopped
   pimiento
1 tablespoon chopped
   capers

Combine all ingredients. Stir vigorously before serving. Serve over the braised onions.

GYPSY SALAD

Zigeunersalat

1 cup drained canned small
   sweet peas
2 cups diced cooked
   potatoes
¼ pound cervelat sausage
   or hard salami, cut into
   thin strips
½ pound sliced Swiss
   cheese, cut into strips

½ cup sliced gherkins
1 cup French dressing
salad greens
1 can flat anchovy
   fillets, drained
3 hard-cooked eggs,
   quartered
3 tomatoes, thinly sliced

Mix the peas with the potatoes, cervelat, cheese and gherkins. Toss with the French dressing. Pile on a platter lined with salad greens. Decorate with the anchovy fillets, eggs and tomato slices.

Note: This salad may also be served in large, scooped-out tomatoes. In this case, omit the tomato-slice garnish.

XIV

Soups

IF I WERE ASKED to single out the one dish that is essential to Swiss living, this dish would be soup. Without soup, the Swiss could not exist. A Swiss family eats soup for supper three, four or more times every week; the soup *is* supper, since the only accompaniments are bread and a bit of cheese, maybe some jam or stewed fruit, and the ubiquitous *Milchkaffee*—coffee with hot milk—that is considered a food rather than a drink. Very often, too, soup will be served as the first course of the main meal of the day at noon. When I asked a number of Swiss people if they did not mind eating soup twice in one day, they looked at me in surprise and said not at all; for one thing, they did not eat the same kind of soup at each meal and, furthermore, without soup a meal would not be a meal.

Except for formal meals, Swiss soups are meant to be hunger appeasers, not appetite titillators. In the old days, as in all European peasant communities, soup was the mainstay of Swiss life, and what we would call a well-balanced meal-in-a-dish, such as the French *pot-au-feu* so popular in Switzerland, is to this day. These "soups" contained vegetables and meat in some form, such as sausage, bacon or smoked meats when fresh meat was not available; the meat was served with the vegetables alongside the soup. But today's Swiss soups no longer simmer for hours at the back of the stove, and the tourist in search of quaint old dishes will be surprised to find soup cubes and packaged soups in the simple kitchens of the most remote Alpine villages.

Switzerland is the country that invented packaged soups, and it perfects them by constantly bringing out new varieties, the number of which staggers the foreigner. Maggi and Knorr are the chief manufacturers, and they run a merry neck-to-neck race to capture the national soup pot with their bouillon cubes, their cubed soups (such as pea) that are simply dropped into boiling water, and their dehydrated soups, all of which can be prepared in less than fifteen minutes. The credit for these soups goes to Julius Maggi, a flour miller.

The inventive Mr. Maggi—and he was a truly remarkable man, well ahead of his time in food matters—noticed in the 1880's the toll the Industrial Revolution was taking of Swiss cooking and the nation's health. Women, who in earlier times had cooked the vitamin-rich, substantial soups that held body and soul together, now worked for long hours in the factories and had little time for their cooking. Maggi succeeded in creating a mixture of ingredients based on flour and seasonings, the ancestor of the Swiss soup cube (as distinguished from the bouillon cube). Later on he perfected a complete dehydrated soup mix which evolved into the soups sold in bags. Julius Maggi also invented the world-famous Maggi seasoning. In the 1880's or so, he managed to extract the flavor essences from a variety of natural grains, and to blend them into an all-purpose liquid flavoring, the first of its kind. This Maggi flavoring became famous all over the world, for, when used in moderation, it is an excellent strengthener of many dishes. But if used too lavishly, as it is in much of Swiss cooking, it makes everything taste the same, as do its various competitors.

All of these ready-to-cook soups are sold in enormous quantities and, as I said, incredible variety, so that the soup-eating Swiss won't get bored. Both Maggi and Knorr have fine, up-to-date, enormous factories which are well worth visiting; they welcome visitors. Tourist offices will tell you how to do this. Both firms promote their products with a vim and a gusto that often make American promotional efforts seem like undernourished violets. They have their own cooking schools, and a flow of excellent recipes for everyone from gourmets to eighth-grade home-economics students, beautifully printed and almost always for free.

The Swiss are a practical people, and the universal appeal of the various prepared soups lies in their saving of time and trouble and their economy. The soups are not only inexpensive but also require little fuel. These qualities, together with the soups' good taste, are irresistible to the thrifty Swiss. To make them taste even better, Swiss cooks add all sorts of refinements such as butter, eggs, cream, fresh herbs, etc.

The original Swiss soups, as I have said, were either substantial one-dish meals or they emerged as an offspring of the gruels made from oats, barley and wheat flour that were standard fare in the olden days. In the land of cheese, the various cantons also developed their own varieties of cheese soup. In its original form, this was usually a thick porridge of stale bread or flour and cheese, cooked with milk or broth, and, frequently, topped with a sauce of onions sautéed in butter. These soups are no longer eaten in the cities, but they are still found in the more remote rural households, especially in the Grisons. The fact that these nonliquid dishes are called soups stems from the use of the word "soup" in Italian, where it means a dish eaten before the main course, and where "dry" soups and soups "in broth" are distinguished. Among the old-fashioned soups that remain popular is the brown flour soup from Basle, a specialty consumed in huge quantities during Carnival, the Basle equivalent of Mardi Gras.

Most homemade Swiss soups resemble German, French, or Italian soups. There is a stress on binding them with flour or egg and cream to thicken them, but bouillon, cauliflower, spinach, lentil, bean and other soups are really not sufficiently different to list them in this book of Swiss specialties. Thus, the recipes that follow are soups of a truly national character. They will make 4 to 6 servings, depending on whether the soup is a main course or the introduction to a meal.

BREAD-AND-CHEESE SOUP FROM THE GRISONS

Käsesuppe

Traditional, and nonliquid.

6 slices firm white bread	*1½ cups hot beef bouillon*
1¼ cups grated Gruyère cheese	*⅓ cup dry white wine*
	2 tablespoons butter

Cut the bread into small cubes. Butter a 1½-quart casserole. Measure 1 cup of the cheese and reserve the rest. Put alternate layers of bread and the 1 cup of cheese into the casserole. Combine the beef bouillon and wine. Pour over the bread and cheese. Dot the top with the butter and sprinkle with the remaining cheese. Bake in preheated moderate oven (350°) for 20 to 25 minutes. Serve with salad or stewed fruit and *Milchkaffee* (*café au lait*). Makes 2 to 3 servings.

BROWNED-FLOUR SOUP FROM BASLE

Basler Mehlsuppe

Traditional. This soup, part of the famous Basle Carnival, is eaten early in the morning, after the first masked parade, which starts at 4:00 a.m. But very similar browned-flour soups are found in other parts of Switzerland, and they go back to the Middle Ages. Swiss people love them, and though my view is somewhat skeptical, they are part of Swiss eating to this day.

7 tablespoons butter	*1 medium onion stuck*
6 tablespoons flour	*with 5 cloves*
7 to 8 cups hot water	*1 bay leaf*
	salt

Melt 6 tablespoons of the butter in a heavy saucepan. Stir in the flour. Cook the butter and flour together over medium heat, stirring constantly with a wooden spoon, until the mixture is smooth and the color of chocolate. This takes about 7 to 10 minutes. Do not let the mixture scorch. Remove from heat and gradually add the hot water, stirring constantly until the mixture is smooth. Add the onion, the bay leaf, and salt to taste. Simmer over the lowest possible heat, stirring occasionally, for 1 hour. Remove the onion and bay leaf before serving. Stir in the remaining 1 tablespoon of butter.

Note: Some Swiss cooks add 1 teaspoon tomato paste to the soup, others 1 or 2 tablespoons of dry Madeira, and others a little grated Swiss cheese.

CABBAGE-AND-RICE
SOUP FROM SCHWYZ

Kabissuppe

Traditional. A very pleasant soup, typical of the cabbage-and-rice soups found in other cantons.

1 small cabbage	*pepper*
1 large onion, thinly sliced	*⅛ teaspoon nutmeg*
2 tablespoons butter	*½ cup rice*
6 cups beef or chicken	*grated Gruyère or*
bouillon	*Parmesan cheese*
salt	

Shred the cabbage as for coleslaw. Wash and shake dry. Combine the cabbage, onion and butter in a 3- to 4-quart kettle. Cook covered over low heat until the cabbage is golden and half cooked. Stir frequently. Add the beef or chicken bouillon. Season with salt and pepper to taste; add nutmeg. Simmer covered for 10 minutes. Add the rice. Continue simmering until the rice is tender. Serve with grated cheese.

LENTEN CHEESE SOUP
FROM EINSIEDELN

Einsiedler Käsesuppe und Fastenspeise

Traditional. Einsiedeln is a magnificent baroque abbey, and one of the great Catholic shrines of Switzerland. This soup is a good example of old European lenten fare, and it makes a good hot dish for a cold summer meal or for a quick pre-theater supper.

1 long loaf crusty French
   or Italian bread, cubed
2 teaspoons salt
2 to 4 cups water

3 tablespoons butter, or
   more as needed
1½ cups grated Swiss
   cheese
2 onions, thinly sliced

Sprinkle the bread cubes with the salt. Add water to cover the bread. Cover and let stand at room temperature for 15 to 20 minutes or until the bread has absorbed most of the water. Drain off the excess water. Melt 1 tablespoon of the butter in a saucepan (add more if necessary). Add the soaked bread. Chop with a fork or potato masher until the bread is smooth. Cook over low heat, stirring constantly. Add the grated cheese a little at a time, stirring after each addition. Simmer for 10 minutes after the last addition, stirring occasionally. Sauté the onions in 2 tablespoons butter until tender. Sprinkle the sautéed onions over the soup. In the old days, this thick soup was served with boiled potatoes on the side.

COUNTRY SOUP FROM THE TICINO

Zuppa del Paes

Traditional.

For each serving:
1 cup beef broth
2 tablespoons butter
1 slice bread

1 egg
1 tablespoon tomato purée
1 tablespoon grated
   Parmesan cheese

Place each cup of beef broth in a small casserole. Melt the butter in a small skillet, and brown the bread on both sides. Place the bread in the beef broth. Break the egg on top of the bread. Spoon the tomato purée over the egg.

Sprinkle with the grated cheese. Simmer over low heat until the egg is set. Serve hot in the casserole.

FRESH MUSHROOM BISQUE

Bisque aux Champignons

¼ cup butter
¼ pound fresh
  mushrooms, sliced
⅓ cup finely chopped
  onion
1 garlic clove, minced
1 tablespoon fresh lemon
  juice

3 tablespoons flour
4 cups chicken consommé
2 teaspoons salt
¼ teaspoon ground black
  pepper
2 cups heavy cream
chopped parsley

Heat the butter and sauté the mushrooms, onion and garlic for 4 to 5 minutes, stirring constantly. Sprinkle with the lemon juice. Blend in the flour. Gradually stir in the consommé and salt and pepper. Cook, stirring constantly, until the mixture is slightly thickened. Stir in the cream and heat thoroughly. Sprinkle with parsley and serve immediately.

OATMEAL SOUP

Hafersuppe

Traditional.

½ cup oatmeal
1 teaspoon salt
½ cup butter
4 to 6 cups water or
  consommé
  (approximately)

2 potatoes, peeled and cut
  into thin slices
2 cups (8 ounces) grated
  Emmentaler cheese
sprinkle of nutmeg
  (optional)

Sauté the oatmeal and salt in half the butter until golden brown. Add the water. Bring to a boil. Cook over low heat, stirring occasionally and adding additional water if necessary, until the oatmeal is cooked into a gruel. This will take about 1½ hours. Add the sliced potatoes. Cook another 30 minutes until the potatoes are tender. Stir in the grated cheese, the remaining butter, and the nutmeg if desired. Add additional hot water if too thick.

SWISS ONION SOUP

Soupe à l'Oignon

Traditional.

6 large onions, finely chopped	½ pound Swiss cheese, grated
½ cup butter	6 slices stale bread, cubed
4 cups milk	salt
2 cups water	pepper
	½ teaspoon paprika

Cook the onions in the butter until they are soft but still white; do not brown them. Stir in the milk and the water. Bring to a slow boil. Add the grated cheese, the bread, salt and pepper to taste, and the paprika. Simmer, covered, over the lowest possible heat for 20 minutes, stirring occasionally.

Note: I have substituted saffron for the paprika with excellent results.

PETITE MARMITE

6 carrots, peeled and sliced	3 tablespoons salt
3 leeks, sliced (use both white and green parts)	½ teaspoon whole black peppercorns
3 white turnips, peeled and quartered	½ teaspoon ground thyme
2½ pounds beef shin	½ teaspoon ground marjoram
2½ pounds soup bones	1 bay leaf
2½ pounds chicken wings and necks	1 quart shredded cabbage
3 quarts cold water	grated Parmesan cheese
	French bread

Place the first twelve ingredients in a large soup kettle. Cover, bring to a full boil, reduce heat and simmer slowly 3½ hours. Skim as necessary. Take out the chicken pieces; remove the meat from the bones, and return the meat to the soup. Add the shredded cabbage; cook another 10 minutes. Serve hot with grated Parmesan cheese and crusty French bread. Makes approximately 4 quarts.

WHITE POTATO SOUP

Weisse Kartoffelsuppe

This basic soup is made everywhere. It is quick and very good.

2 cups peeled and cubed potatoes (cubes should be about ¼ inch in size)	6 cups hot water, or bouillon, or vegetable broth
2 medium onions, thinly sliced	salt
2 tablespoons butter	pepper
	¼ cup chopped parsley

Combine the potatoes, onions and butter in a heavy saucepan. Cover tightly. Over the lowest possible heat, stirring frequently, cook until the potatoes are half done. Add the liquid. Season with salt and pepper to taste. Simmer covered until the potatoes are tender. Sprinkle with parsley.

Variations: Add 1 or 2 thinly sliced leeks (using both the white and green parts) to the potatoes and onions, and increase the butter by 1 tablespoon. Proceed as directed.

Add 1 thinly sliced medium carrot and ½ thinly sliced stalk celery to the soup together with the liquid.

Add a handful of any fresh vegetable, such as shelled green peas, frenched string beans, fresh lima beans or cubed yellow or zucchini squash at the same time with the liquid.

VEGETABLE-AND-TRIPE SOUP FROM THE TICINO

Busecca

Traditional, substantial, and tasty. The original soup is from Lombardy, the Italian province (with Milan as its capital) with which the Ticino is closely related in dialect and customs.

¼ pound lean bacon,
cubed

3 tablespoons butter

1 medium onion, chopped

2 cloves garlic, mashed

2 leeks, chopped (both
white and green parts)

½ cup chopped celery

2 tablespoons chopped
parsley

1 cup white turnip cubes
(about ½-inch cubes)

2 cups chopped cabbage
(preferably savoy
cabbage)

½ cup dried pea beans or
white kidney beans,
soaked overnight

3 tomatoes, peeled and
chopped

1 pound precooked tripe,
cut into julienne strips

8 to 10 cups hot water

2 teaspoons salt

½ teaspoon pepper

1 cup cubed potatoes
(about ½-inch cubes)

1 cup grated Sbrinz or
Romano cheese

In a deep kettle, cook the bacon until it is crisp but not brown. Add the butter. Sauté the onion, garlic, leeks, celery, parsley, turnip and cabbage in hot fat until the vegetables are limp and soft. Drain the beans. Add to the vegetables with the tomatoes, tripe, water, salt and pepper. Cover tightly. Simmer about 1½ hours or until the beans are tender. Add the potatoes. Cook an additional 20 minutes or until the potatoes are tender. Serve hot, sprinkled with cheese. Makes 8 servings.

XV

Fish

THE CHARM OF Swiss fish lies in the fish itself rather than in intricate ways of cooking it. Though Swiss lakes and rivers have an abundance of fish, it has never become a staple food as in other countries, but has remained a prize delicacy.

Generally speaking, Swiss fish is delicate and deliciously flavored. Swiss fish cookery brings out these qualities rather than disguising them with heavy frying or saucing. Depending on variety and size, the fish is sautéed in butter, fried in oil, poached and sauced, or baked with herbs and wine. The sauces remain on the simple side. Or, for elegant meals, a whole fish is served cold, under a blanket of aspic or mayonnaise, with pretty decorations of cooked vegetables cut into fancy shapes.

Most Swiss fish cookery does not differ very much from French fish cookery. Naturally, it is more limited since Swiss fish is, by definition, fresh-water fish, although salt-water seafood of all kinds is becoming more common in Switzerland in this age of refrigeration and fast transportation. Like all fish cookery, the recipes that follow are adaptable to different fish that resemble each other in taste, texture and size.

There really is not a great deal of difference in the taste of the various Swiss fish, with the exceptions of pike, carp and eel. All the other delicate lake and river fish have about the same sweet taste. What makes them superlative is their incredible freshness. In Switzerland the fish you get in the restaurants seems to have really leaped from water to table!

Though few of the Swiss fish are native to American waters, I list the best known for reference so that travelers won't miss them when in Switzerland. Along all the Swiss lakes and rivers there are excellent fish restaurants, matching the local fish with the local wine. The pleasure of sitting on a sunny terrace overlooking water sparkling against mountains, with a carafe of wine on the table, is not to be underestimated, not at all.

Äsche: A kind of trout, caught in the Rhine and other rivers in the fall and winter.

Agone (eel): Eels exist all over Switzerland, but the best-known variety is the small, 6- to-8-inch-long *agone* of Lake Lugano, which is usually cooked in a piquant fashion.

Egli, Perche (perch): A delicate fresh-water fish, excellent as fillets.

Felchen, Fera, Bondelles or *Ballen:* A fish with firm white flesh, found in a number of sizes and varieties in all Swiss lakes.

Forellen, Truites, Trote (trout): These appear on all Swiss menus, mostly cooked *au bleu.* The best trout—and the rarest ones—are those caught in swift, cold mountain streams. Most trout are bred, however, and, though good, they are not as tasty as the wild ones. There are also large trout that live in the lakes and in the Rhine.

XV (*Fish*)

Hecht, Brochet (pike): No different from ours, but far more highly valued.

Rötel: This red-bellied lake fish, a lovely and distant cousin of the trout, is also a fall and winter fish. It is caught only in Lake Zug and the nearby Ägeri See, a mountain lake.

Omble Chevalier: A kind of salmon trout and a very fine fish, caught under this name in Lake Geneva.

BLUE TROUT AND COOKING "AU BLEU"

Truite au Bleu

Traditional, superlative, and probably the national fish dish of Switzerland, to be found on every menu.

In order to cook a trout so that it becomes blue, it is absolutely essential to have fish that have been killed only seconds before cooking. In Switzerland all good restaurants have a tank full of living trout, which are taken out when needed. In America, alas, this best of all fish dishes is available only to people who catch their own trout. Once they've tried cooking *au bleu,* they'll never dip another trout in cornmeal and sauté it in butter or bacon fat; no other way of cooking fish so preserves its essential goodness.

The reason the trout or any fish suitable for cooking *au bleu* must have been killed only seconds before going into the kettle is the following: The fish have a protective coating all over their bodies, and it is this coating that the vinegar in the cooking water and the cooking process itself turn blue. This protective coating dries out very quickly when the dead fish is stored, even if it is refrigerated or kept on ice. For this reason, too, fish that is to be cooked *au bleu* must be handled as little as

(*161*)

possible, so that the coating will not rub off.

All delicate, white-fleshed fish can be cooked *au bleu*. The fish is poached, rather than boiled, in a court-bouillon—that is, a mixture of vinegar, water, spices, and even vegetables and wine.

Large whole fish, weighing over 3 to 4 pounds, are put into a cold court-bouillon, which is brought to a boil. Cooking time, depending on size and fish, is about 10 to 15 minutes to the pound, or until the fish flakes when tested with a toothpick or a fork. A fish cooker is a worthwhile investment if one aims to cook many large fish. Otherwise a deep roasting pan will do. In this case, wrap the fish in a triple layer of cheesecloth, leaving enough cheesecloth on either side to make two handles which can hang outside the cooking vessel. This makes it easier to lift out a whole large fish without breaking it. Unwrap the fish carefully.

Small fish, such as trout—the fish most commonly cooked in this way—are also cooked in a court-bouillon. But they are put into a hot one, and poached just long enough to cook them through, about 4 to 5 minutes for an average 1-pound fish. A good way of doing this is to bring the court-bouillon to a boil and then remove it from the heat. Next, the fish is put into the liquid. The pot with the fish is then put over the lowest possible heat, so that the liquid barely simmers as the fish cooks. Very small fish may be put into the hot liquid when it has been removed from the heat and allowed to stand, covered, for a few minutes, depending on size. Again, easy flaking is the test for doneness.

Big fish that are to be served cold are best cooled in their cooking liquid. Small fish are better taken out of it or they may soften. Again, and it cannot be repeated too often: do not overcook the fish. And the general idea is *never* to have the fish in a violently boiling liquid, but in one that barely simmers.

A fish cooked *au bleu* is served on a dish lined with a linen napkin that will absorb the excess moisture and keep the fish firm and warm. It may be bent into the shape of a U—the classical way of serving blue trout.

SIMPLE COURT-BOUILLON FOR "AU BLEU" FISH COOKERY

Amounts can be doubled, tripled, etc. This quantity will cook 4 medium trout.

2 quarts water	*1 tablespoon salt*
1 cup cider or mild vinegar	*6 to 8 peppercorns*
2 bay leaves	

Combine the ingredients in a saucepan and bring to a boil. Cook for 3 minutes before using.

SWISS COURT-BOUILLON FOR "AU BLEU" FISH COOKERY

Enough for 4 medium fish.

2 quarts water	*1 medium carrot, sliced*
1 cup cider or mild vinegar	*3 large sprigs parsley*
½ cup dry white wine	*3 bay leaves*
1 medium onion, sliced	*¼ teaspoon ground thyme*
white part of 1 leek, or	*1 tablespoon salt*
white part of 3 large	*6 to 8 peppercorns*
scallions, sliced	

Combine all the ingredients. Bring to a boil. Cook, covered, for 15 minutes. Strain before using.

Note: Both court-bouillons may be made ahead, and kept for weeks before using.

HOW TO COOK A BLUE TROUT

4 medium trout, about 12   *1 recipe court-bouillon*
to 16 ounces each

Have boiling court-bouillon ready. Quickly kill and
gut the trout. Plunge the fish into the liquid. Cook over
lowest possible heat, so that the liquid barely simmers,
for about 5 minutes. Or if the fish is small, let it stand
covered in a warm place on the stove (or the campfire
ashes) until it flakes when tested. Place trout on a dish
lined with a napkin to absorb excess moisture. Serve
with melted butter and boiled potatoes and lemon
wedges. Or chill and serve with mayonnaise.

HOW TO BONE COOKED TROUT

Place the trout on a warm platter. Run a thin knife
along the backbone, from head to tail. Cut through the
bottom fillet just in front of the tail. Lift the tail and,
running the knife underneath the backbone, gradually
ease the entire top section from the bottom. Cut through
the bottom fillet at the head and invert the top section
over onto the platter. Repeat the operation with the top
fillet. The whole bone structure should come away in
one piece. The fillets may be put back together again.

SAUCES FOR FISH COOKED
"AU BLEU"

Sauce Amandine

For 4 fish, melt ½ cup butter. Add ½ cup slivered
blanched almonds and cook the almonds until they are

golden brown. Stir in 1 tablespoon of lemon juice and 2 tablespoons of chopped parsley. Pour over trout.

Herb Sauce

For 4 fish, melt ½ cup butter. Add 1 tablespoon lemon juice, ½ teaspoon salt, ¼ teaspoon pepper and ¼ cup of chopped parsley, chives, watercress and/or chervil (use one herb or several, in any desired combination). Pour over trout.

Rosemary Sauce

For 4 fish, melt ½ cup butter. Add 1 tablespoon crushed rosemary, or rosemary to taste, and beat until foamy. Pour over trout.

TROUT WITH CREAM-AND-ALMOND SAUCE

Truite à la Crème et aux Amandes

4 fresh medium whole trout, about 1 pound each, prepared for cooking	*1 cup butter*
	½ cup slivered blanched almonds
	½ to ¾ cup heavy cream
salt	*¼ cup chopped parsley*
flour	

Sprinkle the inside of the trout with a little salt. Coat the fish on all sides with flour. Heat the butter in a large, deep skillet. Sauté the trout in it for about 4 to 5 minutes on each side, or until golden brown. The fish should flake easily when tested with a toothpick or a fork. Do not overcook. Remove the cooked trout to a hot platter and keep warm. Cook the almonds in the butter remaining in the skillet, stirring constantly, until they are golden. Stir in the cream and cook for 2 to 3 minutes, stirring all the time. Pour the sauce over the trout and sprinkle with the parsley. Serve with boiled new potatoes.

FANCY FILLETS OF TROUT

Filet de Truite à la Mode du Patron

This delicious recipe comes from the Goldenes Kreuz, an excellent restaurant in Erlenbach, near Zurich. I give it in the words of the owner, Alfred Lurati, who is also the chef.

Paint a large saucepan with butter and line the bottom with minced shallots. Put the fillet of a fresh trout weighing about 2 pounds on the shallots. Top the fish with minced fresh mushrooms and a few chopped shrimp. Sprinkle with lemon juice and add dry white wine, a little fish broth and salt. Poach gently until the fish is tender.

Place the poached fish in a buttered shallow baking dish. Thicken the pan juices with the mushrooms and shrimp with a little *beurre manié* (flour kneaded with butter) and a little heavy cream. Pour the sauce over the fish and put the mixture for a few moments under a broiler until the top bubbles. Serve with boiled rice or boiled potatoes.

Note: Mr. Lurati uses two kinds of mushrooms, *morels* and *champignons*, adding greatly to the elegance of the dish.

FISH FROM ZUG

Zuger Balchen

Traditional. In Zug this is made with *Balchen*, exquisite lake fish. But fillets or any delicate small fish like trout may be cooked in this manner.

4 tablespoons butter
1 tablespoon minced
   parsley
1 minced shallot, or the
   white part of 2 scallions,
   minced

¼ teaspoon ground sage
2 to 3 pounds fish or fillets
salt
pepper
1 cup dry white wine

Stir the butter until it is soft and foamy. Beat in the parsley, shallot or scallions, and the sage. Beat until the butter is light and fluffy. Spread half of the herb butter on the bottom of a shallow baking dish. Put the fish on it in a single layer. Dot with the remaining butter. Cover with a lid or with aluminum foil. Bake in a preheated moderate oven (350°) for 10 minutes. Remove cover and add salt and pepper to taste and the wine. Cover again and bake for an additional 10 minutes, or until fish flakes when tested with a toothpick or a fork. Fillets may require a shorter cooking time. If the fish is to be served on a heated platter, pour the sauce over it.

PERCH FILLETS POACHED IN WINE

Les Filets de Perche au Fendant du Valais

2 pounds perch or other
   fish fillets
salt
pepper
2 tablespoons butter
1 teaspoon grated onion
1 cup finely chopped
   mushrooms

1 tablespoon chopped
   parsley or fresh dill
1½ cups Fendant or other
   dry white wine
4 tablespoons heavy cream
⅓ cup grated Gruyère
   cheese

Wash fish and dry with paper towels. Sprinkle with salt and pepper. Melt the butter in a large, deep skillet. Add the onion, mushrooms and parsley or dill. Cook,

stirring constantly, for 1 minute. Add the wine and bring
to a boil. Lower the heat and bring the liquid in the
skillet to barely simmering. Put the fish fillets in the
liquid. Simmer, covered, for about 5 minutes, or until the
fish is barely tender. Do not overcook. Butter a shallow
baking dish and carefully place the fish fillets into it.
Keep the fish warm. Bring the skillet liquid to a boil and
reduce it to about 1 cup. Remove the skillet from the
heat and stir in the cream. Pour the sauce over the fish,
and sprinkle with the cheese. Bake in a preheated hot
oven (425°) for about 10 minutes, or place under a
broiler flame until the top is golden brown. Serve with
small parsleyed potatoes.

BAKED PIKE

Gebratener Hecht

Any fish may be prepared in this manner.

2 pounds boned pike	*chopped capers*
(from a 4-pound fish,	*2 anchovy fillets, minced*
approximately)	*2 small onions, minced*
½ cup melted butter	*2 strips bacon, minced*
1 egg, beaten	*2 tablespoons chopped*
1 cup fine dry	*parsley*
breadcrumbs	*½ cup dry white wine*
2 tablespoons drained and	*½ cup heavy cream*

Brush the fish on both sides with about half of the
melted butter. Brush the egg over the top of the fish and
sprinkle with half of the breadcrumbs. Combine the capers, the anchovy, half of the onions, the bacon and the
parsley, and spread this mixture over the fish. Drizzle the
remaining beaten egg over the fish, and top with the

remaining breadcrumbs. Mix the remaining onion with the remaining melted butter, the wine and the cream. Pour the wine and cream mixture into a shallow baking pan. Add the fish. Bake in a preheated hot oven (400°) for 20 minutes, or until the fish flakes when tested with a toothpick or a fork. Serve with boiled potatoes.

PIKE IN TOMATO SAUCE FROM THE TICINO

Luccio alla Ticinese

Any large, coarse fish may be cooked to advantage in this manner.

½ cup olive oil
2 cups finely chopped
   parsley
2 garlic cloves, minced
¼ teaspoon ground sage,
   or sage to taste
¼ cup lemon juice
¾ cups thin, well-seasoned
tomato sauce or tomato
   juice
salt
pepper
1 4- to 5-pound whole
   pike, prepared for
   cooking, or cut into
   1½-inch slices.

Combine the olive oil, parsley, garlic and sage in a saucepan and simmer, covered, for 10 minutes. Stir occasionally. Stir in the lemon juice, tomato sauce, and season with salt and pepper to taste. Heat the mixture. Butter a baking dish and put the fish in it. If the fish is sliced, there should be only one layer. Pour the sauce over the fish. Simmer, covered, over low heat or bake, covered, in a preheated moderate oven (350°) until the fish flakes when tested with a toothpick or a fork. The cooking time depends on the size of the fish and whether it is whole or in slices.

XV (Fish)

PIKE IN THE MANNER OF ZUG

Hecht nach Zuger Art

Any medium or large salt- or fresh-water fish may be cooked in this manner.

¾ cup butter
6 shallots, minced
1 tablespoon minced parsley
1 tablespoon minced fresh chervil or 1 teaspoon dried chervil
1 tablespoon minced fresh tarragon or 1 teaspoon dried tarragon

2 teaspoons minced fresh thyme or ½ teaspoon dried thyme
2 cups dry white wine
1 4- to 5-pound pike, prepared for cooking
salt
pepper
¼ cup heavy cream

Heat ½ cup of the butter in an oblong flame-proof baking dish that will hold the fish. Cook the shallots, parsley, chervil, tarragon and thyme in the butter for 1 minute. Add the wine. Sprinkle the pike inside and out with salt and pepper. Score the sides so that the fish will bend into the shape of a horseshoe, and place the fish on top of the mixture in the baking dish. The fish may also be left whole or cut into slices. Simmer, covered, over low heat for about 10 to 20 minutes, depending on how the fish is cut: if left whole, it will take longer to cook. When done, the fish should flake easily when tested with a toothpick or a fork. Remove the fish to a heated deep serving platter and keep hot. Strain the pan liquid through a fine sieve, or purée in a blender, or leave as is. Beat in the remaining ¼ cup butter by tablespoons and add the cream. Return to low heat and heat through but do not boil. Pour over fish.

PIKE FRIED IN BATTER

Zuger Hechtli

Traditional. Any small fish may be fried in this manner.

Batter:
- *1 cup all-purpose flour*
- *1 teaspoon baking powder*
- *¼ teaspoon salt*
- *2 eggs, separated*
- *⅔ cup milk*
- *2 pounds boned pike, cut into thin slices (from a 4-pound fish— approximately)*
- *salt*
- *pepper*
- *deep fat for frying*

To prepare the batter, sift the flour with the baking powder and the salt. Beat the egg yolks with the milk. Add the egg yolk mixture to the flour and beat until smooth. Beat the egg whites until stiff and fold them into the batter. Sprinkle the fish with salt and pepper. Dip the fish into the batter and shake off excess batter. Fry in deep fat at 380° for 2 to 3 minutes or until the fish slices are puffed and browned. Serve with a tossed green salad.

SAUTÉED RHINE SALMON

Gebackener Rheinlachs

Traditional, from Basle.

- *2 pounds salmon, cut into 1½-inch slices*
- *salt*
- *pepper*
- *4 tablespoons lemon juice*
- *flour for coating*
- *1 cup butter*
- *4 small onions, thinly sliced*
- *¼ cup dry white wine*
- *¼ cup chopped parsley*
- *lemon wedges*

Sprinkle the salmon on both sides with the salt, pepper and lemon juice. Let stand in the refrigerator for 30 minutes. Dry the fish with paper toweling. Coat it on all sides with flour. Heat ¾ cup of the butter in a large, deep skillet. Sauté the salmon in it for about 8 to 10 minutes, or until golden brown. The pieces should not be touching. Turn once during cooking. While the salmon is cooking, heat the remaining butter in another skillet. Cook the onions in it until they are soft and golden. Put the cooked salmon on a heated serving platter and keep warm. Add the wine to the skillet in which the salmon was cooked. Bring to a boil while scraping the bottom of the skillet. Top the salmon with the onions and pour the wine sauce over it. Sprinkle with the parsley. Serve with lemon wedges and parsleyed boiled potatoes.

Note: The salmon may be broiled rather than fried, and then topped with fried onions. There will be no sauce for this version.

HEIDI'S STEAMED FISH WITH SAUCE

Geduenstete Fische nach Heidi's Art

This is a way of making bland fish fillets more interesting.

6 fish fillets (flounder, sole, perch, etc.)
salt
butter
3 tablespoons all-purpose flour
¼ cup minced parsley
½ cup sour cream
1 cup chicken broth
2 tablespoons fresh lemon juice

Sprinkle the fish with salt. Heavily butter a skillet that is suitable to be presented at the table. Place the fillets in it side by side. Sprinkle with the flour and the minced parsley. Spoon the sour cream in a thin layer over the fish. Pour in the chicken broth. Cook uncovered over low heat, without turning, until the fish is flaky. Sprinkle the lemon juice over the fish. Place the skillet under broiler. Broil until barely browned. Serve from the skillet.

SCAMPI À LA FAÇON MÖVENPICK

Since scampi, which are prawns rather than shrimp, are unavailable in the United States, this dish may be made with shrimp.

24 large shrimp	*1½ cups Sauce Américaine*
salt	*(see below)*
4 garlic cloves, mashed	*1 tablespoon flour*
½ cup butter plus 1	*6 small tomatoes, peeled,*
tablespoon	*seeded and chopped*
⅔ cup brandy	*8 large mushrooms, cut*
1⅓ cups heavy cream	*into quarters*

Peel and devein the shrimp. Split the shrimp down the back and sprinkle with salt. Brown the mashed garlic in ½ cup butter in a large skillet. Add the shrimp and sauté them in the garlic butter until they turn pink. Add the brandy and flame. Cook, stirring constantly, until the brandy has been absorbed. Stir in the cream and cook until the cream has been absorbed. Thicken the Sauce Américaine as follows: knead together the flour and 1 tablespoon butter to make a paste, or *beurre manié*. Drop the *beurre manié* into the Sauce Américaine and stir until it has melted and the sauce has thickened. Pour the sauce over the shrimp. Add the chopped tomatoes and mushrooms and cook about 7 to 10 minutes or until the shrimp are tender but firm. Serve with green noodles.

SAUCE AMÉRICAINE

1 tablespoon butter   ¼ *cup brandy*
¼ *cup minced onion*   ½ *cup tomato sauce*
1 cup dry white wine

Heat the butter and cook the onion in it until it is soft. Add ½ cup of the wine and the brandy. Flame the brandy. When the flame dies down, add the remaining wine and the tomato sauce. Cook, stirring constantly, for about 3 to 4 minutes.

GENEVA FISH SAUCE

Sauce Genevoise

5 tablespoons butter   ¼ *cup white wine*
6 tablespoons all-purpose   *2 egg yolks*
   flour   *1½ tablespoons light*
2 cups fish stock   *cream*

Melt 3 tablespoons butter. Stir in the flour. Cook until the paste is golden. Gradually stir in the fish stock and wine. Stir occasionally, and let cook for 15 minutes. Soften the remaining butter. Beat the egg yolks, and beat in the softened butter and cream. While stirring, add the hot fish sauce slowly to the egg yolk and cream mixture. Reheat the sauce to the boiling point. Serve over broiled or baked fish.

XVI

Dumplings, Pasta, Rice and Cereals

THE INFLUENCE OF German, Austrian and Italian cooking on that of Switzerland is nowhere more apparent than in the cereal dishes. (This is least true of western Switzerland, where the cooking is more in the French style.) Swiss housewives, when they follow the truly native tradition, use noodles rather than spaghetti or macaroni, smothering them with fried butter, fried onions and/or cheese, the traditional Swiss garnishes for many foods. But they also cook spaghetti and all the other members of the pasta family in the Italian manner, *al dente* and with tomato sauces. Pasta is so much used in Switzerland as a meat accompaniment, or rather as a stretcher (to which it lends itself ideally), that excellent brands are made locally.

However, the first place in the pasta family is reserved for the tiny dumplings called *Hörnli* or *Spätzli* or *Knöpfli*, which are also extremely popular in southern Germany. Like noodles, they are nowadays bought rather than homemade. The dumplings of Austria, which use up stale bread—and stale bread is a factor in bread-eating Switzerland—also have their place in the diet.

Very often, these pastas make the whole meal, with a salad or a compote.

The Italian influence on the Ticino is seen in the large use of polenta, cornmeal, used as a basic carbohydrate in the daily diet.

As for rice, its consumption has also greatly increased. One of the reasons for this is the Swiss government's encouraging the population to get used to rice as a staple, since it lends itself extremely well to long storage. As the two wars showed, Switzerland has to face the fact that the imports she needs to feed her people may not be available at all times. The Swiss government strongly recommends the hoarding of a basic food supply, which includes rice; the government itself has large food caches stored deep in the mountains to see the Swiss through a crisis. The rice festivals in the Ticino and in other parts of the country have received government support, coinciding happily with the taste of the population.

As stated elsewhere, cereals have been a part of the Swiss people's food ever since there has been a Switzerland. They used to be eaten as gruels, porridges and plain flour dishes, cooked with milk, like the legendary *Fänz*. Now pasta products and rice have taken the place of these old-fashioned foods.

KNÖPFLI OR SPÄTZLI OR HÖRNLI

These are tiny dumplings, and probably the most popular form of pasta in German-speaking Switzerland. Nowadays, most housewives buy them ready-made, like noodles or instant mashed potatoes. *Hörnli* means little horns, *Knöpfli* little buttons and *Spätzli* little sparrows. They all are made from the same basic dough, but *Knöpfli* are made by pressing the dough through a metal colander or a special sieve, whereas *Spätzli* and *Hörnli* are spread on a wooden board and snipped off in tiny pieces. All of them can be served with butter and grated cheese, with gravy, or with any sauce suitable for pasta or rice. The Swiss serve them with meats instead of potatoes, or cooked directly in consommé.

2 ½ to 3 cups flour	*pepper to taste*
¼ teaspoon salt	*½ cup butter, melted*
2 eggs, lightly beaten	*⅔ cup grated Parmesan*
1 cup water	*or Swiss cheese*
3 quarts rapidly boiling	
salted water	

Sift the flour with the salt. Mix the eggs with 1 cup cold water. Stir eggs gradually into the flour, beating until smooth. Let stand for 30 minutes.

To make *Hörnli*, use 2 ½ cups of the flour. Press the dough through a colander into the boiling water. Cook for 3 minutes or until tender. When the *Hörnli* rise to the surface, remove them with a slotted spoon, drain them and place on a hot serving dish. Season with pepper. Pour the butter over them, sprinkle with cheese, and toss.

To make *Spätzli*, use 3 cups of flour. Dampen a small cutting board with water. Put 1 cup of the dough on it and smooth it thin. With a sharp kitchen knife, snip little strips of dough into the boiling water. Dip the knife several times in the water to prevent sticking. Cook and serve as with *Hörnli*.

Note: Since flours absorb liquids differently, it is impossible to give absolutely foolproof quantities. It is best to have a trial run first. If the dough is too thick, it can be made softer with the addition of a little more water—add very little at a time and beat well. Conversely, the dough can be stiffened with a little more flour. The softer the dough, the lighter the end result, but the dough must be firm enough not to disintegrate in cooking. All this sounds far more complicated than it is. As with pancake batter, one gets a feeling for the consistency of the dough after making it a few times.

LIVER DUMPLINGS

Leberknödli

Traditional. Dumplings are eaten throughout German and eastern Switzerland; these are far superior to most and worth making as a main course.

1 pound beef liver	*1 large egg*
¼ pound bacon	*1 teaspoon salt*
2 tablespoons shortening	*¼ teaspoon pepper*
1 medium onion, chopped	*boiling salted water*
2 tablespoons chopped parsley	*⅓ cup grated Parmesan cheese*
1¼ cups soft breadcrumbs	*⅓ cup hot melted butter*

Chop or grind the liver and bacon together; the mixture must be fine. Melt shortening. Cook the onion and parsley in the shortening until the onions are golden brown. Add the onions and parsley, breadcrumbs, egg, salt and pepper to the liver-and-bacon mixture. Blend thoroughly. Let stand 15 minutes. With 2 spoons dipped in water or wetted hands (to prevent sticking), shape dough into 2-inch balls. Drop into boiling salted water. Simmer, covered, for 7 to 8 minutes. Drain. Place on heated serving dish and sprinkle with grated cheese and hot melted butter. Serve with apple or plum sauce.

Note: Or cook the dumplings in hot broth and serve in soup. In this case, omit the cheese and melted butter.

GNOCCHI ALLA TICINESE

2 cups water	*7 tablespoons butter*
1 ½ cups milk	*3 eggs, well beaten*
1 cup cornmeal	*2 cups grated Swiss cheese*
1 ½ teaspoons salt	

Combine the water and milk in a heavy saucepan. Bring to a boil. Gradually stir in the cornmeal and salt, beating constantly to avoid lumping. Cook until very thick, stirring constantly. Remove from heat. Soften 3 tablespoons of the butter; beat in the softened butter, eggs and ½ cup of the cheese. Spread mixture about ¼ inch thick on shallow platter or baking sheet. Cool. Cut into circles or any other desired shape. Place gnocchi in overlapping rows on well-buttered shallow baking dish. If necessary, make two layers. Sprinkle each layer with the remaining 1 ½ cups cheese and dot with remaining 4 tablespoons butter. Bake in preheated moderate oven (350°) for about 30 minutes, or until the top is golden and crisp. Serve with meats in lieu of potatoes, or as a meatless entrée, with a tossed green salad or a vegetable salad.

CORNMEAL FROM THE TICINO

Polenta alla Ticinese

Polenta is a staple dish in the Ticino as in northern Italy, from which the Ticino has adopted so much of its cooking. This is especially true in the rural districts, where polenta is often eaten instead of bread.

Polenta was traditionally cooked in a paiuolo, a tinned copper kettle with a handle which hung over the open hearth on which the peasants cooked. It was stirred with a wooden paddle. Whether polenta is made in this manner, or on a modern stove, one thing is essential for its success—and it is an excellent dish, far superior to our cornmeal mush—it must be constantly stirred with a wooden spoon or paddle until a thin crust forms at the bottom and sides of the kettle (which should be heavy).

4 cups cornmeal   *1 tablespoon salt*
2 quarts boiling water

Drizzle the cornmeal slowly into the boiling salted water with one hand, stirring constantly with the other so that it will not lump. Lower heat. Cook, stirring constantly and slowly for about 30 to 45 minutes, or until the bottom and sides of the kettle crust. Shake the kettle to loosen the polenta. Turn it out on a large platter. Slice it as you would slice bread; the traditional way is to do this with a string so as not to tear the polenta. Serve with any meat or any sauce, or with butter and grated cheese, or with cold milk or buttermilk. Makes about 8 to 10 servings.

Note: Leftover polenta may be sliced and fried in butter or oil. It is entirely possible not to cook the polenta for such a long time. It will be edible, but not quite as good and crisp.

PANCAKES

Omeletten

The German-speaking Swiss call pancakes omelets. Traditional.

1¼ cups all-purpose flour   *4 eggs, well beaten*
1 teaspoon salt   *3 tablespoons shortening*
1 cup milk   *or oil*
1 cup water

Sift the flour with the salt. Gradually add the milk and water to the sifted flour. Beat well until smooth. Beat in the eggs, and continue beating the batter until smooth and shiny. Let stand for 1 hour. Melt the shortening in a skillet. Drop batter by spoonfuls in the shortening or heated oil. Allow to brown on one side. Turn and brown on the other side. Serve with a fruit compote and *café au lait* for a rural supper.

Variation: Cheese Pancakes. Beat 1½ cups grated Swiss cheese into the batter.

LAYERED EGG PANCAKES
FROM THE GRISONS

Gonterser Bock

Traditional. A very old dish that shows what human, or rather Swiss, ingenuity can do with eggs, flour and milk.

3 cups all-purpose flour *3 hard-cooked eggs,*
½ teaspoon salt *shelled and left whole*
3 eggs, well beaten *fat for deep frying*
1¾ cups milk

Sift together flour and salt. Beat in the eggs and milk, beating until the batter is smooth and thick. Let stand for 15 minutes. Dip the eggs into the batter. Fry in deep hot fat (380° on thermometer) for 2 to 3 minutes or until golden brown. Drain. Dip the eggs again into the batter. Fry again until golden brown. Repeat the layering and frying until all the batter is used. There should be 4 to 5 layers on each egg. Cut into slices and serve hot, with a fruit compote.

Note: Whole cored, but unpeeled, apples may be used instead of hard-cooked eggs.

CHOLERMUS PANCAKES

Traditional in Schwyz and other cantons where the cows are tended in the high Alps during the summer. These pancakes are part of the short-order cooking of the "*sennen*," the herdsmen, who are kept busy not only with milking, but with the making of cheese and butter.

½ cup cream	*2 cups all-purpose flour*
½ cup plus 2 tablespoons butter	*1 teaspoon salt*
	sugar
3 eggs, well beaten	

Beat the cream with 2 tablespoons melted butter and the eggs. Pour the liquid into the flour which has been sifted with the salt. Blend until the mixture is smooth. Melt 2 tablespoons butter in a large skillet. Pour large portions (about ⅓ cup batter) into the pan. Brown on one side. Turn and brown on the other side. Keep baked pancakes hot. With two forks, tear the pancakes into bite-size pieces. Melt the remaining butter in skillet. Add pieces of pancake. Brown the pieces until crusty. Sprinkle with sugar and serve hot, with fresh berries or a fruit compote and *café au lait*, if you want a Swiss country supper.

CHERRY PANCAKES

Chriesi Omeletten

Traditional from Zurich.

4 cups small stale bread pieces	*⅓ cup ground almonds*
2 cups hot milk	*2 cups pitted black cherries, well drained*
3 eggs, separated	*⅓ cup butter, melted*
⅓ cup sugar	*sugar*
1 teaspoon cinnamon	

Break the stale bread into small pieces and then measure. Add the hot milk. Stir, and let stand for 10 minutes. Press out the excess milk. Beat well until smooth. Add the egg yolks, sugar, cinnamon, ground almonds and black cherries. Blend well. Fold in the stiffly beaten egg whites. Drop the batter by tablespoonfuls into the hot melted butter. Brown pancakes on each side. Sprinkle with sugar before serving.

WHITE RISOTTO FROM THE TICINO

Risotto in Bianco alla Ticinese

⅓ *cup butter*	*1 cup hot dry white wine*
1 tablespoon minced onion	*salt*
1 cup rice	*pepper*
1 cup hot beef or chicken consommé	*grated Swiss or Parmesan cheese*

Melt the butter in a heavy saucepan. Cook the onion in the butter until it is soft. Stir in the rice. Cook over medium heat, stirring constantly, for 1 to 2 minutes, or until the rice is opaque. Add the hot consommé, the wine, and salt and pepper to taste. Cover tightly. Simmer over the lowest possible heat for about 15 to 20 minutes or until the rice is tender but firm. Serve with grated cheese.

Note: One cup of fresh or thawed frozen peas may be added to the rice when it is half done. Or ½ to ¾ cup finely chopped parsley may be added just before serving time.

COUNTRY RISOTTO
FROM THE TICINO

Risotto Rustico Ticinese

½ *pound green beans*
boiling water to cover the
  beans
6 slices bacon, minced
1 small onion, minced
1 to 2 garlic cloves, minced
1 medium potato, diced
2 medium carrots, diced
1 stalk celery, diced
2 medium tomatoes,
  peeled, seeded and
  chopped

1 leek, sliced (use both
  green and white parts)
3 cups water
2 cups rice
1 cup fresh or frozen peas
2 to 3 cups chopped
  cabbage
salt
pepper
2 tablespoons butter

Cook the beans in boiling water to cover for 5 minutes. Drain. Cook the bacon, onion and garlic together in a large casserole until the onion is soft. Add the beans, potato, carrots, celery, tomatoes, leek and water. Bring to a boil, lower heat and simmer for about 10 minutes. Add the rice, the peas and cabbage. Season with salt and pepper to taste. Cook, covered, over low heat until the rice is tender, about 15 minutes. Before serving, stir in the butter. If desired, serve with grated cheese. Makes 8 servings.

Note: This is the kind of country dish made with what is on hand, so that any other raw or cooked vegetables or leftovers may be added or used.

ARTICHOKE-AND-RICE CASSEROLE FROM THE TICINO

Teglia di Riso e Carciofi alla Ticinese

Traditional.

2 large or 4 small
  artichokes
1 quart water combined
  with 1 tablespoon lemon
  juice or vinegar
3 tablespoons butter
2 tablespoons olive oil
1 medium tomato, peeled,
  seeded and chopped
½ clove garlic, minced
  (*optional*)

¼ teaspoon dried basil, or
  more to taste
2 cups hot chicken
  consommé
1 cup raw long-grain rice
salt
pepper
¼ cup minced parsley
freshly grated Parmesan
  cheese

Pull off the tough outer leaves of the artichokes until the remaining leaves are whitish to pale green—one third to one half the way from the base to the top. Discard. With a sharp knife, cut off the spiky top half or two thirds of the artichoke and discard. Cut off the stem, leaving only about ¼ inch. Peel and trim the base around the stem. Cut artichoke into four parts like an apple. Drop immediately into the acidulated water to prevent discoloration. Take out one piece at a time and cut off the fuzzy part in the center as you would core an apple. Cut into thin slices and return to the acidulated water. In a heavy saucepan heat together 2 tablespoons of the butter and the olive oil. Dry the artichokes on kitchen toweling and put them into the saucepan. Add the tomato, garlic, basil and ½ cup of the consommé. Cook covered over low heat for 7 minutes, or until the artichokes are half done. Stir occasionally. Remove from the heat and keep warm. While the artichokes are cooking, melt the remaining tablespoon of butter in a 1½-quart heavy saucepan or casserole. Add the rice. Cook over medium heat, stirring constantly, until the rice is yellow and translucent. Add the remaining consommé. Simmer, covered, for about 8 to 10 minutes or until the rice is half tender. The cooking time depends on the quality of the rice. Put the artichokes into the pan with the rice and mix. Season with salt and pepper to taste. Simmer, covered, for another 10 minutes or until the rice and artichokes are tender. Stir frequently; if necessary, add a little more hot consommé to prevent scorching. Sprinkle with parsley and serve with plenty of freshly grated Parmesan. Makes 4 servings.

GREEN NOODLES

Grüne Nudeln

4½ cups all-purpose flour	*cooked spinach*
1 teaspoon salt	*4 eggs plus 4 egg yolks*
½ cup well-drained, finely	*boiling salted water*
minced or puréed	

Sift the flour with the salt. Make a well in the center of the flour. Beat the spinach, the 4 whole eggs and the egg yolks together. Pour the mixture into the flour well. Stir until a stiff dough is formed. Knead on a lightly floured board until the dough is stiff and elastic, adding a little more flour if necessary. Divide the dough into small pieces. Roll out each piece on a lightly floured board until it is paper thin. Sprinkle the dough lightly with flour. Roll up like a jelly roll and cut into ¼- to ½-inch

strips. Toss the strips on a board to separate them. Repeat
the process with the remaining dough. Spread the noodles
on a dry cloth to let them dry for at least 2 hours or
overnight. Cook in plenty of boiling salted water for
about 20 minutes or until tender.

ARTICHOKE SPAGHETTI SAUCE

Salsa di Carciofi

3 tablespoons olive oil
1 tablespoon butter
3 medium artichokes,
    thinly sliced
1 medium onion, thinly
    sliced
½ garlic clove, minced

2 cups canned Italian-style
    tomatoes
1 bay leaf
½ teaspoon dried basil
salt
pepper

Heat olive oil and butter. Cook the artichokes in the
oil and butter, stirring constantly, for 3 minutes. Add the
onion, garlic, tomatoes, bay leaf, basil, and salt and pepper to taste. Simmer covered, stirring occasionally, until
the artichokes are tender. Makes enough sauce for about
1 pound spaghetti.

BIRCHERMUESLI

This dish, composed of uncooked oatmeal, milk and
fruits shows as no other the revolution in Swiss eating
that took place around the turn of the century. It was
served at the clinic in Zurich of Dr. R. Bircher-Benner,
who believed that fresh fruits, nuts, raw and cooked
vegetables and cereals were healthier than the rich,
starchy diet of the times. His patients took to the *Muesli*
or porridge with such gusto that they served it in their

homes. Today the *Birchermuesli* has a firm place in the Swiss people's diet, be it humble or splendid. The dish is served in all families and in restaurants throughout Switzerland. I would say that it is far more the Swiss national dish than the fondue.

Birchermuesli is not to be served as a dessert, but as a breakfast or supper, or at the beginning of a meal. It is a perfectly balanced dish, and children (including non-Swiss) and most adults like it very much.

As a matter of fact, *Birchermuesli* is a throwback to the old Swiss country habit of eating a cereal gruel with fruit and milk for supper because these were the foods on hand.

The original *Muesli* was made with apples, but it may be varied with any fresh fruit. It does not contain refined white sugar but sweetened condensed milk. If you do not care for this milk, the *Muesli* may be sweetened with honey. Whole-wheat and other dark breads and butter are the standard accompaniments.

ORIGINAL BIRCHERMUESLI

For 1 serving:
3 tablespoons uncooked oatmeal
3 tablespoons cold water
1 tablespoon lemon juice
1 tablespoon sweetened
condensed milk or honey
1 large unpeeled apple
2 tablespoons chopped nuts

Soak the oatmeal in the cold water until it is soft—preferably overnight. At serving time, stir in the lemon juice and condensed milk. Grate the apple directly into the *Muesli*. Sprinkle with the nuts.

Note: Depending on the oatmeal used, a little more water may have to be added to the *Muesli* to make it the consistency of porridge. Instant oatmeal does not have to be soaked as long, but the *Muesli* is better if allowed to stand for 10 minutes.

FÄNZ

No Swiss cookbook would be complete without this legendary dish of the Swiss herdsmen. In the old days, the herdsmen used to stay on the high Alps for the whole summer, living exclusively on the flour they took with them and on their milk and milk products. During the week they lived on a simple flour-and-milk gruel, but on Sundays and feast days they added their precious butter to the porridge. *Fänz* and similar milk gruels were found in all the cantons with high pastures. The dish is becoming obsolete nowadays, with modern nutrition methods, though I am told that the Glarus herdsmen still eat it. At home, *Fänz* may be made in a chafing dish or fondue pot and served with bread and *café au lait*.

1 ¼ cups butter   *(approximately)*
2 cups all-purpose flour   *4 cups milk, boiling*

Melt the butter in a heavy saucepan. Gradually stir in the flour. Stir in the milk. Put the saucepan on an asbestos plate. Cook, stirring occasionally, over the lowest possible heat for about 15 minutes. The *Fänz* is ready when the butter fat floats on top of the mixture. (The mixture should be of fondue consistency.)

Note: It may be necessary to adjust the proportions of the ingredients a little since flours absorb liquid differently.

XVII

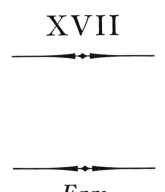

Eggs

E GGS ARE NOT breakfast food in Switzerland, except among the Swiss who copy English or American food habits.

Eggs are chiefly used to make other dishes more palatable and more nutritious. Among per-se egg dishes, fried eggs are the most popular; popularly, they are called *Stierenaugen,* or bull's eyes.

BAKED EGGS

Eier im Förmchen

3 cups grated Gruyère cheese	*pepper*
	nutmeg
6 eggs	*6 tablespoons butter*
6 tablespoons cream	

Butter 6 individual casserole dishes. Sprinkle each casserole with ¼ cup of the cheese. Break 1 egg carefully into each dish. Spoon 1 tablespoon cream over each egg. Sprinkle with pepper and nutmeg. Sprinkle ¼ cup

cheese over each egg. Dot each casserole with 1 tablespoon butter. Bake in a preheated hot oven (400°) for 12
minutes. Serve as an appetizer or an entrée with a vegetable or a salad.

EGGS AU GRATIN FROM BERNE

Berner Zwiebeleier

Traditional.

2 large onions, thinly	1 cup dry white wine
sliced	1 to 2 teaspoons Dijon
5 tablespoons butter	mustard
salt	6 poached eggs, or
pepper	hard-cooked eggs,
2 tablespoons flour	shelled and halved
1 cup consommé	

Cook the onions in 3 tablespoons of the butter over
low heat, stirring constantly, until the onions are soft and
still white. Season with salt and pepper. Stir in the flour.
Combine the consommé, wine and mustard, and stir into
the flour mixture. Cook, stirring constantly, until the
sauce is smooth and thickened. Stir in the remaining 2
tablespoons of butter. Put the eggs into a buttered shallow baking dish. Pour the sauce over the eggs. Put under
the broiler until the eggs are heated through and the
sauce bubbles.

OMELET FROM THE JURA

Omelette Jurassienne

This makes a hearty one-dish meal. It is also a good
way for using leftovers.

For one person:
2 eggs, well beaten
½ cup grated Swiss or
*   other cheese*
½ teaspoon salt
freshly ground pepper
2 slices lean bacon, cubed

2 small new potatoes,
*   cooked in their jackets,*
*   peeled and sliced*
1 shallot, chopped, or 1
*   small onion, chopped*
2 tablespoons chopped
*   parsley*

Combine the eggs, the cheese, and salt and pepper to taste. Over low heat, cook the bacon until just crisp, then add the potatoes and the chopped shallot. Cook until the potatoes are golden. Add the egg mixture and the parsley. Cook over low heat until the eggs are set, stirring occasionally—and carefully—with a fork. Turn the omelet out of the pan onto a warmed plate. Serve at once, with a green salad, a tomato salad or a salad of Belgian endive.

BERNESE LUNCHEON EGGS WITH ONION SAUCE

Berner Eier mit Zwiebelsauce

The canton of Berne loves onions, and every year a big onion fair is held in the city of Berne's picturesque Market Square.

2 big onions, thinly sliced
¼ cup butter
3 tablespoons all-purpose
*   flour*
1 cup hot beef or chicken
*   bouillon*
1 cup hot dry white wine,

such as a Dezaley or a
*   Fendant*
salt
pepper
4 to 6 poached eggs
¼ cup grated Swiss cheese

In a heavy saucepan over the lowest possible heat, cook the onions in 2 tablespoons of the butter until extremely soft; they must remain a pale gold. This will take about 10 minutes. The saucepan should be tightly covered so that the onions can cook in their own juice. Remove the cover frequently and stir to prevent the onions from browning. Turn up the heat to medium and stir the flour into the onions. Blend thoroughly. Combine bouillon and wine. Gradually add to the onion mixture, stirring constantly to avoid lumps. Season with salt and pepper. Simmer, covered, over the lowest possible heat for 20 to 30 minutes, stirring occasionally. Stir in the remaining 2 tablespoons of the butter. Next, butter 2 or 3 individual baking dishes. Place 2 poached eggs in each. Cover completely with the onion sauce. Sprinkle with the grated cheese. Place in a preheated broiler. Broil until the top is slightly browned and bubbly. Serve immediately with the dry white wine used in the dish. A green salad and a slice of cake or fruit and cookies complete the meal.

ONION OMELET FROM THE TICINO

Frittata di Cipolle

Traditional.

½ *cup butter*	*salt*
2 tablespoons olive oil	*pepper*
1 pound onions, minced	*6 eggs, beaten*

Heat the butter and olive oil together in a skillet. Add the onions and cook until they are soft and golden. Season with salt and pepper to taste. Stir in the eggs. Cook over low heat until the omelet is golden on the top side. Turn, and cook on the other side until it, too, is golden brown.

SCRAMBLED EGGS
BAKED WITH CHEESE

Käse Rührei

Traditional.

5 tablespoons butter
5 eggs, well beaten
⅓ cup milk or light cream
½ teaspoon salt
¼ teaspoon freshly ground
  pepper

3 slices Swiss cheese, ¼
  inch thick (about 3
  ounces)
⅓ cup fine dry
  breadcrumbs

Melt 2 tablespoons of the butter. Beat together the eggs, milk, salt, pepper and melted butter. Cook over low heat, stirring constantly, until the mixture starts to set. Pour immediately into a heavily buttered 9-inch shallow baking dish. Let cook slightly. Cover the egg mixture with the cheese slices. Dot with the remaining butter, and sprinkle with the breadcrumbs. Bake in a preheated hot oven (400°) for 10 minutes or until golden brown. To serve, cut into wedges or squares.

CHILDREN'S EGG SUPPER

Plattenmüsli

Traditional. This egg custard is what I—and many Swiss children—were fed for supper with brown bread and butter. We loved it.

6 eggs
3 cups milk

grated rind of 1 lemon
1 tablespoon sugar

Combine all the ingredients and beat together. Pour into a well-buttered shallow baking dish. Bake in a pre-heated moderate oven (350°) for about 30 minutes, or until barely set.

XVIII

Cheese

ALL THAT I think should be said on cheese in this book can be found on pages 48–50 and 112–13.

All cheese dishes should be cooked over low heat to prevent the cheese from becoming tough and stringy.

Gruyère and Emmentaler cheese can be used interchangeably, or jointly, in any desired proportions. The flavor of the dish changes, depending on the cheese used. Dishes made with Emmentaler are milder than those made with Gruyère.

One pound of any Swiss cheese makes 4 cups of grated cheese.

CORNMEAL CASSEROLE FROM THE TICINO

Polenta alla Ticinese

Traditional.

2 cups cornmeal
6 cups water
¼ cup butter
2 cups grated Sbrinz,

Romano or Parmesan cheese
2 teaspoons salt
½ teaspoon paprika
1 cup heavy cream

Blend the cornmeal and 2 cups of the water to a smooth mixture. Bring remaining water to a boil. Gradually stir in the cornmeal mixture. Cook over low heat, stirring frequently, until thick and smooth, or until the mixture clears the sides of the saucepan. Beat in the butter, 1½ cups of the grated cheese, the salt and paprika. Spread the mixture on a buttered cookie sheet to a depth of 1 inch. Chill. Butter a shallow baking dish. Cut cornmeal mixture into fingers, and place in a baking dish. Pour cream over the cornmeal fingers. Sprinkle with remaining cheese. Bake in a preheated moderate oven (350°) for 15 to 20 minutes or until the top is golden brown. Makes 6 servings.

CHEESE CROQUETTES

Croquettes au Fromage

4 tablespoons butter	*1 egg plus 3 egg yolks,*
7 tablespoons flour	*beaten*
1¾ cups milk	*1 tablespoon oil*
salt and pepper to taste	*flour*
½ pound Swiss cheese,	*fine dry breadcrumbs*
grated	*butter for sautéing or fat*
	for deep-frying

Melt the butter over low heat, add 6 tablespoons of the flour and stir until the roux is golden-colored. Add 1½ cups milk and stir until smooth. Cook slowly for about 10 minutes, stirring constantly. Season with salt and pepper and remove from the heat. Add the cheese and stir until melted. Add 3 egg yolks last and stir well. Spread into a well-buttered shallow dish of about 6 x 9 inches. Let cool, then cover with waxed paper and chill for about 2 hours, or until needed. Cut into 18 or 20 equal pieces. Shape into croquettes.

Beat the whole egg with the remaining tablespoon of
the flour, the remaining milk and the oil. Roll each
croquette in flour, dip into the egg mixture, drain well on
waxed paper and then cover completely with fine breadcrumbs. Chill for 30 minutes. Sauté in butter over
medium fire on all sides until golden brown, or fry in
deep fat (this must not be too hot; otherwise they may
split open). Serve with your favorite tomato sauce, or
with stewed tomatoes.

BAKED FARINA DUMPLINGS WITH
SPINACH AND SAUCE

Griessklösschen mit Spinat

A hearty meatless main dish.

1 quart milk	*chopped spinach (very*
¼ cup butter	*well drained)*
1 teaspoon salt	*Sauce:*
⅛ teaspoon nutmeg	*⅓ cup all-purpose flour*
1⅓ cups farina or Cream	*3 eggs, well beaten*
of Wheat	*½ teaspoon salt*
3 eggs, well beaten	*⅛ teaspoon nutmeg*
2 cups grated Swiss cheese	*1¾ cups milk*
1 cup cooked, finely	

Heat the milk. Add the butter, salt and nutmeg. Stir in
the farina. Simmer, stirring frequently, 15 minutes or
until very thick. Remove from heat. Beat in the eggs, 1
cup of the cheese and the spinach. Cool and chill. Grease
a shallow baking dish. Drop the dumplings by the spoonful into the baking dish. Sprinkle with remaining cheese.

To make the sauce, stir the flour into beaten eggs. Beat
until smooth. Add salt, nutmeg and milk. Beat thor-

oughly. Pour over dumplings. Bake in preheated moderate oven (350°) for 25 to 30 minutes or until the sauce is set and the top is golden brown. Makes 8 servings.

SAUTÉED CHEESE DUMPLINGS

Greyerzer Käseklösschen

Traditional.

2⅓ *cups grated Gruyère*	¼ *cup all-purpose flour*
or Emmentaler cheese	½ *teaspoon salt*
¾ *cup commercial sour*	½ *teaspoon dry mustard*
cream	¼ *teaspoon pepper*
4 egg yolks	*butter for sautéing*

Mix together the cheese, sour cream and egg yolks. Beat in the flour which has been sifted with the salt, mustard and pepper. Melt butter in a large skillet to a depth of ½ inch. Add tablespoonfuls of the cheese mixture. Sauté until golden brown; turn and sauté on the other side. Serve hot, with a green vegetable.

CHEESE FRITTERS FROM
THE VALAIS

Walliser Käsechüchli

Traditional.

12 slices Gruyère or	*2 eggs, well beaten*
Emmentaler cheese	¼ *teaspoon pepper*
3 × 2 × ½ inches	*1 cup dry breadcrumbs*
(about ¾ pound)	*fat for deep frying*

Dip the cheese slices into the eggs which have been beaten with the pepper. Shake off any excess egg mixture. Dip in breadcrumbs. Dip again in eggs and breadcrumbs. Fry in deep fat at 380° on thermometer for 1 to 2 minutes or just until golden brown. The center of the fritter should be soft and runny and the outside crisp. Serve immediately with a tomato or mushroom sauce, or with a tossed salad. Makes 6 servings.

CHEESE PIE

Käse Wähe

Traditional.

piecrust for 9-inch pie
½ pound Swiss cheese, grated
1 tablespoon flour

3 eggs, well beaten
1 cup milk (or cream)
salt and pepper to taste

Line the pie plate with the pastry. Dredge the cheese with flour. Distribute the cheese evenly in pie plate. Beat the eggs well, mix with the milk, season lightly and pour the mixture over the cheese. Bake 15 minutes in a hot oven (400°), then reduce heat (300 to 325°), and bake an additional 30 minutes or until a knife inserted in the center of the pie comes out clean. Do not overbake. Serve immediately or warmed over.

BAKED CHEESE PUDDING

Käsepudding

4 eggs, separated
2 cups heavy cream
1 cup grated Swiss cheese

½ teaspoon salt
6 slices firm white bread
¼ cup melted butter

Beat the egg yolks. Mix with the cream, cheese and salt. Beat the egg whites until stiff; fold into the egg yolk mixture. Sauté the bread in the heated butter on both sides until golden. Grease a 9 x 9-inch baking dish. Place overlapping bread slices in it. Pour the cheese mixture over the bread. Place the baking dish into a pan of hot water. Bake in a preheated moderate oven (350°) for 35 to 40 minutes or until the pudding is golden brown and puffed. Serve immediately with a green vegetable. Makes 6 servings.

BAKED CHEESE SANDWICHES FROM THE VAUD

Tranches de Fromage

Traditional. Served as a snack or a supper dish.

6 slices firm white bread	*2 egg yolks*
1 cup dry white wine	*1 teaspoon salt*
⅓ cup melted butter	*¼ teaspoon pepper*
2 tablespoons butter	*½ teaspoon paprika*
2 tablespoons flour	*2 tablespoons melted*
1 cup milk	*butter*
2 cups grated Swiss cheese	

Soak the bread slices in the wine for 5 to 7 minutes; the bread should be drenched but still keep its shape. Grease a 13 x 9-inch shallow baking dish. Place the bread slices in it. Pour the melted butter over the bread. In a saucepan, melt the 2 tablespoons butter. Stir in the flour. Gradually stir in the milk. Cook over low heat, stirring constantly, until the mixture is thick and smooth. Remove from heat. Add the cheese and stir until melted. Beat in the egg yolks, salt, pepper and paprika. Spoon the sauce over bread slices. Drizzle melted butter over the sauce. Bake in a preheated hot oven (400°) for 10 to 15 minutes or until the top is brown and bubbly. Serve hot, with a tossed salad. Makes 6 servings.

CHEESE SLICES WITH MUSHROOMS

Käseschnitten mit Champignons

6 slices firm white bread
½ cup butter
½ pound fresh
  mushrooms, cut in
  quarters
2 tablespoons lemon juice
1 onion, minced
¼ cup flour

1 cup milk
1 cup light cream
1 teaspoon salt
¼ teaspoon pepper
6 slices Swiss cheese
  (about 6 ounces), the
  same size as the bread
6 poached eggs (optional)

Sauté the bread slices on both sides in ¼ cup of the butter until golden. Grease a 13 x 9-inch shallow baking dish. Place the bread slices in it. Sprinkle the mushrooms with lemon juice and mix with the onion. Cook the mushrooms in 1 teaspoon of the remaining butter over low heat until tender. In another saucepan, melt all the remaining butter. Stir in the flour. Gradually stir in the milk and cream. Cook over low heat, stirring constantly, until thick and smooth. Stir in salt and pepper. Add the drained mushrooms and onion. Spoon the sauce over the bread. Top with the cheese slices. Bake in a preheated moderate oven (350°) for 10 to 15 minutes or until the cheese is melted. Top each serving with a poached egg, and serve hot. Makes 6 servings.

SIMPLE FRIED CHEESE SANDWICHES
Einfache gebackene Käseschnitten

6 thick slices Swiss cheese   12 slices firm white bread,
   (about 6 ounces), the   thinly sliced
   same size as the bread   butter

Place 1 slice of Swiss cheese between 2 slices of bread. In a skillet, melt enough butter to cover half the thickness of 1 slice of bread. Sauté sandwiches, pressing bread slices together with a pancake turner. Turn and sauté on the other side. The sandwiches should be golden brown. Makes 6 servings.

BAKED CHEESE SANDWICHES I
Käseschnitten aus dem Ofen

Traditional.

6 slices white bread   6 1-ounce slices
1 cup cold milk   Emmentaler cheese

Dip the bread slices into cold milk. Drain well. Place the bread slices on a well-buttered cookie sheet. Place slices of cheese on the bread. Bake in a preheated hot oven (400°) for 5 to 10 minutes, or until the cheese is melted.

Variations: Sprinkle caraway seeds over the cheese before baking, or place tomato slices and strips of bacon on the bread before placing cheese slices. After baking, sprinkle with paprika or chopped walnuts.

Note: These Baked Cheese Sandwiches are served in

all Swiss restaurants. They are good as snacks, or as a
luncheon dish, with a salad.

BAKED CHEESE SANDWICHES II

Wein-Käseschnitten

Traditional.

6 slices white bread	*2 cups finely grated*
¾ cup dry white wine	*Gruyère cheese*
2 eggs, well beaten	*3 tablespoons butter*

Place the bread slices on a greased shallow 13 x 9
baking pan. Spoon white wine over the bread slices,
allowing the wine to soak into the bread. Add the
well-beaten eggs to the cheese. Blend well. Spread the
cheese mixture on the bread slices. Dot the cheese with
butter. Place on a greased cookie sheet. Bake in a
preheated moderate oven (350°) for 10 to 15 minutes or
until the cheese is golden brown.

CHEESE SANDWICHES, MOUNTAIN FASHION

Käseschnitten nach oberländer Art

A flavorful ham should be used for this dish.

6 slices firm white bread	*boiled ham (about ¾*
¼ cup butter, melted	*pound)*
6 thick slices (4 × 4	*6 thick slices (4 × 4*
inches) smoked or	*inches) Swiss cheese*
	(about 6 ounces)
	6 poached eggs

Sauté the bread slices on both sides in heated butter. Place the bread on a baking sheet. Top the bread slices with the ham, and then top ham with the cheese slices. Bake in a preheated moderate oven (350°) for 10 to 15 minutes or until the cheese is melted. Place a poached egg on the cheese and serve immediately.

PUFFY CHEESE SANDWICHES

Feine Käseschnitten

2 eggs, separated
½ pound Swiss cheese
  (about 2 cups, grated)
½ teaspoon salt

¼ teaspoon pepper
12 slices firm white bread,
  thinly sliced
butter

Beat the egg yolks. Blend with the cheese, salt and pepper. Fold the egg whites into the cheese mixture. Spread on 6 of the bread slices. Top with the remaining bread slices. Press together. Sauté in ¼ inch of hot butter on both sides until golden brown.

BAKED CREAM CHEESE SANDWICHES

Rahmkäse Schnitten

6 slices white bread,
  toasted
6 tablespoons butter,
  softened

1 8-ounce package cream
  cheese
cayenne pepper
18 walnut or pecan halves

On each slice of toast, spread 1 tablespoon of the butter. Cut the cream cheese into ¼-inch cubes. Sprinkle the cheese cubes over the buttered toast. Sprinkle the cheese with cayenne pepper. Place the bread slices on a buttered baking sheet. Bake in a preheated moderate oven (350°) for 10 to 15 minutes or until the cheese is melted. Decorate each slice of bread with 3 nutmeats. Serve immediately.

SIMPLE CHEESE SKEWERS

Emmentaler Käse Spiessli

Metal knitting needles will do when there are no skewers.

Swiss cheese   butter
stale bread

Cut the cheese and bread into matching square pieces. Each piece should be about ½ inch thick and 2 inches square. Thread alternate pieces of bread and cheese on skewers. Melt the butter in a heavy skillet (to the depth of ½ inch). Cook the skewers in the butter, turning frequently, until the cheese melts. Good for luncheon or supper, with a salad.

CHEESE SKEWERS II

Käse am Spiesschen

12 thin slices pumpernickel, square shape	1 cup milk
	1 cup flour
12 slices Swiss cheese, same size and shape as bread	4 egg yolks, well beaten
	fat for deep frying

Cut each slice of bread into 4 triangles. Cut the cheese into triangles to match the bread. Thread alternate slices of bread and cheese on skewers. Each skewer should have 8 bread triangles and 8 cheese triangles, alternately placed. Dip the skewers into milk, then flour, then egg yolks. Fry in deep fat at 380° on thermometer for 5 minutes or until golden brown and puffed. Serve immediately with a spicy tomato sauce.

CHEESE SOUFFLÉ

Soufflé au Fromage

Traditional.

4 tablespoons butter	*2 cups (½ pound)*
4 tablspoons flour	*shredded or grated*
1½ cups milk, heated	*Swiss cheese*
salt	*4 eggs, separated*
1 teaspoon Dijon mustard	

Melt the butter over low heat and stir in the flour. Cook, stirring constantly, until the mixture is smooth. Stir in the hot milk, all at once. Cook, stirring all the time until the mixture is smooth and thickened. Remove from heat. Stir in salt to taste and the mustard. Add the cheese and stir until it is melted. Beat in the egg yolks, one at a time. Cool mixture. Beat the egg whites until they are stiff. Fold them into the cheese mixture. Put the mixture into a greased or ungreased 2-quart soufflé or baking dish with straight sides. Bake in a preheated moderate oven (375°) for about 30 to 40 minutes, or until the soufflé has risen and is browned on the top. Serve immediately.

Note: A richer soufflé may be made with 6 eggs. To make a "top hat" on a soufflé, run the tip of a teaspoon around in the mixture 1 inch from the edge of the baking dish, making a slight track or depression. This will make the top hat as the soufflé bakes and puffs up.

FARINA-CHEESE SOUFFLÉ

Gratin Montagnard

Traditional.

4 cups (1 quart) milk	*shredded Emmentaler or*
2 tablespoons butter	*Gruyère cheese*
⅔ cup farina	*1 teaspoon salt*
½ pound (2 cups)	*4 eggs, separated*

Heat the milk. Add the butter and gradually stir in the farina. Cook until the mixture is thickened. Add the shredded cheese and salt, and stir until the cheese is melted. Cool, then add the yolks. Beat well. Fold in the stiffly beaten egg whites. Pour into a well-buttered 2-quart baking dish. Bake in a preheated moderate oven (350°) for 40 minutes or until golden brown. Serve hot with a salad.

POTATO-CHEESE SOUFFLÉ

Soufflé aux Pommes de Terre

Traditional.

2 pounds potatoes	*1 teaspoon salt*
boiling water	*¼ teaspoon nutmeg*
¼ cup all-purpose flour	*1⅔ cups milk*
4 eggs	*2 tablespoons butter*
2 cups grated Swiss cheese	

Peel the potatoes and cut them into quarters. Cook or steam the potatoes in boiling water until they are tender. Press through a sieve or a food mill. Cool slightly. Beat in the flour, eggs, grated cheese, salt, nutmeg and milk. Spoon into a well-buttered 1½-quart mold. Dot the top with butter. Bake in a preheated moderate oven (375°) for 10 minutes. Lower temperature to 325° and bake an additional 30 minutes. Serve as a meatless entrée with mushroom or tomato sauce, or with a well-sauced meat dish.

CHEESE SOUFFLÉ WITH SHRIMP

Soufflé au Fromage aux Scampi

An elegant Swiss hotel dish.

1 cup Portuguese Sauce (see below)	*⅛ teaspoon cayenne pepper*
1½ cups chopped cooked shrimp	*2 teaspoons cornstarch*
3 tablespoons butter	*3 tablespoons water*
3 tablespoons flour	*6 eggs, separated*
1 cup light cream	*¾ cup grated Swiss cheese*
½ teaspoon salt	*paper-thin slices of Swiss cheese, cut in diamonds, to cover soufflé*

Combine the Portuguese Sauce and the shrimp, and place in a well-buttered 3-quart soufflé dish. Melt the butter and stir in the flour. Stir in the cream, then cook over low heat, stirring constantly, until the mixture thickens. Stir in the salt and cayenne. Mix the cornstarch with water to a smooth paste and stir it into the mixture. Remove from heat and beat in the egg yolks, one at a time. Return to heat and cook for about 1 minute. Remove from heat, and stir in the grated cheese. Beat the egg whites until stiff. Fold them into the cheese mixture. Pour the mixture over the shrimp. Decorate the top with

cheese slices cut into fancy shapes. Bake in a preheated
moderate oven (375°) for 30 to 40 minutes or until well
puffed and golden brown. Serve immediately.

Portuguese Sauce

2 tablespoons butter
1 teaspoon minced shallot
  or onion
¼ cup dry white wine
3 tomatoes, peeled, seeded
  and chopped

⅓ cup tomato sauce
⅓ cup canned beef gravy
⅓ cup Madeira or dry
  sherry
2 teaspoons chopped
  parsley

Melt the butter and cook the shallot or onion in it until
soft. Add the wine and simmer, uncovered, over low
heat until the wine is reduced to one third its original
volume. Add the tomatoes and cook until they are soft.
Stir in the tomato sauce, canned beef gravy, Madeira or
sherry, and the parsley. Bring to a boil. Use without
straining. Makes about 1 cup sauce.

SPINACH SOUFFLÉ

Spinatauflauf

2 pounds spinach, or 1 cup
  finely chopped cooked,
  well-drained spinach
3 tablespoons butter
4 tablespoons flour
½ teaspoon salt

¼ teaspoon pepper
⅛ teaspoon nutmeg
1 cup hot milk
1 cup (¼ pound) grated
  Swiss cheese
4 eggs, separated

Cut the coarse stems off the spinach. With scissors, cut
the leaves—this makes chopping easier later. Wash carefully in several changes of water. Cook in the water

clinging to the leaves. Drain extremely well, pressing spinach with hands. Chop finely. Melt the butter. Blend in the flour and seasonings. Gradually add the hot milk. Cook over low heat, stirring constantly, until the sauce is thickened and smooth. Add the cheese and spinach. Cook, stirring constantly, until the cheese is melted. Cool. Beat the egg yolks until thick, then add to the spinach mixture. Beat the egg whites until very stiff. Carefully fold them into the spinach mixture. Pour into a buttered 1½-quart baking dish. Bake in a preheated slow oven (325°) for about 50 minutes or until inserted tester comes out clean. Serve immediately. Makes 4 servings.

CHEESE TART

Käsewähe

Traditional.

Dough:
3 cups all-purpose flour
1 teaspoon salt
¾ cup butter or

homogenized shortening
or lard
7 tablespoons water
1 tablespoon vinegar

Filling:
½ pound Emmentaler
cheese, cut into ¼-inch
slices
1⅔ cups milk

2 tablespoons flour
2 egg yolks
1 teaspoon salt
¼ teaspoon nutmeg
2 egg whites

To make the dough, sift the flour with the salt. Cut in the shortening until the particles are the size of small peas. Add the water and vinegar. Stir until the dough clears the bowl. Knead on a lightly floured board. Let the dough rest for 30 minutes. Roll out thinly to fit the bottom and sides of a 15 x 10 jelly roll pan. Prick the crust with a fork.

After the pan has been prepared, place slices of cheese over the crust. For the filling, add the milk gradually to the flour. Beat in the egg yolks, salt and nutmeg. Fold in the egg whites which have been stiffly beaten. Pour the mixture evenly over the cheese. Bake in a preheated hot oven (400°) for 20 to 25 minutes or until golden brown. Cut into squares and serve hot.

XIX

Fondues and Raclette

FONDUE comes from *fondre*, the French verb for *to melt*, and a fondue is a melted dish, or a dunk. It is amusing to think of the fondue's progress from a humble peasant dish to a *haut-monde gastronomique* production. Fondue goes back to the patriarchal days when the meal for the whole family was cooked in one dish which was then put in the middle of the scrubbed wooden kitchen table. Porridges, gruels, potato and cheese dishes were prepared in this simple and expedient manner. With spoons, pieces of bread or boiled potatoes everybody scooped up some of the dunk until the paterfamilias stopped eating, the signal that the meal was finished. The luxury of individual plates came at a later date, or was reserved for the rich and mighty.

Fondues were a product of necessity. The cheese and the bread that formed the staple diet of Switzerland were made in the summer and the fall and had to last all winter. Naturally, both became very hard. That the bread would be dunked we can understand from the way the Swiss peasants still dunk their bread in their milk, *café au lait* or wine. As for the cheese, who knows who discovered that it too would melt? I imagine that a piece of cheese was left lying on the open hearth and started melting in the heat.

Fondues, besides tasting good, are a parlor game and an icebreaker at the table. These qualities, plus the fact that fondues are easy to prepare and not expensive, has made them irresistible to adventurous cooks. I have found them very useful for feeding unexpected guests, or during hot weather when a large meal would pall, or late in the evening as a snack rather than the usual sandwiches.

CLASSIC FONDUE

Fondue Neuchâteloise

The chief thing to remember about a cheese fondue is that the cheese must cook over very low heat or it will become stringy. It must also be kept hot, but over low heat, so that it will not heat too much and become tough.

Equipment:

In Switzerland, a fondue is made in a round metal or earthenware pot called a *caquelon*. But a heavy earthenware or cast-iron casserole will serve as long as it holds the heat and is round in shape. The *caquelon* is put in the middle of the table on a fondue-warmer, which may be a mild alcohol flame, a candle-warmer or an electrical hot plate. A heavy chafing dish makes a good fondue receptacle.

Long-handled fondue forks are necessary to hold the bread that will be dunked into the cheese. In a pinch, metal skewers or even knitting needles will do.

The cheese:

The choice of the cheese is of the greatest importance.

For a good fondue, you must have a well-matured Swiss cheese. American Swiss cheese, though good in taste, is seldom, if ever, sufficiently matured to make a proper fondue. It is really worth investing in the Swiss cheese that comes from Switzerland, which can be recognized by the red trademark SWITZERLAND.

For the mildest fondue, use all Emmentaler cheese. For a medium fondue, use half Emmentaler and half Gruyère. If you like a stronger flavor, use two thirds Gruyère and one third Emmentaler. The strongest fondue is made from well-matured Gruyère.

As for the preparation of the cheese: Experience has proved that cheese cut into small dice melts better and more smoothly than grated cheese. The latter tends to form lumps when cooking. If you are in a hurry, shred the cheese but do not grate it.

The wine:

Choose a light, sparkling, slightly acid wine, preferably a Swiss one such as Neuchâtel wine. The acidity of the wine helps to liquify the cheese and to make the melted cheese homogenous. Wines with little acidity are not suited to a fondue. If you think that the wine is not sufficiently acid, add a little lemon juice, which will help prevent the formation of lumps. *One teaspoon of lemon juice for each 6 to 7 tablespoons (3½ liquid ounces) of wine will serve.*

Proportions of cheese and wine:

Count on about 6 to 7 tablespoons of wine for each 6 ounces of cheese. Since cheese, depending on its kind and age, absorbs liquids differently, you may have to adjust these quantities a little. Start with less wine rather than more—you can always add some.

How to cook the fondue:

Rub the fondue pan with a cut garlic clove. Pour in the wine. Put the pan on low heat on the kitchen stove if the fondue is to be made in the kitchen and then taken to the warmer at the table or placed over the heat of the chafing dish. Warm the wine, but do *not* boil it. Dredge the cheese with the flour. Add the cheese gradually, stirring constantly, not clockwise but in the shape of the figure 8. Increase the heat to moderate. Keep on stirring and don't worry if the cheese does not thicken at once. Flavor the fondue with pepper and nutmeg to taste; most likely it won't be necessary to salt it since the cheese itself will be salty enough. Stir a little Kirsch (or, *faute de mieux*, another spirit such as brandy, gin or whisky) into the fondue until the mixture is smooth and creamy. If you want to, add a pinch of baking soda which will make for a lighter fondue.

Now bring the fondue to the table if it has been cooked in the kitchen and is to be put on a warmer. Once the fondue has been made, it must be kept bubbling. Regulate the flame of the warmer so that the fondue keeps on simmering while it is being eaten. A candle-warmer or an electric hot tray at low heat is good for keeping fondues warm.

Toward the end of the meal, some of the melted cheese in the caquelon will form a brown crust at the bottom of the pot. At this stage, keep the heat as low as possible, because an earthenware pot might crack otherwise. The crust can be lifted out with a fork and it is justly considered a special treat.

How to eat the fondue:

Spear a piece of bread with a fork, going through the soft part first and securing the points in the crust. The idea is not to lose your bread when you dip it into the fondue ("First loser pays for the works," say the Swiss). Dunk the bread in the fondue in a stirring motion until your neighbor takes over to give you a chance to enjoy your morsel. While each one takes his leisurely turn in rotation, the stirring helps maintain the proper consistency of the fondue and will assure that each piece is thoroughly coated with melted cheese.

Care of the fondue:

It is essential that the fondue keeps *bubbling lightly* at all times. This is done by regulating the heat, or by turning it off and on.

If the fondue should become lumpy, or the liquid separate from the fat, the following should be tried: put the fondue back onto the stove, stir it thoroughly with a wire whisk and again add ½ teaspoon cornstarch. According to the quantity of the fondue, the cornstarch may be diluted with up to ½ glass of wine. This should bring the fondue mass back to a thick creamy consistency.

It may cheer you to know that if the fondue does turn lumpy despite the care you have taken in following the instructions it is not your fault. Cheese that is not well matured tends to become lumpy and to form "threads." Both these can be avoided by using more Gruyère cheese than the Emmentaler.

If the fondue becomes too thick because of the continuous cooking and evaporation of the liquid, it can be thinned by adding some wine which must be warmed first. For this purpose, put the fondue back onto the stove. Be very careful with the quantities, and if the mass does not amalgamate, add ½ teaspoon cornstarch (diluted) again.

Care of the fondue eater:

Do as the Swiss do: do *not* drink cold or iced drinks, including wine, during the fondue eating. A pony of

Kirsch or of the spirit used in the fondue may be served in the middle of the meal. The Swiss call this *le coup du milieu* and serve the Kirsch in special little containers shaped like a fondue *caquelon*.

Finish your meal with a cup of hot coffee or tea; the true Swiss fondue-lovers prefer tea.

What to eat with a fondue:

A fondue is a meal in itself, but the Swiss like to serve a little smoked ham or sausage afterward, followed by crisp fruit such as apples.

BASIC CHEESE FONDUE

1 pound Switzerland Swiss cheese or half Emmentaler and half Gruyère, shredded or diced; or the equivalent in slices, finely cut

3 tablespoons flour, or 1½ tablespoons cornstarch

1 garlic clove

2 cups dry white wine such as Neuchâtel or any light dry wine of the Rhine (Riesling) or Chablis type

1 tablespoon lemon juice

3 tablespoons Kirsch or brandy

nutmeg, pepper or paprika, to taste

2 loaves Italian or French bread, cut in cubes, crust on each side

Dredge the cheese lightly with the flour. Rub the cooking pot with garlic; pour in the wine; set over moderate heat. When air bubbles rise to surface, add lemon juice. Then add the cheese by handfuls, stirring constantly with a wooden fork or spoon until the cheese is melting. Add the Kirsch and spices, stirring until blended. Serve and keep bubbling hot over burner. Spear the bread cubes through the soft side into the crust, dunk and swirl in the fondue. Serves 4.

LOCAL FONDUE VARIATIONS

There are a number of different fondues in western Switzerland, and their chief difference depends on the cheeses used. Very often, two varieties of the same cheese are used—i.e., a young cheese and a well-matured one. Or two different kinds of cheese may be used. These local cheeses, such as the Vacherin from Fribourg and the Gomser, Bagnes and Orsière cheeses from the Valais have a flavor all of their own which naturally goes into the fondue. Unfortunately, they can seldom, if ever, be found in this country. Of course, all the local fondues use the local wines.

The fondue from Fribourg is different from the classic fondue in as much as no wine nor Kirsch is used in the dish. Hot water is substituted in their stead. The procedure is the same, except that in Fribourg, Vacherin cheese would be used and boiled potatoes substituted for the bread. This fondue is suited for people who do not like alcohol, though in cooking, all alcohol evaporates, leaving only the flavoring of the drink.

The fondue from the Valais uses the local cheeses, and hot milk to melt the cheese in.

The fondue from Geneva occasionally has a handful of peeled, seeded and chopped fresh tomatoes added with the cheese.

FANCY FONDUE VARIATIONS

Egg Fondue:

When the cheese in the fondue pot is reduced to one third its original volume, add 1 to 2 eggs, stirring vigorously with a fork. Some salt may be needed for seasoning.

Fondue with Mushrooms:

Cook some chopped mushrooms (about ¼ pound for each ½ pound of cheese) with a little minced onion in hot butter until their liquid has evaporated. Add the mushrooms to the fondue when it is ready to eat.

Fondue with Truffles:

Cook the chopped truffles in a little hot butter, and add them to the fondue when it is ready to eat.

Fondue with Ham:

Cut cooked ham into dice (about 3 slices for each ½ pound of cheese) and cook the ham in a little hot butter. Add it to the fondue when it is ready. Or cut cooked ham into 1- to ½-inch cubes and use the ham for dunking in the fondue instead of the bread.

Fondue with Champagne:

Use dry champagne instead of the wine, for great results.

Fondue Flambée:

Heat ¼ cup Kirsch (or Kirsch to taste) in a ladle. Pour the hot Kirsch over the bubbling fondue. Flame, and eat when the flame has died down.

LA FONDUE BOURGUIGNONNE

This Swiss table amusement consists of cubed meat, cooked in hot fat, dipped in various sauces and accompaniments. Each guest cooks his own at the table, in a special small, deep saucepan set over a spirit or electrical warmer or in a chafing dish. Strictly speaking, it is not a fondue since nothing melts in this dish. Nor is it "*bour-*

guignonne" since it neither uses red wine nor comes from Burgundy. The charm of Fondue Bourguignonne is that it gives people something to do at the table and that the hostess can prepare the whole thing ahead of time.

To set the table for a Fondue Bourguignonne, place the heating unit in the middle of the table, within easy reach of the guests. Place salt and paprika shakers, pepper mills, sauces and other fondue accompaniments around it. Or, use a Lazy Susan. For each guest, allow two forks, a plate with the prepared meat, a salad plate, a finger bowl with lukewarm water and a slice of lemon, and napkins.

To prepare the Fondue Bourguignonne, allow about ½ pound lean sirloin or other tender beef for each serving. Cut the meat into ¾- to 1-inch cubes, and place it on small wooden or china plates decorated with greens. In the kitchen, half-fill the fondue saucepan with salad oil or clarified butter. (Some Swiss prefer peanut or other salad oil, others butter—but the butter must be clarified. See below.) Heat to the boiling point and set on a heating unit. Put in a small piece of bread to prevent sputtering.

To cook and eat the Fondue Bourguignonne, each guest first helps himself to sauce and other accompaniments, which he puts on his salad plate. He then spears a piece of meat with the first fork and dips it into the boiling fat, cooking it to his liking. Since the fork will be very hot by this time, the guest transfers his meat to the second fork and dips it into the sauce of his choice on his plate. While he is eating, the first fork will have cooled, and he will use it to cook the next piece of meat.

A Fondue Bourguignonne should be served with a variety of sauces and side dishes. The following are suitable:

Béarnaise or Hollandaise Sauce (a must)

Chutney

Cumberland Sauce

Freshly grated horseradish or bottled horseradish

Horseradish cream (cold or hot)

Hot and mild mustards

Mushroom catsup

Mustard Sauce

Pickled mushrooms

Pickled onions

Olives

Sauce Diable

Tomato mayonnaise

Tomato catsup

Mushroom and radish salads, made by slicing vegetables thinly and marinating them in olive oil and lemon juice with salt and pepper to taste are also good accompaniments.

How to Clarify Butter

Melt the butter over low heat or in the top of a double boiler over boiling water. When it is completely melted, remove it from the source of heat. Allow the milk solids to settle at the bottom. Strain the butter through a very fine sieve or through cheesecloth into a jar. The butter will be clear and ready to use. Cover the jar tightly. Keep it like any other butter in the refrigerator. It will keep for 3 weeks.

Note: Clarified butter is the secret of first-class sautéing, butter sauces, basting and baking. The milk sediments in ordinary, unclarified butter brown and burn quickly when butter is heated, and make for a speckled appearance of the food and a bitter taste.

LA FONDUE ORIENTALE

This table game resembles the Fondue Bourguignonne except for the fact that the meat is cooked in boiling hot bouillon rather than fat. It is better for people on a diet, though not quite as tasty.

For a Fondue Orientale, substitute beef or chicken bouillon for the hot fat. The bouillon must continue to boil throughout the meal.

The meats can be varied, and can include lean veal and pork besides beef. Lamb or veal kidneys may also be used. Kidneys should be soaked in cold water for ½ hour before using (change the water three times, drain and dry), and all the hard cores should be removed.

Have the butcher slice the meats into wafer-thin, bite-size pieces. Or slice the meats at home, freezing them slightly to make the job easier.

Beef, veal and kidneys should be lightly cooked in the boiling bouillon, but pork *must* be well cooked.

Serve the Fondue Orientale with the same sauces and accompaniments listed for the Fondue Bourguignonne.

CHOCOLATE FONDUE

This latest of all fondues was invented in New York by an enterprising public relations lady by the name of Beverly Allen. It caught on like wildfire at the Swiss Chalet Restaurant on New York's 48th Street and found its way back to Switzerland, where the citizens also like it very much.

Normally I am not a lover of food stunts, but this chocolate fondue, though very rich, is surprisingly good, especially with fruit. It is an excellent thing for teen-age parties.

The fondue is made with Toblerone, a Swiss milk chocolate with honey, crushed almonds and flavorings.

3 bars Toblerone (3 ounces each)	*cream*
½ cup light or heavy	*2 tablespoons Kirsch, brandy or Cointreau*

Break the Toblerone into separate triangular pieces. Combine all the ingredients in a saucepan or a small chafing dish. Stir over *low* heat until the chocolate is melted and smooth. Serve in a chafing dish over low heat.

For dunkables serve each fondue-er an individual plate with one or a combination of the following:

Angelfood cake or ladyfingers, cut in chunks
Orange or tangerine slices, strawberries, bananas, pineapple chunks (fruit should be well drained)
Profiteroles of cream-puff pastry, 10 to 12 per person

Spear the dunkables on fondue forks or skewers, and dunk into the chocolate as you would with any fondue. Makes 4 servings.

Teen-age Variation: Omit the Kirsch, and flavor the fondue instead with 1 tablespoon instant coffee or ¼ teaspoon each ground cinnamon and cloves.

LA RACLETTE

A traditional country dish of melted cheese, made in many parts of Switzerland but known under this name in the Valais. Heidi's grandfather made raclette before his open fire. The word comes from the French *râcler*, to scrape.

The best raclette is made in the Valais from the local Bagnes or Gomser cheeses which melt easily and have a flavor all their own. Unfortunately they are seldom found in American cheese stores. Semi-soft cheeses that will melt, such as Münster, Tilsiter and California Jack, may have to be used instead, though they are not nearly as good for the purpose.

Raclette is made by holding a whole section of cheese before an open fire or, more recently, before a special electric grill. When the cheese starts to melt, the melted part is scraped off with a knife and placed on an extremely hot plate to prevent the cheese from becoming gummy. (For easier handling, the hot plate is put on a cold one.) Each serving of raclette is accompanied by a boiled potato, sour pickles and sour onions, and plenty of white wine or beer. The number of servings consumed at one sitting can be astonishing because raclette is very good indeed, especially with several glasses of a Fendant du Valais.

From Switzerland also comes an acceptable substitute method of making raclette without a special grill or open fire. This method can be used in an American home kitchen. The Swiss restaurants use it when they don't want to turn on the electric raclette stove for one or two customers.

Preheat the oven to 450°. On a metal or other oven-proof plate, place 2 or 3 paper-thin slices of cheese (this will make one serving). Pop into the hot oven until the cheese is melted. Serve immediately with a boiled potato, pickles and sour onions.

XX

Meats

LARGE ROASTS of meat, such as we know in America and in England, are not traditional in Switzerland. The usual way of cooking big pieces of veal, beef, kid (young goat) or venison is not to roast them in the oven, but to pot-roast them with butter, seasonings, consommé and/or wine, and to thicken the gravy with cream. The Swiss in general like their meat sauced; small pieces, such as cutlets, steaks, etc., are usually served with a wine or a cream sauce. Only recently have the *rotisseurs*—restaurants where the meat is broiled or roasted on a spit—become fashionable. These restaurants are elegant and expensive.

The Swiss eat a good deal of stewed meat of all kinds. In German Switzerland, these equivalents of veal *blanquette* or *boeuf bourguignon* are called *Kalbsvoressen* or *Rindsvoressen,* the words meaning "veal-befores" and "beef-befores." The canny housewives served these less expensive cuts of meat before the main dish of pot-roasted meat at dinners in the country so that the guests would eat their fill and go easy on the main course.

Another very Swiss way of serving meat is to put it in a pastry case and bake it as a pie. Some of these dishes can be very good, but on the whole I find them tiresome. After all, those *pâtés-en-croûte* that are so admired are basically a product of necessity. The famous Lucerne *Kügelipastete* is nothing but veal sausage meat, mushrooms and sweetbreads in a rich sauce cooked in pastry. I don't give the recipe because I really don't believe that any American would ever make the dish.

As a thrifty nation, the Swiss also use the innards of critters, such as tripe, heart and tongue, a good deal. But there is nothing in their way of cooking these meats that makes them different from the French and German methods.

Until recently, before chicken became less expensive because of large imports (also from the U.S.A.), chicken was a great delicacy, and served at important meals without fail. It was roasted or sautéed in the usual manner; hence a scarcity of original chicken recipes. In German Switzerland, chickens are known affectionately as *Guggeli* or as *Mistkratzerli*, which means "little manure scratchers."

Switzerland is a sausage-eating country par excellence. There are any number of superb sausages made from beef, veal and/or pork, prepared in local communities or marketed nationally as ready-to-cook sausage. Their composition and spicing is the secret of their makers. Enough to say that a good sausage has made many a Swiss butcher rich and famous.

The best-known sausages to eat as is, for snacks, include *Cervelas*, *Schübling*, *Landjäger*, *Lyoner*, *Mettwurst*, *Salami* and *Salsiz*. For cooking, there are *Bratwurst*, *Cipolata*, *Berner Zungenwurst*, *Saucisson du Vaud*, *Saucisses au foie* and so on.

Two German Swiss specialties are *Brät* and *Fleischkäse*. *Brät* is sausage meat usually made from veal. The housewife shapes it into little balls, which she poaches in simmering water for 10 minutes. Then she makes a sauce with a little butter, some of the sausages' cooking water and perhaps a little wine, and adds a little heavy cream to it. This is served with rice or noodles. Our own pork sausage meat is too rich to lend itself to this preparation.

Fleischkäse is a meatloaf, composed according to the butchers' wisdom, which is often excellent. Butchers' shops will sport notices: Hot FLEISCHKÄSE AT 3 O'CLOCK, which bring the housewives flocking for the freshly prepared meatloaf. *Fleischkäse*, like scrapple, is usually sautéed in hot butter on both sides, and served with pickles and a salad for supper.

THE ART OF ROASTING VEAL IN THE SWISS MANNER

A juicy, tender veal roast is one of the glories of Swiss cooking, found in restaurants and homes alike as a festive dish. It is not difficult to make, provided certain principles are observed. However, one word of warning: an American veal roast will never be as good as a Swiss one because our veal is inferior to Swiss veal. Fine veal comes from a very young animal fed exclusively on milk; the meat is almost white, with just a pinkish tinge, and very bland. American veal, on the other hand, comes usually from adolescent calves which have frolicked on grass and thus coarsened their meat to a reddish pink. No matter how carefully cooked, it will never be as delicate and tender as Swiss veal. Still, a very good veal roast can be made with American veal.

I think veal is best roasted in a covered saucepan, which should be just large enough to contain the meat. Very little liquid should be added to the meat, the idea being that it should cook in its own juices. A container that just fits the meat makes this easier; a larger container dispels the juices. The reason for cooking the meat covered is to prevent its drying out, which happens easily with veal, especially when, as in this case, there is not enough liquid in the pan to baste it with.

Veal is a bland meat even in America, and it profits from being roasted with a *mirepoix*—that is, a mixture of vegetables such as onions, carrots and celery, that will add to the flavor. The best liquid to use is dry white wine, bouillon, meat glaze or beef drippings diluted with water, which will add character to the meat. These liquids can be used singly, or in combination.

To my mind, the best gravy for veal is made by puréeing the pan juices and vegetables in a blender, or by straining them through a fine sieve. The gravy should not be thickened with flour; the puréed vegetables give it body. Depending on the consistency you want the gravy to have, the puréed mixture can be diluted with a little more liquid (wine, bouillon or diluted drippings, *hot*, never cold). Or, if it is too thin, the gravy can be boiled down; the evaporation of the liquid will thicken it.

Another advantage of cooking veal this way is that a small roast, which would shrink to nothing if oven-roasted in the conventional manner, can be used satisfactorily.

SWISS VEAL ROAST

Kalbsbraten

3- to 4-pound boneless veal roast, tied, at room temperature
1 ½ teaspoons salt
½ teaspoon pepper
¼ cup butter
½ cup minced carrot
½ cup minced onion
½ cup minced celery

¼ cup minced bacon
1 bay leaf
½ garlic clove, minced
½ teaspoon ground thyme
¾ to 1 cup dry white wine or bouillon or diluted beef drippings
parsley sprigs

Make sure that the veal roast is *not* barded—that is, wrapped in sheets of fat. If it is, remove the barding. Rub meat with salt and pepper. Heat butter in a heavy casserole just big enough to contain the meat. Over high heat, brown the meat on all sides; it should be chestnut-colored. Push the meat aside, and add the carrot, onion, celery, bacon, bay leaf, garlic and thyme. Still over high heat, cook until the vegetables are browned. Lower the heat and add wine or other liquid. Simmer, covered, over low heat. Or better, cook in preheated slow oven (325°) about 30 minutes to the pound, or 1½ to 2 hours. The meat should be tender, and its juices a clear yellow color, without a trace of pink. Check occasionally for moisture. If there is a danger of sticking and scorching, add a little more *hot* liquid. There should be about 1 inch of liquid at the bottom of the pan during cooking-time. Turn the meat three times during the cooking-time, to ensure even cooking.

When the meat is done, remove it to a hot serving dish and keep hot. Purée the pan liquid and vegetables in a blender. Return to pan. To achieve desired consistency, thin with a little more of the liquid used for cooking and heat through. Or if the gravy is already too thin, boil it down. Slice the meat and arrange it in overlapping slices on a platter. Dribble a little gravy around the meat—not over it—and serve the remainder separately. Decorate the platter with parsley.

To garnish veal roast in the Swiss manner:

Do not dribble any gravy around the meat. Surround it with asparagus tips and broiled tomato halves, arranged alternately. Decorate with parsley sprigs. Serve with mashed or hashed potatoes.

Flavor Variation: An excellently flavored veal roast is

obtained by rubbing the meat with 2 teaspoons to 1 tablespoon of ground cardamom before rubbing it with salt and pepper.

ROAST VEAL FROM GENEVA

Veau à la Genevoise

2 pounds boneless veal shoulder or leg	1 rib celery, chopped
2 strips lean bacon, cut into strips	4 sprigs parsley
1½-inch slice salt pork, cut into strips	1 bay leaf
¼ cup all-purpose flour	¼ teaspoon crumbled thyme
¼ cup butter	1½ cups water
1 onion, sliced	½ cup white wine
1 carrot, sliced	1½ teaspoons salt
	1 cup sour cream

Lard the veal with the lean bacon underneath and the salt pork on top. Roll the meat in flour. Melt the butter in a Dutch oven. Brown the meat on all sides. Add the onion, carrot, celery, parsley, bay leaf and thyme, water, white wine and salt. Cover tightly. Place in a preheated moderate oven (350°) for 1½ hours, or until the meat is tender. Baste occasionally. Remove the meat to a hot platter and slice. Keep hot. Remove the bay leaf, then stir the sour cream into the pan drippings. Reheat slightly. Do not boil. Serve the sauce over the meat slices.

Note: If you do not have a larding needle, cut narrow little pockets into the meat with a thin, sharp kitchen knife. Push the bacon and salt pork strips into the meat with a knitting needle.

ROAST VEAL FROM ST. GALL

St. Gallner Kalbsbraten

This is a specialty of Mrs. Werner Boos, an excellent cook.

3-pound boneless roast of veal (loin or rump)	*1 tablespoon grated onion*
2 tablespoons salt	*⅔ cup beef or veal drippings, or 1 tablespoon meat glaze*
½ teaspoon freshly ground pepper	*10 slices lean bacon*
1 garlic clove, mashed	

Cut the meat in half lengthwise, but do not cut through it completely. It should be attached to the depth of about 1 to 1½ inches. Open up the meat without tearing it apart. Rub salt, pepper, garlic and onion over half of the meat. Spread the drippings or meat glaze over the other half. Press the two halves together. Wrap the bacon slices around the meat, covering it completely. Tie them in place with string or secure them with toothpicks or tiny skewers. Place the meat on a rack in a shallow pan. Roast in a preheated moderate oven (350°) for 1¼ hours to 1½ hours, or until the meat is completely cooked through. Serve with creamed spinach and *Kartoffelrösti*.

Note: The roasting time depends on the tenderness of the veal, which is determined by the age and feed of the animal. A general guide is to roast for 25 to 30 minutes to the pound, or until a meat thermometer registers 165 to 170°.

MARGOT SCHWARZ'S VEAL WITH MUSHROOMS

Margot Schwarz's Kalbsbraten mit Champignons

From a distinguished Zurich hostess.

4-pound boneless leg of
   veal
1 teaspoon salt
½ teaspoon pepper
2 tablespoons butter
6 shallots, minced
1 pound mushrooms, sliced

1 bay leaf
⅛ teaspoon marjoram
1 cup dry white wine,
   preferably Neuchâtel,
   Dezaley, etc.
½ cup heavy cream
1 egg yolk

Rub the meat with salt and pepper. Heat the butter in a Dutch kettle or casserole. Brown the meat in it over high heat. Lower the heat and add the shallots, mushrooms, bay leaf, marjoram and wine. Simmer, covered, for about 1½ to 2 hours or until the meat is tender. Remove the meat to a serving dish and slice. Keep hot in a low oven. Continue cooking the sauce until it is reduced to about half its volume. Beat the cream and egg yolk together. Stir the mixture into the sauce in the casserole. Cook over low heat, stirring constantly, for about 2 minutes. Pour the sauce over the veal slices. Serve with *Knöpfli* and green peas.

Note: This dish may also be made with 2½- to 3-pound frying chickens, cut into serving pieces.

MINCED VEAL BELLEVOIR FROM ZURICH

Zürcher Geschnetzeltes Bellevoir

Traditional and, like the *Berner Platte*, a national dish. This recipe is by far the most delicious; it was developed by Herr Direktor Hammer, who runs the famous Belle-voir hotel school in Zurich. Swiss butchers sell the veal for this dish already minced; they do the mincing in special machines which produce even julienne strips about ¼ inch wide. The dish must be prepared quickly and just before serving time or the meat will toughen.

1½ pounds veal cutlets	*¼ teaspoon white pepper*
6 tablespoons butter	*1⅓ cups dry white wine,*
3 tablespoons minced	*heated*
shallots	*1 cup heavy cream, heated*
¼ cup brandy	*1 tablespoon minced*
¼ cup flour	*parsley*
½ teaspoon salt	

Trim the meat of all fat and gristle. Cut against the grain into strips ¼ inch wide and 1 inch long. Heat the butter in a large skillet or chafing dish. Add the shallots and cook 3 minutes, or until soft and golden. Add the veal. Cook, stirring constantly, for 2 minutes. Flame with the brandy. When the flame has died down, sprinkle the flour over the veal. Stir in the salt and pepper. Add the hot wine and heated cream. Cook over low heat, stirring constantly, until the mixture comes just below the boiling point and thickens. Sprinkle with the minced parsley. Serve immediately. The classic accompaniments are *Kartoffelrösti* and a tossed green salad.

VEAL WITH CREAM SAUCE

Rahmschnitzel

Traditional.

1½ pounds boneless veal	*⅓ cup butter*
salt	*1 cup consommé*
pepper	*½ cup heavy cream*
juice of 1 lemon, or 2	*paprika*
tablespoons brandy	

Cut the meat into slices ¼ inch thick; they should be all the same size. Sprinkle with salt and pepper and the lemon juice or brandy. Let stand for 10 minutes. Heat the butter and sauté the meat in it for 3 to 4 minutes on each side, or until golden brown. Remove the meat to a heated serving dish and keep hot. Stir the consommé into the pan juices. Bring to a boil and reduce by about one fourth. Stir in the cream and reduce the sauce again until it is shiny and the consistency of heavy cream. Put the meat back into the sauce for 2 minutes to heat it through. Return to the platter and pour the sauce over the meat. Sprinkle with paprika. Serve with green peas and mashed potatoes.

VEAL PICCATA FROM THE TICINO

Piccata alla Ticinese

Traditional. This famous recipe is nothing but our old Italian friend scaloppine, which the Ticinese took over from their Italian neighbors.

1 ½ to 2 pounds veal scaloppine	*juice of 1 lemon*
salt	*flour*
pepper	*⅓ to ½ cup butter*
	½ cup dry white wine

Pound the scaloppine between 2 sheets of waxed paper to make them as thin as possible. Sprinkle with salt, pepper and lemon juice. Let stand for 10 minutes. Dip the scaloppine lightly in flour. Heat the butter, and over high heat, sauté the meat until the scaloppine are golden brown on each side. Remove them to a heated serving dish; keep hot. Stir the wine into the remaining pan juices. Bring the sauce to a boil, and pour it over the scaloppine. Serve with sautéed mushrooms and polenta.

VEAL CUTLETS FROM OUCHY

Veau à la Façon d'Ouchy

I had this exquisite dish in a restaurant on Lake Geneva.

4 tablespoons butter,
* softened*
1 tablespoon anchovy
* paste*
1½ pounds veal scaloppine
thin slices of boiled ham

thin slices of Gruyère
* cheese*
1 egg, beaten with 1
* tablespoon water*
flour
butter for sautéing

Mix the butter with the anchovy paste. Trim the meat so that the slices are all of the same size. Spread the anchovy butter on half of the meat slices. Top each with a slice of boiled ham and cheese. Cover with the remaining veal as if making sandwiches. Secure each meat sandwich with a toothpick or tie with a string. Take care that the cheese is well covered by the meat, or it will ooze out during the cooking. Dip the meat sandwiches in the beaten egg and then in the flour. Sauté in hot butter for about 3 to 5 minutes on each side or until golden brown. Serve very hot with any green vegetable.

Note: The meat for this dish must be very thin.

VEAL CUTLETS À LA STORCHEN

Escalopes de Veau à la Storchen

The Storchen is a lovely old hotel overlooking the river Limmat in Zurich. The food there is superb.

6 very small green peppers
¾ cup cooked rice
6 tablespoons smoked ham
   or Canadian bacon,
   minced
5 tablespoons small cooked
   green peas
2 small tomatoes, peeled,
   seeded and chopped
6 large Italian-style veal
   cutlets (about 1½
   pounds)

salt
pepper
⅔ cup butter
6 tablespoons Madeira
   wine
1½ cups dry white wine
1½ cups Espagnole Sauce
   or beef gravy
3 cooked chicken livers,
   minced

Slice the tops from the peppers. Remove the seeds and membranes. Combine the rice, ham, peas and tomatoes; stuff the peppers with this filling. Pound the veal cutlets until they are large enough to wrap around the peppers. Sprinkle lightly with salt and pepper. Wrap the cutlets around the stuffed peppers. Tie with thread. Melt ⅓ cup of the butter in a large skillet. Add the meat rolls and brown them on all sides. Combine Madeira and white wine. Add ¼ of the wine mixture to the meat rolls. Cover and simmer over low heat about 1¼ hours. Add the remaining wine during cooking-time to prevent the meat from sticking to skillet. Uncover, and cook until all the pan juices have evaporated. Add the Espagnole or beef gravy. Stir in the chopped livers and the remaining butter. Stir until the butter is melted. Place on a heated platter, and garnish each meat roll with 2 tips of cooked asparagus tied with red pimiento strips.

THE COUNCILLORS' CASSEROLE
FROM ZURICH

Zürcher Ratsherrntopf

Traditional, and a one-dish meal. This is one of several versions.

1 pound boneless veal, cubed	*1½ pounds cabbage, shredded*
1 pound boneless pork, cubed	*4 medium potatoes, peeled and cubed*
1 tablespoon salt	*4 white turnips, peeled and sliced*
½ teaspoon pepper	*water or consommé*
1 onion, chopped	

Place a layer of half the veal and pork, and half the salt, pepper, onion, cabbage, potatoes and turnips in a Dutch oven. Top with a second layer of the remaining ingredients. Add sufficient water or consommé to fill the Dutch oven halfway. Cover tightly. Simmer over low heat about 1½ to 2 hours, or until the pork is very tender. If necessary, cook the last 20 minutes uncovered to let the excess liquid evaporate. Serve with a tart cucumber salad.

THE COUNCILLORS' POT FROM BERNE

Berner Ratsherrntopf

1 meaty shin of veal, cut by the butcher into 4 slices	*1 teaspoon ground sage (optional)*
salt	*flour*
pepper	*¼ cup butter*
	1 cup dry white wine
	consommé

Rub the meat with the salt, pepper, and the sage if desired. Dip lightly in flour. Heat the butter in a skillet, and brown the meat on all sides. Arrange the meat in a casserole so that each side stands up; this will keep the flavorful marrow in the meat. Stir the wine into the pan juices in the skillet. Bring to a boil, then pour over the meat. Add enough consommé to come to the top of the meat. Simmer, covered, over the lowest possible heat for about 1 to 1½ hours, or until the meat is very tender. Remove the meat to a hot platter and keep hot. Degrease the sauce. Bring to a boil and reduce to the consistency of heavy cream. Pour over the meat. Serve with green peas and *rösti* potatoes. Serves 2 to 3.

BRAISED LIVER FROM BELLINZONA

Fegato in Umido di Bellinzona

3 tablespoons olive oil	*½ stalk celery, diced*
2 tablespoons butter	*2 slices prosciutto or*
1 medium onion, minced	*bacon, minced*
2 teaspoons flour	*2 bay leaves*
1½ pounds calf's liver, in	*1 cup dry white wine*
one piece	*salt*
1 medium carrot, diced	*pepper*

Heat the olive oil and the butter, and cook the onion until it is soft. Sprinkle with the flour. Add the liver and brown lightly. Add the carrot, celery, prosciutto or bacon, bay leaves and wine. Simmer, covered, for about 1 hour. Add salt and pepper to taste. Place the liver on a warm platter. Strain the pan gravy through a sieve or purée it in a blender. If it is too thin, reduce to desired consistency. Slice the liver and pour the gravy over it. Serve with mashed potatoes and braised onions.

LIVER SKEWERS FROM ZURICH

Zürcher Leberspiessli

Traditional, and a Swiss favorite. The flavor combination of sage and liver is excellent. Fresh leaf sage is best for the dish; dried leaf sage, found in herb shops and Italian grocery stores, ranks next. But an acceptable dish can be made with dried ground sage.

1 ½ pounds calf or beef liver	*12 slices lean bacon, cut into halves lengthwise*
24 pieces leaf sage, or 1 to 2 teaspoons dried ground sage	*¼ cup butter*
	2 medium onions, thinly sliced
	salt

Cut the liver into 24 finger-length pieces. Top each piece with 1 sage leaf. Wrap ½ slice of bacon around the liver and sage. Using 6 skewers, spear 4 pieces of bacon-wrapped liver on each skewer. Melt the butter in a large, heavy skillet, and cook onions until golden brown and soft. Place skewers in the skillet side by side. Over low heat, cook uncovered for 15 minutes or until the bacon is crisp yet still soft. Sprinkle with salt before serving; the amount depends on the saltiness of the bacon. (Do not salt the liver or it will toughen in cooking.) Serve skewers on buttered green beans, with *Kartoffelrösti* on the side.

FLAMED VEAL KIDNEYS

Rognons de Veau Flambés

A chafing-dish specialty prepared and served at the table in many fine Swiss restaurants.

4 medium veal kidneys	*pepper*
3 tablespoons sweet butter	*⅓ cup brandy or Kirsch*
3 tablespoons olive oil	*1 teaspoon Dijon mustard*
flour	*juice from ½ lemon*
salt	

Remove most of the fat and all the membrane from the kidneys. Wash the kidneys and soak for ½ hour in cold water. Change the water twice. (This removes the strong flavor.) Dry the kidneys thoroughly. Cut into ½-inch slices. Heat the butter and oil in a chafing dish or skillet. Dust the kidneys with flour. Brown quickly on all sides. Season with salt and pepper. Pour brandy or Kirsch into a ladle that is hot, or hold a ladle briefly over the burner. Pour heated spirits over the kidneys and flame. Do not flame longer than 1 minute or kidneys will be tough. (The flame can be extinguished by beating it down with a spoon.) Remove the kidneys to a hot serving plate and keep hot. Stir the mustard and lemon juice into the pan juices. Spoon over kidneys if they are to be served from the serving plate, or return kidneys to the chafing dish and toss lightly. Serve with hot buttered rice.

Note: 1 medium veal kidney makes about 1 serving.

POT ROAST WITH MARSALA
FROM LUGANO

Stufato alla Luganese

1 large onion, minced	*salt*
¼ cup chopped prosciutto or bacon	*pepper*
	1 tablespoon flour
1 tablespoon butter	*3 bay leaves*
4 to 5 pounds chuck or round of beef	*½ cup consommé*
	1 cup dry Marsala

Cook the onion, prosciutto and butter together until the onion is soft. Rub the meat with salt, pepper and the flour. Brown the meat over high heat on all sides. Add the bay leaves and consommé. Cook, covered, in a slow oven (275°) for 3 to 4 hours, or until the meat is tender. Remove the meat from the gravy and keep it warm in the oven. Degrease the sauce. Over high heat, reduce it to 1 cup. Add the Marsala and bring to a boil. Slice the meat and drizzle a little gravy over the meat. Serve the remaining gravy in a sauceboat.

Note: The degreasing is best done with a bulb baster. Insert the baster into the pan gravy and bring up the non-fat part of the gravy which rests under the fatty top. Squeeze out the baster into a bowl and repeat until there is only a layer of fat in the pot. Wash out the pot, put the degreased gravy in it and reduce (see above).

POT ROAST WITH MUSHROOMS

Gedämpfter Rindsbraten mit Pilzen

The amount of mushrooms may seem excessive, but it is necessary to saturate the meat with the mushroom flavor. This dish must be cooked in a heavy casserole with a tight-fitting lid.

4 pounds beef pot roast, chuck, round or rump, at room temperature
¼ cup butter
2 pounds mushrooms, sliced
1 small onion, stuck with 3 cloves

1 teaspoon salt
¼ teaspoon pepper
dry white wine (if necessary to prevent scorching)
sweet or sour cream (optional)

Trim the meat of all fat and gristle. Heat the butter in a heavy casserole until it begins to brown. Over high heat, brown the meat on all sides. The meat should be thoroughly browned. Add the mushrooms and onion.

Cook over high heat 2 minutes. Lower the heat as much as possible. Add the salt and pepper. Cover tightly. Simmer over the lowest possible heat 2 to 3 hours, about 30 minutes to the pound, or until the meat is tender. The natural juice of the mushrooms should provide sufficient liquid to cook the pot roast in. But check occasionally for moisture; if necessary to prevent scorching, add a little dry white wine, a couple of tablespoons at a time. Slice the pot roast; place on a hot platter and keep hot. If desired, thicken the mushroom gravy with sweet or sour cream or pour gravy as is over the meat slices. Serve with plain boiled new potatoes or buttered noodles.

Note: The moisture content of mushrooms varies, and therefore it is impossible to say how much wine will be needed or if any will be needed at all. If the gravy is too thin, boil up to let the excessive moisture evaporate to the desired consistency; if too thick, thin with a little additional dry white wine.

BEEF CASSEROLE

Carbonades

1½ to 2 pounds chuck, round or pot-roast meat
salt
pepper
⅓ cup olive oil
1 to 2 tablespoons flour
2 tablespoons butter

1 medium onion, minced
1 medium carrot, minced
¼ cup chopped parsley
1 cup dry red wine
hot water or hot consommé

Trim the meat of all fat and cut into 2- to 3-inch pieces the thickness of ¼ to ½ inch. Sprinkle with salt and pepper. Heat the olive oil in a skillet. Brown the meat over high heat for 2 minuts on each side. Remove the meat to a casserole and sprinkle it with the flour. Pour off the fat from the skillet. Heat the butter in the skillet in which the meat was browned. Cook the onion, carrot and parsley until the onion is soft. Add the wine and bring to a boil. Pour the sauce over the meat, scraping the bottom of the skillet. Add enough hot water or consommé to barely cover the meat. Cook, covered, in a preheated medium (350°) oven for about 1 hour. Place the meat on a hot platter and keep hot. Strain the sauce through a fine sieve or purée in a blender. If it is too thin, reduce to the consistency of heavy cream. Put the meat back in the sauce for 2 to 3 minutes to heat through. Serve from the casserole with plain boiled rice or mashed potatoes.

BEEF STEW FROM THE TICINO

Stufato alla Chiassese

Traditional.

3 to 4 pounds beef, bottom round
4 slices bacon, cut into strips
2 to 4 cloves garlic, slivered
½ cup flour
⅔ cup butter

2 large onions, coarsely chopped
1 cup red wine
water
8 to 10 medium potatoes, peeled and cubed
3 cups tomatoes

Cut slits into the entire surface of the meat. Poke slivers of bacon and garlic into each slit. Roll the meat in the flour. Melt the butter in a large Dutch oven. Brown the meat on all sides. Add the onions and red wine. Simmer, covered, for 1½ hours or until the meat is almost tender. Add water, if necessary to keep the meat from sticking. Add the potatoes and tomatoes. Cook, covered, for 30 more minutes or until the meat and potatoes are tender. Remove the meat and slice. Serve with potatoes or noodles and pan gravy.

JOST SCHMID'S SAVORY BERNESE BEEF STEW

Berner Rindsvoressen

A very good family recipe from the manager of one of Switzerland's great hotels, the Bellevue Palace in Berne. The hotel's cuisine is as memorable as the view over the Alps from the dining terrace.

1 ½ pounds beef chuck or round, cut into 1-inch pieces
½ pound bacon, cut into ½-inch pieces
1 large onion, thinly sliced
3 tablespoons all-purpose flour
4 cups hot beef consommé
1 large carrot, chopped
1 medium stalk celery, chopped

2 tomatoes, peeled and chopped, or 1 tablespoon tomato paste
2 bay leaves
salt
pepper
1 ½ to 2 pounds potatoes, peeled and cut into 1-inch cubes
½ cup chopped parsley

In a heavy skillet, combine the beef, bacon and onion. Cook together over high heat, stirring constantly, until well browned. With a slotted spoon, transfer them to a casserole. Stir the flour into the remaining fat in the skillet. Cook, stirring constantly, until medium brown. Gradually add hot consommé. Cook until the sauce is smooth. Pour the sauce over the meats and onion. Add the carrot, celery, tomatoes, bay leaves, and salt and pepper to taste. Simmer, covered, for about 1 hour or until the meat is almost tender. Stir occasionally. Add the potatoes. Cook until the potatoes are soft. If the stew is too liquid, simmer, uncovered, until it reaches the right consistency. If too thick, add a little more hot consommé. Sprinkle with parsley before serving.

TOURNEDOS FLAMBÉS MÖVENPICK

The taste of this dish depends on the flavor combination of the wines and brandy.

4 tournedos, 1 to 1½ inches thick	*Dijon or other mild mustard*
¾ teaspoon salt	*1¼ cups Pinot Noir or other dry red wine*
½ teaspoon freshly ground pepper	*6 tablespoons dry Madeira*
½ teaspoon ground thyme	*¼ pound mushrooms, sliced*
5 tablespoons butter	*⅔ cup heavy cream*
⅓ cup minced shallots	*2 tablespoons chopped parsley*
¼ cup brandy	

Have the butcher tie the tournedos with string so that they won't come apart in cooking, or secure them yourself with toothpicks. Sprinkle the meat on both sides with the salt, pepper and thyme. Heat 4 tablespoons of the butter in a large, heavy skillet. Cook the shallots in it until soft and golden, but do not brown. Push the shallots to one side of the skillet. Add the tournedos. Cook over high heat for 1 minute on each side. Sprinkle with the brandy, and flame. When the flame has died down, transfer the meat to a heated platter. Spread both sides with just a touch of mustard. Keep warm. Pour the wine and Madeira into the skillet liquid. Cook uncovered until reduced to ¾ cup liquid. Meantime, sauté the mushrooms in the remaining tablespoon of butter for about 2 minutes; they must remain white and firm. Add the mushrooms, cream and parsley to the reduced skillet liquid. Correct seasonings. Return the tournedos to the skillet. Cook uncovered over medium heat for 8 to 10 minutes or to desired doneness. Turn once. Serve with boiled new potatoes and a tossed mixed green salad.

Note: Do not cook more than 4 tournedos at one time. If more are needed, use two skillets.

BERNER PLATTE

Traditional. This assortment of meats, sauerkraut, potatoes and string beans is the Swiss equivalent of a *choucroute garnie*. It is one of the Swiss national dishes. The full *Berner Platte* is a party dish for robust eaters, but for a smaller group, it can be made with fewer meats. A full *Berner Platte* is best prepared in four pots.

First pot:

- 2 tablespoons lard or bacon fat
- 1 large onion, chopped
- 2 cups sauerkraut, drained
- 8 juniper berries, crushed
- 1 cup dry white wine
- 6 smoked pork chops (about 3 pounds)
- ½ pound Canadian bacon, in one piece
- 1 12-inch mild Italian or Polish sausage

Melt the lard in a Dutch kettle. Cook the onion until soft and golden brown. Add the sauerkraut, juniper berries and dry white wine. Put the pork chops and Canadian bacon on the sauerkraut. Simmer, covered, over the lowest possible heat for 1½ hours. Add sausage, and simmer for 1 more hour.

Second pot: 2 teaspoons salt
3 pigs' hocks   ½ cup diced celery
6 pigs' ears and 2 pigs'   2 large leeks, white and
   tongues, or 1 small fresh   green parts, chopped, or
   or smoked beef tongue,   1 medium onion,
   ready to cook   chopped
2 quarts water   1 carrot, sliced

Combine all the ingredients in a Dutch kettle. Simmer, covered, over the lowest possible heat for 1 to 2 hours, or until the meats are tender.

Third pot: boiling salted water
6 medium potatoes, peeled
   and quartered

Cook the potatoes in boiling water until just tender. Drain, and return to the pot. Shake over the lowest possible heat until the potatoes are dry and mealy. Cover with a clean kitchen towel and keep hot.

Fourth pot: ¼ cup butter
1 pound green beans   ½ teaspoon salt
boiling salted water   ¼ teaspoon pepper

Cook the beans in boiling salted water until almost tender. Drain; return to saucepan. Add the butter, salt and pepper. Cook over low heat, stirring frequently, until the beans are tender. Keep hot.

To serve:

Heat 2 large platters. Slice all meats. Place the sauerkraut on the first platter. Top with the pork chops, sliced Canadian bacon and sliced sausage, arranged in overlapping rows. Put the string beans on the second platter.

Arrange the pigs' ears, hocks and sliced tongue on top of the beans. Serve the potatoes separately. Have a choice of hot and mild mustards and different pickles on the table, as well as rye bread and sweet butter. Dry white wine or beer are suitable drinks. Makes 6 to 12 servings, depending on whether the diners are Swiss or foreigners.

MARGOT SCHWARZ'S BAKED LOIN OF PORK

Margot Schwarz's Schweinsfilet im Ofen

4-pound loin of pork,
   boned and cut into
   1-inch slices
½ cup lemon juice
salt
pepper
flour
¾ cup butter
1½ cups chopped onion
1 cup chopped parsley

1 teaspoon ground thyme
1 teaspoon ground sage
as many ¾-inch slices of
   firm tomatos as there are
   meat slices
½ cup grated Parmesan
   cheese
Madeira Sauce (see
   page 266)

Place the pork slices in a bowl and sprinkle them on all sides with lemon juice. Let stand for 3 hours. Drain and dry the meat. Sprinkle the meat with salt and pepper and dip in flour. Heat ½ cup of the butter in a skillet. Sauté the pork slices until they are golden brown. Arrange them side by side in a shallow baking dish. Cook the onion, parsley, thyme and sage in the skillet juices until the onion is soft, stirring constantly. Put a layer of this mixture on each pork slice. Top with a tomato slice. Dot with the remaining butter and sprinkle with Parmesan cheese. Bake in a preheated slow oven (325°) for about 1 hour or until tender. Serve with Madeira Sauce and dry boiled rice.

PICKLED PORK

Schweinebraten aus der Sulz

Traditional. A good company dish.

4 pounds fresh pork loin, boned	1 tablespoon sugar
½ cup salt	1 teaspoon saltpeter
4 to 6 juniper berries	3 cups water
2 to 3 peppercorns	⅓ cup lard, bacon fat or shortening
1 large onion, chopped	½ cup hot water

Cut the pork into slices and pound thin. Sprinkle the meat with half of the salt. Pound the juniper berries and peppercorns and rub them into the meat. Sprinkle the chopped onions over the meat. Combine the remaining salt, sugar, saltpeter and water. Bring the mixture to the boiling point. Remove from the heat and let cool. Pour the mixture over the meat and let stand in a cool place 8 to 14 days. Drain the meat, and sauté slices in ⅓ cup hot lard until golden brown. Add ½ cup hot water. Cook, covered, over a low heat an additional 1½ hours or until the meat is tender. Serve with potatoes and vegetables. Makes 8 servings.

PORK STEW

Schweinsfrikassee

Traditional. This meal is generally prepared when a pig is killed.

2 pounds fresh pork, cut
   into small cubes
2 cups vinegar
3 slices bacon, cubed
¼ cup butter
12 small white onions,
   peeled

4 tablespoons flour
5 tablespoons fresh pig's
   blood (to keep blood
   from clotting add 1
   teaspoon vinegar)
1 cup light cream

Cook the pork in the vinegar ¾ to 1 hour or until almost tender. Brown the bacon cubes in the butter. Add the onions to the bacon and sauté until they are brown. Remove bacon and onions and reserve. Drain the meat, reserving 1 cup of the broth. Brown the meat in the fat in which the onions were cooked. Sprinkle the meat with flour. Add 1 cup of the broth left after the meat was drained. Stir well, and let simmer until the sauce is thickened and the meat is tender. Stir in the pig's blood and cream. Add onions and bacon. Reheat slightly, but *do not boil*. Serve with boiled potatoes.

Note: Needless to say, this dish can be made without pig's blood. In this case, use heavy cream instead of the light cream.

CHESTNUTS WITH PORK FROM URI

Gedörrte Kastanien mit Rauchfleisch

Traditional, and good. This dish can be made with the dried chestnuts that are available in Italian grocery stores during the winter season, or with fresh chestnuts. Dried chestnuts should be soaked in cold water for several hours as for dried beans.

1 pound chestnuts
2 pounds smoked pork

tenderloin
hot water, to cover meat

With a sharp knife, score the chestnuts on the flat side. Place the chestnuts in cold water. Bring to a boil and boil 5 minutes. Drain. Remove the shells and brown skin. Cover the smoked tenderloin with water. Simmer, covered, over low heat for 1 hour or until almost tender. Add the chestnuts, and simmer an additional 20 minutes or until the chestnuts are tender. Add a little hot water to prevent scorching. Cut the meat into slices, and serve hot with the chestnuts.

HAM STEAKS WITH ALMONDS

Le Jambon aux Amandes

6 slices cooked ham, at least ½ inch thick	*chopped blanched almonds*
1 garlic clove	*butter for sautéing*
2 egg yolks, beaten	*1 cup heavy cream*
1½ to 2 cups slivered or	*1 teaspoon Dijon mustard or more to taste*

Rub the ham slices with the garlic clove. Dip in beaten egg yolks to which almonds have been added. With a spatula, tap the almonds onto the meat so that they will stick. Sauté on both sides in a skillet in hot butter until the almonds are golden brown. Put the ham slices on a hot serving dish and keep hot. Mix the cream and the mustard. Stir this mixture into the pan juices in the skillet. Heat through and pour the sauce over the ham. Serve with mashed potatoes and buttered green beans.

Note: Pork or veal chops and even fish fillets may be cooked in the same manner.

BRATWURST

Traditional. These veal sausages are one of the favorite Swiss dishes and they bring nostalgia to any Swiss's heart. In this country they are known as *Weisswurst* or white sausages, and they can be bought in German butchers' shops.

To cook *Bratwurst,* put the sausage into a skillet with enough boiling salted water to cover. Bring the water to a boil and lower the heat so that the water is just below the boiling point. Simmer for 10 minutes. Remove the sausages from the water and pat dry between kitchen toweling. Roll the sausages in a little flour and brown in butter. (The rolling in flour is not strictly necessary, but it makes for a crisper sausage.) If a sauce is desired, pour a little dry white wine into the skillet. Serve the *Bratwurst* topped with onions fried in butter and with mashed potatoes.

FRIED CERVELAS SAUSAGE

Gebratene Cervelas

A traditional dish from Zurich. *Cervelas* is a pork sausage, cured and dried, that the Swiss eat at all times. (There is also fresh *Cervelas,* but this is less popular in Switzerland.) *Cervelas* is very savory, and lends itself both to eating as is and cooking. German-type sausage stores carry it, and in a pinch, the Polish *Kolbasi* sausage can be substituted for *Cervelas.*

6 Cervelas sausages	*2 large onions, coarsely*
½ cup flour	*chopped*
⅓ cup shortening	*¼ cup chopped chives*

Cut the sausages in half lengthwise. Score in two or three places to prevent curling during cooking. Dip the cut edges in flour. Melt the shortening in a skillet. Place the sausages, floured side down, into the hot fat. Add the onions and chives. Cook over low heat until the sausages are crisp. Serve very hot, with the fat and onions from pan. Potato salad, tossed green salad or boiled potatoes are traditional accompaniments for a typical Swiss supper.

LAMB CASSEROLE FROM THE GRISONS

Beckibraten

Traditional.

2 pounds boneless lamb	6 small white turnips,
salt	peeled and halved
pepper	½ cup celery, cut into
¼ cup shortening	1-inch pieces
1 cup dry white wine	2 onions, coarsely chopped
6 medium potatoes, peeled and cubed	¼ cup chopped parsley

Rub the lamb with salt and pepper. In a deep, heavy pan, melt the shortening. Brown the meat on all sides. Add the white wine, potatoes, turnips, celery and onions. Cover tightly. Bake in a preheated moderate oven (350°) for 1¼ to 1½ hours or until the meat is tender. Check occasionally for dryness; if necessary, add a little more wine. Remove meat before serving. Slice and return the meat to the vegetables. Heat through again. Sprinkle with parsley. Serve with a salad and a dessert.

Note: This dish may also be made with pork.

MARY'S ROAST LEG OF MUTTON OR LAMB

Mary's Hammelschlegel

A recipe from the owner of Mary's Old-Timers' Bar in Zurich, which has offered comfort to many a homesick American, from G.I. to V.I.P.

*5-pound leg of mutton or
    lamb*
*6 garlic cloves, cut in
    halves or quarters*

salt
pepper
*prepared mustard,
    preferably Dijon*

Remove the outer papery covering or fell from the
meat, and trim off all the fat. With a pointed knife, cut
small pockets into the meat and insert garlic pieces. Rub
with salt and pepper. Spread all over with mustard, covering all the meat. Return to refrigerator for 24 hours.
Remove from the refrigerator at least 1 hour before
cooking. Place the meat on a rack in a baking pan. Roast
uncovered in a preheated hot oven (450°) for 10 minutes. Turn the heat down to 350°. For well-done meat,
roast about 25 minutes to the pound, from the time the
meat has been put into the oven, or until a meat thermometer registers an internal temperature of 175°. For
less well-done mutton or lamb—preferred in Europe—
roast 15 to 20 minutes to the pound, or to an internal
temperature of 160° to 165°. For rare mutton or lamb,
roast for 10 to 15 minutes to the pound, or to an internal
temperature of 145° to 150°. Remove the roast when
the thermometer registers the minimum temperature,
since it will go on cooking a little longer on its own accord. Do not baste. Serve with white beans and a tossed
green salad. Makes 6 to 8 servings.

Note: Serve the mutton or lamb on hot plates since fat
congeals when cold.

SCHWYZ LAMB-AND-CABBAGE
CASSEROLE

Häfelichabis

Traditional. Nourishing and inexpensive family fare
from Schwyz, one of the three original Swiss cantons, a
non-touristy part of Switzerland to this day.

¼ cup shortening
2 pounds boneless cubed
   stewing lamb, trimmed
   of excess fat

6 cups shredded cabbage
1 teaspoon salt
boiling water or bouillon

Melt the shortening in a Dutch oven. Brown the lamb cubes on all sides. Add the shredded cabbage and salt. Add water or bouillon to the depth of ½ inch. Cover tightly and cook over low heat 1 to 1½ hours or until the meat is tender and the cabbage golden. It may be necessary to add additional water or bouillon, but the liquid should be kept at a minimum.

Variation: Add 1 pound cubed boneless pork to the above ingredients, and increase the cabbage to 8 cups. Cook as directed.

CHICKEN IN A POT

Poulet im Topf

A traditional restaurant dish.

2 3-pound chickens, cut
   into quarters, or 1
   6-pound fricassee
   chicken, cut into
   serving pieces
¼ cup butter
salt and pepper
paprika
1 cup hot water
1 tablespoon cornstarch

dissolved in ¼ cup
   water
2 pounds peas, shelled and
   cooked
6 medium carrots, sliced
   and cooked
1 small head cauliflower,
   broken into flowerets
   and cooked
6 small potatoes, cooked

Brown the cut chickens in butter in a large Dutch oven. Sprinkle with salt, pepper and paprika. Cover tightly and cook slowly until tender. Add a little water from time to time. Remove the chickens. Add the hot water to the pan drippings. Stir in the cornstarch dissolved in ¼ cup water. Cook, stirring constantly, until smooth and thickened. Pile the chicken in the center of the pot. Surround with the peas, carrots, cauliflower and potatoes. Replace the lid. Reheat for 10 minutes. Serve at once.

SAUTÉED CHICKEN BREASTS WITH CHEESE FROM THE JURA

Suprêmes de Volaille Jurassienne

2 *whole chicken breasts*	2 *eggs, lightly beaten*
½ *cup flour*	¾ *cup breadcrumbs*
¼ *teaspoon grated nutmeg*	¼ *cup grated Swiss cheese*
salt	⅓ *cup melted butter*
black pepper, freshly	4 *lemon wedges*
ground	

Have the chicken breasts split in half and boned. Remove and discard the skin. Season the flour with nutmeg, salt and pepper. Dredge the breasts lightly in the flour mixture, then in the eggs, then in a mixture of breadcrumbs and Swiss cheese. Brown on all sides in the melted butter. Serve hot with lemon wedges. Makes 4 servings.

CHICKEN BREASTS CLARIDENHOF

Suprêmes de Volaille Claridenhof

A specialty from one of Zurich's finest restaurants. It can be made successfully at home.

4 large chicken breasts

6 tablespoons butter

3 large egg yolks

1 cup heavy cream

¾ teaspoon salt

¼ teaspoon freshly
  ground pepper

¼ teaspoon ground

cardamom (optional)

½ cup brandy

½ cup Kirsch

buttered baby peas

sautéed mushroom caps

toast triangles

parsley sprigs

Ask the butcher to skin, bone and cut the chicken breasts into halves. Divide the butter and melt it in two large skillets. (Two skillets are needed to cook the chicken breasts which must not touch each other while cooking; no one skillet is large enough to accommodate 8 halves. Furthermore, the breasts must be cooked at the same time to be equally fresh and warm.) Over medium heat, cook the chicken breasts in hot butter for about 6 to 10 minutes on each side, or until golden brown and done. The cooking-time depends on the thickness of the breasts. Transfer the chicken to a hot serving platter, preferably a silver one. Keep warm. Combine the skillet juices into one skillet, scraping up the brown glaze at the bottom of the pans. Beat together the egg yolks, cream, salt, pepper and cardamom. Add brandy and Kirsch to the skillet juices. Heat and flame spirits. As the flame gradually dies down, lower the heat. Stir the cream mixture into the skillet. Over the lowest possible heat, heat through thoroughly, but do not boil or the sauce will curdle. Spoon the sauce over the chicken breasts. Alternate little mounds of buttered baby peas and sautéed mushroom caps around the rim of the platter. Garnish with toast triangles and parsley sprigs. Serve hot, on heated plates.

Note: An added note of elegance can be achieved by sprinkling 2 medium minced truffles over the chicken breasts.

CHICKEN WITH LEMON-EGG SAUCE

Pollo alla Ticinese

Traditional.

2½- to 3-pound frying chicken, cut into serving pieces	3 tablespoons butter
	2 teaspoons flour
	1 cup consommé
salt	1 egg
pepper	juice of 1 lemon
1 tablespoon olive oil	

Skin the chicken and trim off all the fat. Sprinkle with salt and pepper. Heat the olive oil and the butter together in a casserole. Cook the chicken pieces over high heat until they are golden on all sides. Lower heat. Sprinkle the chicken with the flour. Add the consommé. Simmer, covered, over low heat for 30 minutes or until the chicken is tender. Check for moisture; if necessary, add a little more consommé. Remove the chicken from the casserole and keep it warm. Beat the egg and lemon juice together. Stir into the liquid in the casserole. Put back the chicken pieces and heat through for 2 minutes. Serve with dry boiled rice and a tossed salad. The recipe serves 2 to 3.

CHICKEN QUAI DES BERGUES

Poulet Quai des Bergues

A recipe from my youth as a student in Geneva, where I had it in my *pension*. The trick of the dish is to use coarse and fresh breadcrumbs, or, rather, bread shreds and plenty of sweet butter. The breadcrumbs are best made by trimming the crust from sliced bread and tearing the slices apart with the fingers.

2 2½- to 3-pound frying chickens, cut in serving pieces	2 cups sweet butter or more
salt	1 loaf fresh white bread, shredded into crumbs
pepper	

Skin and trim the chicken pieces. Sprinkle them with salt and pepper. Cream the butter until it is very soft. Spread the chicken pieces with the creamed butter on all sides. Put the chicken pieces into a large buttered baking dish. Dot with more butter. Bake in a preheated moderate oven (350°) for about 30 to 40 minutes or until the chicken is tender and the crumbs golden and crisp. Serve with watercress or Belgian endive vinaigrette.

SAUTÉED CHICKEN FROM THE TICINO

Pollo in Padella alla Ticinese

2 2½- to 3-pound frying chickens, cut into serving pieces	1 cup dry white wine (approximately)
½ pound bacon, diced	salt
6 spring onions	pepper
1 tomato, peeled and chopped	½ teaspoon crumbled rosemary or ground thyme (optional)

Put the chicken and the bacon into a heavy casserole. Cook, covered, over low heat, stirring frequently, until the chicken pieces are golden. Add all the other ingredients. Simmer, covered, for about 25 to 30 minutes or until the chicken is tender. Put the chicken on a heated serving dish. Degrease the sauce. Pour a little of the sauce over the chicken pieces. Pour the remaining sauce over a dish of spaghetti or plain boiled rice.

POT-ROASTED KID FROM LOCARNO

Capretto alla Locarnese

Young kid (goat) is a popular Swiss meat, and a very tasty one. But this recipe, which is rather a method of cooking, can be applied to lamb or venison or beef. The meat may be left whole, cut into steaks or into small pieces. The cooking-time depends on the kind and size of the meat. The taste of the dish depends on the combinations of seasonings.

2 pounds boneless kid, lamb or venison, whole or cut as desired
salt
pepper
3 tablespoons butter
1 to 1½ teaspoons ground sage
6 juniper berries, crushed
½ teaspoon dried mint, or

1 tablespoon chopped fresh mint
⅛ teaspoon ground cinnamon
⅛ teaspoon ground nutmeg
1 cup dry white wine (approximately)
1 cup heavy cream
1 tablespoon rum

Sprinkle the meat with the salt and pepper. Heat the butter in a casserole, and add the sage, juniper berries, mint, cinnamon and nutmeg. Cook, stirring constantly, for 3 minutes. Add the meat and brown on all sides. Lower the heat and add the wine. Simmer, covered, until the meat is tender. Remove the meat and keep warm. Strain the sauce. Put the sauce back into the casserole, and stir in the cream and the rum. Bring to a boil and reduce to the consistency of heavy cream. Return the meat to the sauce and heat through. Serve with dry boiled rice and green peas.

VENISON STEAK MIRZA

Rehschnitzel Mirza

From the first-class station restaurant in Zurich. Veal or pork may be cooked in the same manner, either in one piece or as boneless cutlets.

1½-inch-thick slice of venison, weighing about 1½ pounds	*2 teaspoons crumbled rosemary*
salt	*flour*
pepper	*4 tablespoons butter*
2 teaspoons paprika	*1 cup dry red wine*
	½ cup heavy cream

Rub the venison with the salt, pepper, paprika and rosemary. Dip lightly in flour. Heat the butter, and brown the meat quickly on both sides. Add the wine. Simmer, covered, over low heat until the meat is tender; the cooking-time depends on its age. Remove the meat to a heated platter, slice and keep hot. Stir the cream into the pan juices and bring to a boil. Pour the sauce over the meat. Serve with stewed apples and cranberry sauce.

XX (*Meats*)

MEAT FRITTERS

Fleischkräpfli

Traditional.

Dough:

¼ cup olive oil

6 tablespoons lukewarm water

3 eggs

4½ cups all-purpose flour

1 teaspoon salt

Filling:

1 cup ground cooked veal

1 cup ground cooked pork

2 slices white bread, broken into fine soft crumbs

¼ cup milk (approximately)

1 egg, well beaten

½ teaspoon salt

¼ teaspoon pepper

1 tablespoon chopped chives

deep fat for frying

For the dough, beat the olive oil and water together. Beat in the eggs. Sift the flour with the salt. Add the liquid to the flour. Stir until a stiff dough is formed. Knead on a floured board for 1 minute until dough is smooth. Let stand covered for 20 minutes.

To make the filling, grind the meat together, then add soft breadcrumbs and blend well. Add the beaten egg and enough milk to form a paste that can be spooned. Blend in the salt, pepper and chives.

Roll out dough to ⅛-inch thickness. Brush half of the dough with water. On this half of the dough, place teaspoonfuls of the meat mixture about 1 inch apart. Cover the balls with the second half of the dough. Press dough together around each ball of filling. Cut into squares or diamonds with a pastry cutter. Fry in deep fat

(263)

at 370° for about 3 to 4 minutes or until golden brown. Serve with a salad or whortleberries.

MEAT PIE FROM CHUR

Churer Fleischtorte

Traditional. Meat pies of this kind turn up in almost all the Swiss cantons, as a savory way of making a little meat go a long way. This is the Grisons version as eaten in Chur, the canton's capital, a ravishing medieval mountain town.

Dough:

3 cups sifted all-purpose flour

½ teaspoon salt

¾ cup butter

⅓ cup lukewarm milk or water

1 egg yolk

Filling:

¼ pound boneless raw veal, ground twice

¼ pound boneless raw pork, ground twice

4 strips bacon, diced

1 tablespoon butter

⅓ cup chopped onions

2 tablespoons chopped parsley

4 slices stale white bread, crusts removed

1 cup milk or beef broth (approximately)

1 teaspoon salt

½ teaspoon pepper

¼ teaspoon ground nutmeg

To make the dough: Sift the flour with the salt. Cut the butter into the flour until the particles are the size of small peas. Beat together the milk and egg yolk. Add to flour. Stir until dough cleans the bowl. Knead lightly on a floured board. Roll out two thirds of the dough. Roll out thinly enough to cover the bottom and sides of a well-greased 8-inch layer cake pan. Allow dough to overhang slightly.

To make filling: Combine the veal, pork and bacon. Heat the butter in a small skillet and cook the onions and parsley until the onions are soft and golden. Soak the bread in milk or broth; chop with a fork. Add the onions, parsley, bread, salt, pepper and nutmeg to the meats. Blend thoroughly. The mixture should be the consistency of a thick purée; if necessary, add a little more milk or broth. Pour mixture into pastry-lined pan. Roll out the remaining dough to fit the top of the pie. Place dough on top of meat. Overlap the two layers of dough and pinch the edges together. Brush with slightly beaten egg white and milk. The pie should be about 1½ to 2 inches thick. Bake in a preheated moderate oven (350°) for about 50 minutes to 1 hour. Serve, in the Grisons manner, with a compote of dried apples or prunes, or with a tossed green salad.

MEAT PIE FROM URI

Urner Plattenpastete

1 pound thinly sliced round steak
1 pound thinly sliced veal cutlet
½ pound thinly sliced fresh ham
2 hard-cooked eggs
1 head lettuce cut into 6 wedges
½ cup butter
2 teaspoons salt
½ teaspoon pepper
1 recipe piecrust for 1 9-inch pie shell
1 egg, well beaten

Remove all sinews from the meat. Pound the meat and cut it into 2-inch squares. Place the meat, hard-cooked eggs and lettuce in layers in a well-greased 2-quart casserole. Dot each layer with butter. Place the ham on top. Sprinkle with salt and pepper. Roll out the piecrust to fit the top of the casserole. Make sure that the dough fits tightly over the filling and the edges are sealed to prevent drying. Brush with beaten egg. Bake in a preheated moderate oven (350°) for 1½ hours or until the meat is tender and the crust is golden brown.

MADEIRA SAUCE

2 tablespoons butter
2 tablespoons minced
    shallots
1½ cups canned beef

gravy or brown sauce
⅓ cup dry Madeira
2 tablespoons brandy
½ cup heavy cream

Melt the butter and cook the shallots until they are tender. Stir constantly. Add the canned gravy, the Madeira and the brandy. Bring to a boil, lower the heat and simmer for 2 minutes. Stir in the cream and heat through, but do not boil. Makes about 2⅓ cups sauce.

XXI

Vegetables

VEGETABLES have always been an integral part of the Swiss diet, among all classes of society. This healthy habit antedates the modern knowledge of vitamins, and it is due to the fact that other foods were scarce and that the people were poor and had to eat what they could grow.

All the vegetables that Americans know are eaten in Switzerland, and pretty much in the same fashion as we eat them. The vegetable dishes characteristic of Switzerland are those in which different vegetables are combined in a dish; used as meat stretchers; or cooked with a starch, such as rice, or with cheese, to make for a more substantial dish.

ARTICHOKE BOTTOMS WITH CHEESE

Fonds d'Artichauts au Fromage

12 artichoke bottoms, cooked fresh or canned	*½ teaspoon paprika*
¾ cup finely diced Swiss cheese	*¾ cup soft breadcrumbs*
	½ cup melted butter

Place the artichoke bottoms in a buttered shallow baking dish. Pour a few tablespoons of water into the bottom of the dish, just enough to prevent the artichoke bottoms from sticking during the baking. Mix the cheese and paprika. Fill the artichoke bottoms with the mixture. Sprinkle the breadcrumbs over the cheese. Drizzle 2 teaspoons of butter over the breadcrumbs in each artichoke bottom. Bake in a preheated moderate oven (350°) for 10 minutes or until the cheese is melted and the crumbs are browned. Serve as a vegetable course or with plain roasted poultry or meats.

BAKED CAULIFLOWER MOUNTAIN FASHION

Blumenkohl nach Oberländer Art

This is a good main dish for meatless days.

½ cup finely grated dry
  pumpernickel
  breadcrumbs
2¾ cups grated Swiss
  cheese
1⅓ cups light cream
3 egg yolks

¼ teaspoon ground
  nutmeg
½ teaspoon salt
¼ teaspoon pepper
1 large head cauliflower
boiling salted water
¼ cup melted butter

Combine the breadcrumbs, grated cheese, cream, egg yolks, nutmeg, salt and pepper. Break the cauliflower into flowerets. Cover with boiling salted water. Cook until tender. Drain. Put the cauliflower into a heavily buttered shallow baking dish. Spoon the cheese mixture over the cauliflower. Dribble the melted butter over the cheese mixture. Bake in a preheated moderate oven (350°) for 15 to 20 minutes, or until the cheese is crusty and browned. Serve with a tossed green salad or a green vegetable.

CHEESE SOUFFLÉ BAKED IN TOMATOES

Tomates Soufflées Jurassiennes

12 firm medium tomatoes	*½ cup light cream*
salt	*6 eggs, separated*
pepper	*1 ¾ cups grated Swiss*
3 tablespoons butter	*cheese (about 7 ounces)*
2 tablespoons flour	

Slice off tomato tops. Scoop out tomatoes, but do not break the shells. Sprinkle with salt and pepper. Melt butter and stir in flour. Gradually stir in the cream, 3 of the egg yolks, ½ teaspoon salt and ¼ teaspoon pepper. Cook over low heat, stirring constantly, until smooth and thickened. Remove from heat. Beat in the grated cheese and the remaining egg yolks. Cool. Beat the egg whites until stiff. Fold into the egg and cheese mixture. Spoon into the tomatoes; fill each about three quarters full. Place the tomatoes in a buttered shallow baking pan. Bake in a preheated moderate oven (350°) for 15 to 20 minutes, or until the soufflé has risen and is golden brown. Serve immediately. As a main dish, use 2 tomatoes for each serving. Or use as a garnish for fish, poultry and meats.

CHESTNUT PURÉE

Purée de Châtaignes

Chestnuts are much used as a vegetable in western Switzerland.

1 pound chestnuts
1 teaspoon oil
boiling water
3 stalks celery
1 small onion, sliced
2 to 4 tablespoons butter

salt to taste
¼ teaspoon freshly
    ground black pepper
¼ cup heavy cream,
    heated

Make a gash on the flat side of each chestnut. Place the chestnuts in a pan with the oil and shake them until they are coated with fat. Transfer to a preheated moderate oven (350°) and heat until the shells and skins can be removed easily. Cook the chestnuts in boiling water with the celery and onion until they are tender. Drain; discard celery and onion. Purée or mash the chestnuts. Season with salt and pepper. Beat in the butter and cream. Serve with game, or pork.

LEEKS AU GRATIN

Lauchgratin

2¼ pounds leeks
1 cup water
½ teaspoon salt

2 cups grated Swiss cheese
1 cup julienne strips ham

Trim the leeks. Cut them into finger-length pieces and wash them thoroughly in at least three changes of cold water to remove all earth and grit. Add 1 cup water and the salt. Cook, covered, over low heat until the leeks are tender but firm, about 10 to 20 minutes. Drain. Reserve ½ cup of the water in which the leeks were cooked. Place the leeks in one layer in a well-buttered shallow baking dish. Top with 1 cup of the cheese and all of the ham strips. Add the ½ cup vegetable water. Sprinkle the remaining cheese over the top. Bake in a preheated moderate oven (350°) for about 20 minutes or until golden brown. Serve with fried fish or any hot or cold meats.

LETTUCE AND BACON

Lattich und Speck

Traditional from Berne and Neuchâtel, and very good.

6 small heads Romaine
   lettuce
boiling water
½ *pound lean bacon,*
   diced
1 *large onion, minced*
1 *tomato, peeled and*

   seeded (*optional*)
½ *teaspoon salt*
¼ *teaspoon freshly*
   ground pepper
hot bouillon or water (*if*
   necessary to prevent
   dryness)

Trim the lettuce heads and leave them whole. Wash under running cold water and shake dry. Plunge the lettuce into boiling water and cook the heads about 2 to 3 minutes, or until they are barely tender. Drain. In a deep skillet, cook the bacon until crisp. Pour off about half of the fat. Add the onion and tomato, if desired, and cook until the onion is tender. Add the lettuce. Sprinkle with salt and pepper. Cook, covered, over low heat about 10 minutes. Check for dryness; if necessary, add a little hot bouillon or water, a tablespoon at a time. The lettuce should be dry when cooked. Serve hot, with roast meats or poultry.

BASLE ONION TART

Basler Zwiebelwähe

Traditionally served during carnival time.

Dough:
2 cups all-purpose flour
½ teaspoon salt
Filling:
1½ tablespoons butter
6 large onions, thinly
    sliced
½ teaspoon salt
⅓ cup diced bacon

½ cup butter
4 tablespoons ice water
    (approximately)

2 cups milk
3 tablespoons all-purpose
    flour
2 eggs, well beaten
2 cups shredded cheese

To make the dough, sift the flour with the salt. Cut in the butter until the particles are the size of small peas. Add the ice water. Stir until a stiff dough is formed. Knead quickly on a lightly floured board. Roll out to fit the bottom and sides of a well-buttered 10-inch layer cake pan. Prick the dough several times with a fork.

To make the filling, heat the butter in a pan and sauté the onions. Add the salt and diced bacon. Cook over medium heat until the onions and bacon are golden brown. Add the milk gradually to the flour. Stir until smooth. Beat in the eggs and cheese. Add the sautéed onions and the bacon, including the fat in which they were sautéed.

Pour the mixture into the dough-lined pan. Bake in a preheated moderate oven (350°) for 30 minutes. Raise oven temperature to 400° and bake 5 minutes longer, or until the top is browned and crisp. Cut into wedges; serve hot.

FRENCH-FRIED PARSLEY

Prezzemolo Fritto

This is delicious when properly done. The parsley must be stemmed, washed and dried between kitchen towels until it is absolutely dry—but it must not be bruised in the drying. The fat must be at the proper temperature—just at the smoking point. If the fat is not hot enough, the parsley becomes limp, if too hot, it will be the color of olives. There should be about 4 inches of fat in the frying kettle for each cup of parsley.

1 cup fresh, stemmed, washed and well-dried parsley
salad oil or frying fat

Put parsley in frying basket or strainer. Immerse in hot oil or fat. Fry for about 1 to 2 minutes or until no hissing noise is heard. Drain on paper toweling and serve immediately with any meats.

FRIED POTATO CAKE

Kartoffelrösti

Traditional: the national potato dish of German-speaking Switzerland, where it is eaten daily. The potatoes are shredded on a special shredder which is standard kitchen equipment. It is best to cook the potatoes a day ahead.

2 pounds potatoes	*¾ teaspoon salt*
4 tablespoons butter	*2 tablespoons hot water*

Boil the potatoes in their skins and cool. Peel and shred, or cut the potatoes into julienne strips. Heat the butter in a large skillet. Gradually add the potatoes and salt. Cook over low heat, turning frequently with a spatula, until the potatoes are soft and yellow. Press the potatoes with a spatula into a flat cake. Sprinkle with hot water. Cover, and cook over low heat until the potatoes are crusty and golden at the bottom, about 15 to 20 minutes. Shake the pan frequently to prevent scorching and, if necessary, add a little more butter to prevent sticking. Turn into a hot serving dish crusty side up and serve immediately.

BERNESE RÖSTI

Berner Bauernrösti

Use lard instead of butter to cook the potatoes in. Cook 3 slices diced bacon with 1 small minced onion until the onion is soft and add them to the potatoes. Do not brown the bacon or the onions.

CHEESE RÖSTI

Käserösti

Add ½ cup diced Gruyère or Emmentaler cheese to the potatoes.

DRIED-PEAR- OR DRIED-APPLE-AND-POTATO CASSEROLE

Schnitz und Erdäpfel

Traditional, and very old. Home-dried fruits were and still are part of the rural Swiss diet.

2 tablespoons lard or
  butter
1 large onion, coarsely
  chopped
3 cups cubed raw potatoes,
  washed and drained

1 cup dried pears or apples,
  cored, soaked for 2
  hours
½ teaspoon salt
2 tablespoons honey
  (optional)

Melt the lard in a covered saucepan. Add the chopped onion, and sauté until transparent. Add the potatoes, drained pears, salt and honey, if desired. Add water to cover the contents of the pan. Replace the lid and cook over a low flame about 30 minutes or until the potatoes and pears are tender. Serve with beef, pork or smoked meats.

POTATOES FROM FRIBOURG

Pommes de Terre Fribourgeoises

2 pounds potatoes
⅓ cup butter
2 teaspoons salt

1½ cups milk
2 eggs
½ cup grated Swiss cheese

Peel the potatoes and cut them into ⅛- to ¼-inch slices. Heat the butter in a deep skillet. Add the potatoes and sprinkle them with the salt. Cook, stirring constantly, for about 2 minutes. Cook, covered, over lowest possible heat until the potatoes are tender. Stir frequently. Beat together the milk, eggs and cheese. Pour the mixture over the potatoes, distributing it evenly. Cover again and cook for another 10 minutes or until a golden crust has formed at the bottom. Serve on a hot platter, crust side up.

POTATO CAKES FROM THE GRISONS

Kartoffelplätzli

Traditional. They can be prepared beforehand, refrigerated and cooked when needed.

2 pounds potatoes
2 eggs, well beaten
⅓ cup all-purpose flour
2 cups grated cheese
1 teaspoon salt
¼ teaspoon ground

nutmeg, or ½ teaspoon
*   ground marjoram*
½ cup flour
½ cup shortening or
*   cooking oil, heated*

Peel the potatoes and cut them into cubes. Steam or cook in the smallest amount of water possible to prevent scorching. Drain. Press the potatoes through a sieve or a ricer. Cool. Add the eggs, flour, grated cheese, salt, nutmeg or marjoram. Blend well to form a soft dough. Shape the dough on a lightly floured board into a roll measuring 2 inches in diameter. With a sharp knife, cut into slices ¾ inch thick. Dip slices into the ½ cup flour. Brown on both sides in hot shortening. Serve hot with fish, meats or vegetables.

BAKED POTATO CAKE

Kartoffelkuchen

Traditional.

4 large potatoes or 6
*   medium potatoes, peeled*
*   and cubed*
boiling salted water
½ cup potato stock
1 teaspoon salt

2 eggs
¾ cup cream
½ pound (2 cups) grated
*   Emmentaler, or 1 cup*
*   Emmentaler and 1 cup*
*   Parmesan cheese*

Cook the potatoes in boiling salted water. Drain, reserving the stock. Press the potatoes through a ricer. Add the stock. Beat well, with the salt. Spoon the potatoes into a well-buttered 8-inch square pan. Smooth the top. Beat the eggs with the cream. Blend with grated cheese. Pour the egg and cheese mixture over the potatoes. Bake in a preheated moderate oven (350°) for 25 to 30 minutes.

PURÉE OF POTATOES
AND KNOB CELERY

Kartoffel und Sellerie Purée

This is frequently served with pork. Knob celery, celery root or celeriac is the only kind the Swiss know; our own stalk celery is a rarity.

2 large knob celery	*4 tablespoons butter*
(celeriac)	*salt*
2 large potatoes	*pepper*
boiling salted water	*⅓ to ½ cup heavy*
	cream

Peel the knob celery and cut it into eighths, as you would an apple. Peel the potatoes into the same size pieces. Cover with boiling salted water. Cook over medium heat until the vegetables are tender. Drain. Strain the vegetables through a fine sieve or a food mill. Beat in the butter and salt and pepper to taste. Add the heavy cream. Return to heat and beat until hot and fluffy.

POTATOES WITH LEEKS
FROM FRIBOURG

Les Pommes de Terre aux Poireaux
à la Mode de Fribourg

2½ pounds potatoes
boiling salted water
2 tablespoons butter
¾ pound leeks, thinly
   sliced

2½ cups grated Swiss
   cheese
3 eggs, well beaten;
1⅓ cups milk
1 teaspoon salt
1 teaspoon nutmeg

Peel the potatoes. Cook them in boiling salted water until tender. Drain and cool. Cut the potatoes into ⅛-inch slices. Melt the butter. Cook the leeks in the butter until golden. Butter a 2-quart casserole or baking dish generously. Measure 2 cups of grated cheese. Place a layer of potatoes, then leeks, then grated Swiss cheese (from the 2 cups), ending with a layer of potatoes. Beat the eggs with the milk, salt and nutmeg. Pour the mixture over the layers in the casserole. Sprinkle with the remaining ½ cup grated cheese. Bake in a preheated moderate oven (375°) for 20 to 30 minutes or until the eggs are set and the top is golden brown.

SCRAMBLED SUPPER POTATOES
FROM THE GRISONS

Maluns

Traditional. This is a very old dish, and typical rural family fare. *Maluns* brings the tears into the eyes of the

Bündner Leute, or folks from the Grisons who are far away from home.

6 medium potatoes	*⅔ cup butter*
2 cups all-purpose flour	*(approximately), or*
2 teaspoons salt	*lard*

Cook the potatoes until they are tender. Chill. Peel and grate finely. Sprinkle with flour and salt, and mix well. Heat about ½ cup of the butter in a heavy skillet. Add the potato mixture. Stir until small balls are formed. Over very low heat, cook for about 35 minutes, stirring frequently. Add the remaining butter during the cooking process, a tablespoon at a time. The potato mixture should be the size of peas, golden-brown in color, and soft inside. In the Grisons, the dish is served for supper with a dried fruit compote and oceans of *café au lait* or milk.

COUNTRY MASHED POTATOES
WITH PEARS

Kartoffelstock mit Birnen

Traditional rural food in all of German-speaking Switzerland.

6 pears or apples,	*1 teaspoon ground*
quartered, stems	*cinnamon*
removed and cored	*1 whole clove*
½ cup water	*grated rind of ½ lemon*
½ cup white wine	*6 cups mashed potatoes*
½ cup sugar	*2 cups soft breadcrumbs*
	⅓ cup butter, melted

Combine the pears, water, white wine, sugar, cinnamon, clove and grated lemon rind. Bring to a boil and
simmer until the pears are tender. Remove the clove. In a
greased 3-quart serving dish place a layer of mashed
potatoes. Add a layer of pears and 2 spoonfuls of the
sauce. Repeat, ending with the mashed potatoes and the
remainder of the sauce. Brown the breadcrumbs in the
melted butter. Spoon over the mashed potatoes. A good
dish for children.

MASHED POTATOES BAKED
WITH BACON

Unterwäldner Ofentori

Traditional.

2 pounds potatoes	2 tablespoons minced
¼ cup butter, softened	onion
2 eggs	½ pound thickly sliced
⅓ cup heavy cream	bacon, cut into ½-inch
salt	strips
pepper	

Boil potatoes in their skin. Peel, and while still hot,
force them through a sieve or a food mill. Beat in the
butter. Beat the eggs with the heavy cream and beat into
the potatoes. Season with salt and pepper to taste; the
amount of salt depends on the saltiness of the bacon. Add
the onion and mix thoroughly. Place in a buttered 1½-
or 2-quart baking dish. Smooth the top with a knife or
spatula. Stick the bacon strips into the potatoes to resemble the quills of a porcupine. Bake in a preheated moderate oven (375°) until the potatoes are browned and
bacon-crisp. Serve with a mixed green salad, and if you

want to be like a Swiss farmer, with *café au lait* for supper.

CHEESE POTATOES FROM SCHWYZ

Käsekartoffeln

Traditional—an old Swiss variation on mashed potatoes.

6 large potatoes	*⅓ cup butter*
boiling salted water	*2 large onions, chopped*
3 cups grated Swiss cheese	*1½ cups hot milk*

Peel the potatoes and cut them into cubes. Cook in boiling salted water until tender. Drain. Place layers of potatoes and grated cheese in a 2-quart casserole. Melt the butter. Add the chopped onions and sauté until golden brown. Add the hot milk, stir, and pour the entire mixture over the cheese and potatoes. Serve at once very hot, with a tossed salad, for luncheon.

POTATO DIP

Stupfete

Traditional and typical of the simplicity of former Swiss living. The family sat around the table and dipped their potatoes. *Café au lait* was served with it. With a salad, this makes a surprisingly tasty simple supper.

18 small new potatoes, scraped	*2 medium onions, finely chopped*
boiling salted water	*2 teaspoons salt*
¾ cup salad oil	*½ teaspoon pepper*
1¼ cups cider vinegar	

Cook the potatoes until tender in boiling salted water. Combine oil, vinegar, onions, salt and pepper in an enamel saucepan. Cook over low heat until the onions are soft and transparent. Place the sauce on a warmer at the table. Dunk potatoes in the hot sauce and eat while hot.

RICE AND CABBAGE FROM URI

Reis und Kraut

Traditional, and a very good dish of its kind.

1 medium head cabbage	*3 cups cooked rice (1 cup*
boiling salted water	*uncooked)*
½ cup melted butter	*½ teaspoon nutmeg*
	2 cups grated Swiss cheese

Core the cabbage. Cook in boiling salted water until tender. Drain, and chop finely. Add the melted butter, cooked rice, nutmeg and grated cheese. Toss lightly. Reheat, and serve immediately.

SQUASH AU GRATIN

Le Gratin de Courgettes

From the Canton de Vaud.

3 large or 6 small Italian	*1 ½ cups milk*
squash (zucchini)	*1 tablespoon flour*
2 tablespoons butter	*¼ teaspoon pepper*
1 teaspoon salt	*⅔ cup grated Gruyère or*
½ teaspoon pepper	*Swiss cheese*
4 eggs, well beaten	

Peel and dice the squash. Melt the butter in a heavy saucepan, and add the squash. Sprinkle with salt and pepper. Cover, and cook over very low heat, stirring from time to time, until the squash is soft and mushy. Beat together the eggs, milk, flour and pepper. Drain the squash and add to the egg mixture. Beat well. Pour the mixture into a 2-quart buttered baking dish and sprinkle with cheese. Bake in a preheated hot oven (400°) for 20 minutes or longer until the top is brown and the casserole is slightly puffed.

SPINACH-AND-LEEK TART
FROM THE TICINO

Smeazza

Traditional. Cornmeal is much used in the Ticino, either as polenta or to make other dishes more substantial.

1 pound fresh spinach, well washed	*½ cup water*
	salt
10 medium leeks (use both white and green parts)	*pepper*
	¼ pound Gruyère cheese, cut into thin strips
3 eggs	
½ cup cornmeal	*4 tablespoons butter*

Finely chop the spinach and the leeks. Beat together the eggs, cornmeal and water. Combine this mixture with the vegetables, and season with salt and pepper to taste. Mix well. Add the cheese. Butter a 1½-quart baking dish and place the mixture in it. Dot with the 4 tablespoons of butter. Bake in a preheated moderate oven (350°) for 15 to 20 minutes, or until set and golden brown.

SPINACH AND RICE AU GRATIN

Epinards et Riz au Gratin

3 cups cooked rice
3 cups cooked drained
   coarsely chopped
   spinach
1 onion, finely chopped
   and sautéed in 1
   tablespoon butter

1 cup grated Emmentaler
   cheese, mixed with
1 cup grated Gruyère
   cheese
3 tablespoons butter

Place a layer of half the rice in the bottom of a well-greased 2-quart shallow baking dish or casserole. Mix the spinach with the sautéed onions. Sprinkle with ½ cup of the cheese mixture. Add a layer of spinach. Sprinkle with another ½ cup cheese. Repeat layering once more. Dot the top with butter. Bake in a preheated moderate oven (350°) for 20 minutes. Serve with tomato sauce.

WHITE TURNIPS, LUCERNE STYLE

Weisse Luzerner Rüben

Traditional.

12 small or 6 medium
   white turnips
boiling salted water

¼ cup cubed bacon
1 large onion, chopped
½ teaspoon salt

Peel the turnips and cut them into matchstick-size. Cook them briefly in boiling salted water until they are barely tender. Drain. In a skillet, fry the bacon until limp. Add the onion and cook until golden brown. Add the drained turnips and salt. Sauté over low heat about

20 minutes, stirring occasionally, or until the turnips are golden brown. Serve with boiled beef.

HEIDI'S BRAISED WATERCRESS

Heidi's gedämpfte Kresse

The slightly bitter flavor resembles that of dandelion greens. It makes an excellent vegetable for rich meats, such as duck, pork or ham.

4 large bunches watercress　*¼ cup hot chicken*
3 tablespoons butter　　　　　*bouillon*
½ teaspoon salt　　　　　*sour cream* (*optional*)

Remove the heavy stems below the leaves of the watercress. Wash thoroughly and remove any wilted leaves. Place in a saucepan. Cook, covered, with the water clinging to the leaves for about 7 minutes. Stir in butter, salt and hot bouillon. Cook until the watercress is on the dry side and is the consistency of chopped spinach. Serve hot with a bowl of sour cream on the side.

The following two recipes from the Ticino, where I spent my childhood, are examples of rural ingenuity in the kitchen. They taste surprisingly good.

POTATOES AND BEANS FROM THE VALLE-MAGGIA

Patati e fasöl fregiei

Cook equal quantities of green beans and peeled and cut-up potatoes together in salted water. Drain and mash as for mashed potatoes, with lots of butter, salt and pepper and a little thyme.

SWISS CHARD FROM THE VAL DI BLENIO

La Scarpaza di Blenio

Chop or cut Swiss chard into fine pieces. Butter a baking dish and sprinkle it with fine dry bread crumbs. In this dish, put alternate layers of Swiss chard, thinly sliced Swiss cheese and a sprinkling of flour and salt. Sprinkle the top layer with more breadcrumbs and dot with butter. Bake in a preheated moderate oven (350°) for about 15 minutes or until the vegetable is tender.

XXII

---◄◆►---

---◄◆►---

Cakes and Cookies

---◄◆►---

T HERE IS no end to the wonderful cakes and cookies that delight native and foreigner alike in Switzerland. After all, what greater pleasure is there than taking a scenic walk through fragrant woods and flowering meadows, the blue horizon limited by the snowy Alps, and ending up at a *Konditorei, confiserie* or *pasticceria* full of the most delectable goodies? No pleasure is greater, I declare. The coffee and chocolate, hot or iced, and the ice creams crowned by whipped cream made by cows and not chemical labs as only too frequently in the United States, are the perfect accompaniments to all the *Kuchen, Torten, Schnitten, tartes, pastes, mille-feuilles* and so on, almost *ad infinitum*.

The most elegant Swiss cakes are, and have always been, baked by professional pastry cooks. Even in small rural towns, the pastry cooks produce goodies with the finest ingredients that would do the Ritz proud. No Swiss home cook feels compelled, or is expected, to be a *confiseur:* on the contrary, when she wants to honor her family or guests, she will buy her cakes at the best pastry shop she knows.

Swiss housewives have an advantage over American
ones in as much as bakeries sell excellent uncooked puff
paste, *pâte brisée* or tart pastry, yeast dough, and even
doughs for various kinds of cookies. Today, few Swiss
cooks will make anything from scratch if they don't
have to, and all these prepared doughs are extremely
popular. In the case of puff paste, the advantage is overwhelming because puff-paste creations are among thé
most elegant and tricky pastries.

Cakes and tortes serve as desserts, and they are also
eaten in the afternoons when the ladies—and often the
gentlemen—meet in the cafés and *confiseries* for their
afternoon chats. At four in the afternoon, all these places
are jammed beyond belief, with everyone stuffing himself or herself on irresistible goodies. I admit, however,
that the Swiss ladies are now more concerned about their
figures than they were in my childhood, when a visit to
the local *confiserie* was the highlight of the family Sunday-afternoon walk or the acknowledged birthday treat.

About every cake or pastry in France, Germany,
Austria and Italy is known and admirably made in Switzerland. Even among the indigenous pastries, there are
many that I would have liked to put into this book, if
space had permitted. Thus I beg forgiveness if a reader
misses some splendid confection that he or she loved
above all others when in Switzerland. *C'est la vie.*

As I said elsewhere, professional Swiss pastry cooks
have been famous for centuries wherever people lived
well. This made it unnecessary for the Swiss housewife
to go in for elaborate bakings. But there are several
homemade pastries which are very Swiss indeed. One of
them is the fried cookie or the fritter, cooked in deep fat
such as lard or vegetable oil, deliciously crisp and not at
all greasy; they are excellent with a glass of wine or a cup
of coffee. Alas, these fried cookies, of rural origin, are
becoming obsolete except for special occasions like New

Year's, Carnival, weddings and christenings. There used to be dozens and dozens of varieties in every canton. There were the Bernese *Strübli*, where the batter was pushed through a funnel into the boiling fat (this cookie is still popular with our Pennsylvania Dutch); the Bernese *Schenkeli*, little thighs, so called because of their shape; the *Salbeiküchlein* from Zurich, sage fritters; the *Kniescheiben*, where the dough was pulled wafer-thin over the cook's knee, which gave the cookie its name; the long thin cookies called apron strings, grassworms, and so on. I don't believe that many Americans would make these cookies, so I have limited myself to a few samples such as the *Eieröhrli* which are made at Carnival time in Zurich.

Very Swiss, too, and dating back for many centuries, are the fruit breads filled with dried apples, pears, almonds and any other fruit that was at hand. These also arose from necessity, utilizing the local bounty and keeping edible for a long time. Here again, there are any number of varieties of these breads, depending on canton and locality. Some blend the fruit into the dough, others encase it in a dough shell. Some of these breads are small, in the shape of buns, and others are baked in the shape of long loaves. I have included one of the recipes (page 305) which I consider best. I make it frequently and give it away for Christmas presents instead of the traditional American fruit cakes.

Spice cakes made with honey, plain or filled with almonds, called *Lebkuchen* or *Biber* are very traditional in Switzerland, though their ancient origin goes back to the times when Nuremberg was the capital of the Central European spice trade. They have a firm place in Swiss hearts, but they really are far better made by professionals, as any Swiss will admit.

As with cakes, all of Europe's cookies are known and loved in Switzerland. Home baking flourishes particularly at Christmastime, though there is not the orgy of festive baking that can be found in Germany, Denmark or Norway. The cookies that follow are the most popular ones, though the *Leckerli* or honey or marzipan cookies are usually bought rather than homemade.

As for breads, not many Swiss housewives bake their own any longer as they used to do. Switzerland has always had a splendid selection of very different breads, light, dark or a mixture of the two, and made with different flours. These breads vary from canton to canton and even locally, in flavor, texture and in shape. They all are excellent. Generally speaking, the German-speaking Swiss favor dark or semi-white breads, and the French- and Italian-speaking Swiss the white breads.

Perhaps the two most famous Swiss breads are the butter rolls, eaten at breakfast or for snacks, which vary in shape in different cities like Zurich, Basle or Neuchâtel, and the braided loaves from Berne, for which there is a recipe on page 320. These braided loaves are still baked at home, and it is said that for the two weeks around Christmas no self-respecting Bernese will eat anything but their *Zöpfe*.

Switzerland, like so much of Europe, used to be a cereal-eating country, using cereals in all sorts of forms. Today, it is interesting to see how modern nutrition, food distribution and a high standard of living have increased the use of vegetables, meats, eggs and similar foods, even among the populations of the distant Alpine villages.

HOW MANY SERVINGS IN A CAKE?

The number of servings in a cake varies, depending on the kind of cake and the use it is put to: if it is to be a dessert at the end of a meal or served alone with a beverage. The following table gives an approximate number of servings in a cake of a given size:

8-inch round layer cake makes 8 servings
9-inch round layer cake makes 8 to 10 servings
8-inch square cake makes 6 servings
9-inch square cake makes 6 to 8 servings
13 x 9 x 2 cake makes 24 2-inch squares and 12 3-inch squares
9-inch or 10-inch spring-form cake or torte makes 10 to 12 servings

BLACK ALMOND CAKE

Schwarze Mandeltorte

½ *pound almonds (about* 1½ *cups)*	1 *teaspoon ground cinnamon*
1 *cup sugar*	8 *eggs*

Do not blanch the almonds. Grate or grind them finely. Add the sugar and cinnamon. Add the eggs, one at a time, beating well after each addition. Pour the batter into a well-greased 9-inch spring-form pan. Bake in a preheated slow oven (325°) for 45 to 50 minutes.

ALMOND PIE

Gusstorte

6 *eggs*	*tablespoons water (approximately)*
1 *cup sugar*	1 *cup mashed cooked dried*
1½ *cups blanched almonds, ground*	*fruit (prunes, apricots,*
pastry, using 1 cup flour, ⅓ *cup butter, 2*	*pears, peaches)*

Beat the eggs until they are thick and lemon-colored. Beat in the sugar gradually, 1 tablespoon at a time. Fold in the nuts. Roll out the pastry dough to fit the bottom of a well-greased 9-inch spring-form pan. Spread the dough with the cooked dried fruit. Pour the nut mixture over the fruit. Bake in a preheated moderate oven (350°) for 30 to 40 minutes, or until the eggs are set.

ALMOND PIE FROM FRIBOURG

Gâteau d'Amandes de Fribourg

Traditional.

Dough:	½ *cup butter*
2 cups all-purpose flour	*6 tablespoons water*
½ *teaspoon salt*	(*approximately*)
Filling:	*7 tablespoons water*
2 cups blanched almonds,	¼ *cup butter*
ground	½ *teaspoon salt*
⅔ *cup sugar*	*1 egg yolk, beaten*

For the dough, sift the flour and the salt together. Cut in the butter until the particles are the size of small peas. Add the water gradually, stirring with a fork until the dough cleans the bowl. Knead lightly. Chill for 15 minutes.

To make the filling, combine the almonds, sugar, water, butter and salt. Heat quickly in a saucepan, stirring constantly until the mixture boils. Cool to room temperature.

Roll two thirds of the dough to fit the bottom of a well-buttered 8-inch spring-form pan. Spread with the nut mixture. Roll the remaining dough and cut into

¾-inch strips. Form a lattice over the filling. Brush with the egg yolk. Bake in a preheated hot oven (400°) for 15 to 20 minutes or until golden brown.

CARROT CAKE

Aargauer Rübli Torte

Traditional. This is a somewhat lighter version of a famous old cake.

⅔ cup grated raw carrots, firmly packed
1⅔ cups finely ground unblanched almonds
¾ cup fine dry breadcrumbs
½ teaspoon ground mace
½ teaspoon ground cinnamon
1 teaspoon ground ginger
1 teaspoon double-acting
baking powder
6 large eggs, separated
1¼ cups sugar
2 teaspoons grated lemon rind
3 tablespoons Kirsch or fresh lemon juice
Confectioners' Sugar Glaze (see below)
candied fruits for garnish

Combine the carrots and almonds in a mixing bowl. Mix the breadcrumbs with the spices and baking powder, and blend with the carrots and almonds. Beat the egg yolks until they are thick and lemon-colored. Gradually beat in the sugar, lemon rind and Kirsch or juice. Beat until thick. Stir into the carrot mixture. Beat the egg whites until they are stiff. Fold them into the carrot mixture. Line an 8-inch spring-form pan with waxed paper. Grease and sprinkle the bottom and sides with fine dry breadcrumbs. Turn the mixture into the pan. Bake in a preheated moderate oven (350°) for 1 hour or until a cake tester inserted into the center comes out dry and clean. Cool. Remove from the pan. Spoon Confectioners' Sugar Glaze over the sides and top of the cake. Garnish with candied fruits. Store in a tightly covered cake box. This cake improves with age.

Confectioners' Sugar Glaze

1 cup sifted confectioners' sugar	*1 tablespoon water* *¼ teaspoon vanilla extract*

Blend the sugar and water together until smooth. Add the vanilla extract.

BERNESE CAKE

Bernerbrot

Traditional.

1⅓ cups cream	*2 teaspoons baking powder*
2 eggs	*½ cup jam (prune,*
1¼ cups sugar	*apricot, strawberry)*
3½ cups flour	

Beat the cream with the eggs and sugar. Sift the flour and baking powder together. Add the flour to the cream mixture. Beat well for a smooth dough. Butter a 7-inch spring-form pan and spread it with half the dough. Spread the jam over the top of the dough. Bake in a preheated moderate oven (350°) for 15 minutes. Remove from the oven and spread with the remaining dough. Replace and bake for another 15 to 20 minutes or until brown. One-day-old *Bernerbrot* tastes better than fresh.

MAX BAUMANN'S CHOCOLATE CAKE

Schokoladentorte à la Baumann

I had this delicious cake at the house of Max Baumann, who is an executive of Chocolats Tobler. His wife, an accomplished cook and a handsome and elegant woman as well, makes it with the firm's Berna, a dark, sweet chocolate, which is available in the U.S.A.

½ *pound Tobler Berna, or other dark, sweet chocolate*	*1 teaspoon vanilla extract, or ½ teaspoon almond extract*
½ *cup butter, at room temperature*	*1 cup sifted all-purpose flour*
1 cup sugar	*1 teaspoon baking powder*
5 eggs, separated	*sifted confectioners' sugar*

Grate the chocolate on a cheese grater. Place in the top part of double boiler over boiling water. Stir in the butter and sugar. Stir until butter and sugar are melted and the mixture is smooth. If the top part of the double boiler is large, it may be used as a mixing bowl. Otherwise, pour the mixture into a mixing bowl. Beat in egg yolks, one at a time, beating well after each addition. Stir in the vanilla extract. Sift the flour with the baking powder. Stir into the chocolate mixture. Beat the egg whites until stiff. Fold into dough. Grease a 9-inch spring-form pan and line it with wax paper. Pour dough into pan. Bake in preheated moderate oven (350°) for 40 to 45 minutes, or until cake tests done. Cool on a rack. Place a 9-inch lace paper doily on top of the cake. Sift confectioner's sugar over it. Remove doily; there will be a lacy pattern on the cake. Or serve the cake with a side dish of whipped cream.

EASTER TART

Osterfladen

Traditional in the German-speaking parts of Switzerland.

⅔ cup blanched almonds, ground
⅔ cup sugar
1 ¾ cups light cream
⅔ cup milk
1 tablespoon cornstarch
or rice flour
4 eggs, separated
½ cup raisins, plumped
1 tablespoon Kirsch (optional)
1 9-inch pie shell, unbaked

Mix the almonds with the sugar and the cream. Beat until smooth. Combine the milk and cornstarch to make a smooth paste. Beat into the almond mixture. Add the egg yolks, one at a time, beating well after each addition. Stir in raisins and Kirsch. Just before baking, beat egg whites until stiff and fold them into the mixture. Pour into the unbaked pie shell. Bake in a preheated slow oven (325°) for about 1 hour or until browned and set. Serve cooled, but not chilled.

Note: The filling may also be baked in a 9-inch spring-form pan lined with puff paste. This makes for a richer and fancier tart.

ENGADINER NUSSTORTE

Traditional and very famous.

1 cup sweet butter
⅔ cup granulated sugar
1 tablespoon rum
1 egg plus 1 egg yolk
⅛ teaspoon salt
grated rind of 1 lemon
4 cups sifted all-purpose flour

Filling:
1 ⅓ cups granulated sugar
1 cup heavy cream, heated
3 tablspoons honey
2 tablespoons Kirsch

2 ¾ cups (11 ounces)
   coarsely chopped
   walnuts
1 egg yolk beaten with 1
   tablespoon cream

For the dough, have the butter at room temperature. Put all the remaining ingredients into a bowl and work with the fingers until all the particles combine and form a dough. Chill the dough for 20 minutes. Press one third of the dough into the bottom of an 11-inch spring-form pan. Divide the remaining dough into three parts. Press one part up onto the sides, making them 1 inch high.

To make the filling, cook the sugar over low heat in a large skillet until it liquefies and becomes golden brown. Gradually stir in the hot cream. Stir over low heat until the sugar blends with the cream. Scrape the bottom of the skillet to loosen all the sugar syrup. Stir in the honey and Kirsch. Fold in the nuts. Cool slightly.

Spread the filling in the pastry-lined pan. Roll the second part of the dough with the fingers into strips and place the strips about 1 inch apart over the top of the nut filling, forming a lattice. Roll the remaining dough and use it to form an edge around the outside of the torte. Brush the lattice and edge with egg beaten with cream. Bake in a preheated moderate oven (350°) for 45 minutes or until richly browned. Bake the torte on the bottom shelf of the oven. Makes one 11-inch torte.

FILBERT TORTE

Haselnusstorte

Traditional, from Zurich. The cake is easy to make and keeps well. Don't be alarmed if it sinks in the middle; this is its nature.

½ pound (about 1½
  cups) filberts, blanched
  and finely ground
1 cup sugar
7 eggs

grated rind of 2 lemons
1 tablespoon Kirsch or
  brandy
fine dry breadcrumbs

Combine the ground filberts and sugar. Beat in 1 whole egg. Separate the remaining eggs. Beat in the egg yolks, one at a time, beating well after each addition. Stir in the lemon rind and Kirsch. Beat egg whites until stiff. Fold into the nut mixture. Butter a 9-inch spring-form pan thoroughly. Coat with breadcrumbs. Pour dough into it. Bake in a preheated slow oven (325°) for 45 minutes to 1 hour or until the cake tests done. Cool on a rack. Serve in narrow wedges with ice cream or a fruit compote.

Note: This cake is usually not iced. But if desired, it can be iced with a mixture of fresh lemon juice and sifted confectioners' sugar. The mixture should be thin enough to make a thin glaze.

HOLIDAY GÂTEAU

Gâteau Grande Fête

1 Almond Cake (see
  below)
¼ cup cognac
1 recipe Swiss Broyage (2
  baked circles—see
  below)

¾ cup apricot jam
1 recipe Chocolate Cream
  (see page 300)
½ cup coarsely chopped
  toasted almonds
confectioners' sugar

Sprinkle the Almond Cake with cognac. Let it stand for ½ hour. Place one Broyage layer on a large serving plate. Spread with half of the jam. Set the cake on top; spread with the remaining jam. Top with the second Broyage layer. Reserve ½ cup Chocolate Cream; spread the remainder on the sides of the torte. Press chopped almonds on the sides. Decorate the top with a border of tiny rosettes made from the reserved Chocolate Cream. Dust with confectioners' sugar. Makes 12 servings.

Note: This torte may be made one day in advance.

Almond Cake

3 eggs plus 2 egg yolks	*¾ cup sifted flour*
½ cup sugar	*⅓ cup blanched almonds, ground or finely grated*
1 teaspoon grated lemon rind	*¼ cup butter, melted and cooled*
½ teaspoon vanilla	

Combine the eggs, egg yolks, sugar, lemon rind and vanilla. Beat until the mixture is thick and fluffy. Sprinkle the flour and almonds over the mixture; fold in gently. Stir in the butter. Spread evenly in one buttered and floured 9-inch layer cake pan. Bake in a preheated moderate oven (350°) for 20 to 25 minutes, or until firm and golden brown. Cool on a rack.

Swiss Broyage

3 egg whites (6 tablespoons)	*dash salt*
1 teaspoon vanilla extract	*¾ cup sugar*
⅛ teaspoon cream of tartar	*⅓ cup sifted cornstarch*
	¼ cup blanched almonds, ground or finely grated

Grease and flour 1 large or 2 medium cookie sheets. Press the rim of a 9-inch layer cake pan lightly into the flour to make 2 guide circles for the Broyage. Combine the egg whites, vanilla, cream of tarter and salt in a large bowl. Beat until soft peaks form when the beater is raised. Gradually add ½ cup sugar, beating constantly until stiff peaks form. Combine the remaining ¼ cup sugar, cornstarch and almonds. Fold into the egg white mixture. Place half in each circle on a cookie sheet, and spread evenly to fill the circle. Bake in a preheated slow oven (325°) for about 25 minutes, or until sandy colored and dry. Remove carefully from cookie sheet. Cool on rack. Makes two Swiss Broyages.

Chocolate Cream

½ *cup butter*	*1 egg yolk*
6 ounces semi-sweet	*1 tablespoon cognac*
chocolate, melted	½ *teaspoon vanilla*
and cooled	

Cream the butter. Beat in the chocolate, egg yolk, cognac and vanilla.

APPENZELL HONEY CAKES

Appenzeller Biberfladen

Traditional. As I said elsewhere, the best *Biber* are made by professionals, who guard with their lives the secret of their spicing and the way they combine honeys of different kinds and various kinds of flours. This recipe is of necessity a simplified Swiss version, but then, few people in Switzerland would make *Biber* at home when the ones they can buy are so much better.

⅔ cup sugar
¾ cup honey, lukewarm
1 egg
1 teaspoon ground
   cinnamon
½ teaspoon ground cloves
½ teaspoon ground
   coriander

½ teaspoon ground anise
½ teaspoon nutmeg
½ cup milk or Kirsch
4½ cups all-purpose flour
   (approximately), sifted
   with
2 teaspoons baking powder

Beat the sugar, honey, egg, spices and milk or Kirsch until smooth and well blended. Stir in the flour (which has been sifted with the baking powder) until a stiff dough is formed. Knead lightly on a floured board. Cover the dough and let rest 1 hour. Roll dough to ½ inch thickness. Cut into 3-inch rounds. Brush with milk. Bake on a greased cookie sheet in a preheated slow oven (325°) for 15 to 20 minutes or until lightly browned. Makes about 6 dozen.

HONEY CAKE

Lebkuchen

Traditional.

1 cup honey
½ cup strong coffee
1 cup cream
2 tablespoons Kirsch
⅔ cup sugar
1 teaspoon nutmeg

1 teaspoon crushed anise
   seeds
2 teaspoons cinnamon
4 cups flour
   (approximately)
1½ teaspoons baking
   powder
1 teaspoon baking soda

Blend the honey with the coffee, cream, Kirsch, sugar and spices. Add the flour which has been sifted with the baking powder and baking soda. Beat until smooth. The dough should be sticky. Turn the batter into a well-buttered 15 x 10 baking pan, spreading evenly to the corners. The dough should be ¼ to ½ inch thick. Bake in a preheated moderate oven (350°) 30 to 40 minutes. Cut into bars.

MERINGUE TORTE

Vacherin Chantilly

Traditional. A *vacherin* may be different things: one of several cheeses from French-speaking Switzerland or a meringue dessert. Dessert *vacherins* are a specialty of the fine *confiseurs*, who, depending on their fancy, decorate them in many different ways by coloring the whipped cream with chocolate or food colorings, and with candied violets, angelica and the like.

8 egg whites, at room temperature
¼ teaspoon salt
¼ teaspoon cream of tartar
2 cups sugar
1 teaspoon vanilla, or ½

teaspoon almond flavoring
2 cups heavy cream, whipped and sweetened to taste with confectioners' sugar

Preheat the oven to 225°. Lightly grease and flour 2 large baking sheets. Line with waxed paper. With a pencil, trace the outline of a 9-inch layer cake pan four times, twice on each baking sheet. There should be four circles. Beat the egg whites until frothy. Add the salt and cream of tartar and beat thoroughly. Add the sugar, one tablespoon at a time, beating constantly. Add the vanilla or almond flavoring, and beat until the meringue is stiff and glossy, but not dry. Divide the meringue into four parts, one part for each meringue circle. Fill a pastry bag with the meringue mixture. Press out a pencil-thick strip of meringue around the outer rim of each waxed-paper circle. Then make a lattice by pressing four strips of meringue horizontally and four strips vertically across the waxed-paper circle, touching the meringue rim. Make similar lattices on the next three waxed-paper circles. Bake until firm and dry but still white, about 45 minutes. Cool the meringues a little, but remove from the paper while they are still warm, using a broad spatula.

Divide the whipped cream into two parts. Reserve one. Place one meringue lattice on a serving dish. Spread lightly with some of the whipped cream. Top with the second layer and repeat the process until all the four layers are used, but do not spread whipped cream on the last layer. Fill the pastry bag with the reserved whipped cream. Pipe decorative swirls on the sides of the *vacherin* and a row of rosettes around the top. Fill the lattice cavities with candied violets, candied cherries or with large fresh strawberries. Keep refrigerated until serving time, but serve as soon as possible after decorating with the whipped cream.

Note: The *vacherin* may also be baked in four ordinary layers, but it won't look as pretty.

VACHERIN AUX VERMICELLES

Make a *Vacherin*, page 302, but decorate the sides with Chestnut Purée, page 269, piped from a pastry bag with a small tube.

RURAL PIE FROM URI

Urner Bauernpastete

Traditional. Country treat, served in the farmhouses for special occasions, and as old a dish as the canton of Uri.

Dough:
4 cups sifted all-purpose
  flour
½ cup sugar
1 ½ teaspoons salt
1 cup butter, softened

1 egg, well beaten
1 cup cold cider,
  approximately, or ½
  cup cider, ½ cup
  applejack

Filling:
½ cup yellow raisins,
  plumped
½ cup black raisins,

  plumped
¼ cup sugar
½ teaspoon cinnamon
1 egg yolk, well beaten

For the dough, sift the flour with sugar and salt. Stir in the butter, egg and enough cider to make a firm dough-like pie crust. Knead on a lightly floured board. Chill the dough overnight. Cut the dough in half. Roll out each piece to ¼-inch thickness and 11 inches in diameter.

Fit the dough into the bottom and ½ inch up on the sides of a well-buttered 10-inch layer cake pan. Sprinkle with the yellow and black raisins and sugar and cinnamon. Top with a second round of pastry. Pinch the edges together. Prick the top well. Brush with the beaten egg yolk. Bake in a preheated moderate oven (375°) for 25 to 30 minutes or until the pastry is golden brown.

Note: To plump raisins, cover with boiling water. Let

stand 15 minutes. Drain and dry thoroughly on kitchen towels.

SPICY PEAR BREAD

Old Swiss cookery features many breads filled with dried pears, once a staple of rural households. Most cantons have their own variety, differing usually in the spicing. The recipe from Berne that follows is one of the nicest, and it can also be made with dried apples. This bread tastes best when about a week old (it will keep 3 weeks in an airtight container) and served with a glass of wine.

Pastry:
¼ cup butter
¾ cup milk
½ cup sugar
2 teaspoons salt

1 egg, well beaten
2 packages active dry yeast
¼ cup lukewarm water
*5 to 6 cups all-purpose
    flour (approximately)*

Filling:
1 pound dried pears or
    apples
½ pound pitted prunes
½ cup raisins
¾ cup figs
½ cup coarsely chopped
    walnuts
juice of 1 large lemon

*¼ cup finely chopped
    citron*
½ teaspoon cinnamon
1 teaspoon nutmeg
½ cup sugar
¼ cup Kirsch
*¾ cup dry red wine
    (approximately)*

2 eggs, well beaten

To make the pastry, heat the butter and milk to lukewarm. Stir until the butter is melted. Add the sugar, salt and egg. Cool to lukewarm. Dissolve the yeast in lukewarm water. Stir into the first mixture. Beat in enough flour to make a soft dough. Knead on a lightly floured board. Put in a deep bowl and cover. Let rise in a warm place until doubled in bulk.

To make the filling, cook the pears and prunes until tender. (If unpitted prunes have been used, pit the prunes). Put the pears, prunes, raisins and figs through the coarse knife of a meat grinder. Add the walnuts, lemon juice, citron, cinnamon, nutmeg, sugar and Kirsch. Blend thoroughly. Add enough red wine to make a very thick jam.

To assemble, punch down the risen dough and divide into two pieces. Roll out each piece into a 12-inch square. Spread each square with half of the filling. Turn in the ends and roll like a jelly roll. Prick the surface several times. Brush with beaten eggs. Place on greased cookie sheets. Let rise until doubled in bulk. Bake in a preheated moderate oven (350°) for 30 minutes or until golden brown. Cool thoroughly before cutting. Makes two loaves.

WINE TART FROM NEUCHÂTEL

Sèche au Vin de Neuchâtel

Traditional.

*pastry for a 2-crust 9-inch
   pie*
¼ cup sugar
¼ cup all-purpose flour

*1 cup dry white wine
   (approximately)*
*1 teaspoon ground
   cinnamon*
¼ cup sweet butter

Roll out the pastry to a 13-inch square. Put it on a buttered and floured baking sheet. Pinch up the edges to

9 4

form a ½-inch rim. Prick the pastry liberally with a fork. Blend the sugar with the flour. Sprinkle the mixture evenly over the pastry. Pour in enough white wine to fill the pastry without overflowing the sides. Sprinkle with cinnamon. Dot with butter. Bake in a preheated hot oven (400°) for 15 to 20 minutes or until golden brown. Cut into squares.

WHITE CAKE FROM ZURICH

Zürcher Eiweisstorte

1 cup butter
1⅔ cups sugar
7 egg whites

2 cups all-purpose flour
½ teaspoon salt

Cream the butter until light. Gradually beat in the sugar. Beat with an electric beater until very light, about 5 to 10 minutes. Beat in 2 of the egg whites. Stir in the flour. Beat the remaining egg whites with salt until stiff but not dry. Fold into the flour mixture. Pour into a well-greased 9-inch spring-form pan. Bake in a preheated slow oven (325°) for 30 to 40 minutes or until golden brown.

Variation: Butter the pan and sprinkle with ¼ cup finely diced blanched almonds. Brush the top of the cake, when cool, with ¼ cup apricot preserves. Glaze the top with 1 cup confectioners' sugar combined with 2 tablespoons water.

The following five recipes for Hungarian Chocolate Cake, Chocolate Chestnut Tarts, Lace Wafer Cones, Fudge Cake Squares and Filled Chocolate Cupcakes are examples of the chocolate cakes found in Swiss *confiseries*. I followed the custom of the creators of these recipes and used Tobler's alkali-processed cocoa (though other Dutch-processed cocoa may be used) because this kind of cocoa gives better results than ordinary cocoa. The Swiss don't go in for as much chocolate cookery as we do; when they do, they use cocoa for baking.

The other cakes, St. Gall Monastery Torte, Japonais, Schwarzwälder Kirschtorte, Zuger Kirschtorte, Pine Cone and Engadiner Nuss Torte, are all famous cakes which in Switzerland would be ordered from a *confiserie* rather than be made at home.

These cakes taste like their Swiss prototypes, but they don't quite look like them. Professional Swiss pastry cooks decorate many of their cakes with exquisite colorful landscapes, figures and patterns made from sugar so that the cake looks like an elegantly dressed lady. My readers need not despair: these coverings are made by specialists and sold to the *confiseurs*. They look like flat lids to be clamped on the top of the cakes.

HUNGARIAN CHOCOLATE CAKE

Ungarische Schokoladen Torte

5 eggs, separated	*1 package vanilla pudding*
¼ teaspoon salt	*(not instant)*
1 cup sifted confectioners'	*2 cups light cream*
sugar	*Chocolate Glaze (see*
¼ cup cocoa	*below)*
1 teaspoon vanilla extract	*blanched almonds*
	candied cherries

Beat the egg whites with the salt until stiff but not dry. Beat in the sugar, 1 tablespoon at a time. Fold in the cocoa. Beat the yolks until thick and lemon-colored, and fold into the cocoa mixture. Add the vanilla. Spread the mixture into a 15 x 10 x 1-inch pan, greased, waxed-paper-lined and greased again. Bake in a preheated moderate oven (350°) for about 20 minutes. Turn out on a rack covered with waxed paper. Remove the top paper. Cool; cut in quarters. While the cake is baking, cook the pudding with the cream until it is smooth and thick. Chill. Spread three layers of the cake with cooled vanilla pudding. Stack the layers, topping the pudding with the last layer. Spread with Chocolate Glaze and decorate with blanched almonds stuffed into candied cherries.

Chocolate Glaze

¼ cup melted butter	2 tablespoons boiling water
⅓ cup cocoa	1 teaspoon instant coffee
1 cup confectioners' sugar	1 teaspoon vanilla extract

Combine all the ingredients and blend well until they are smooth and runny. (It may be necessary to add more boiling water to reach the desired consistency.) Spread thinly over the top and sides of the cake. Chill the cake until ready to serve.

CHOCOLATE CHESTNUT TARTS

Tartelettes aux Marrons

Dough:	½ teaspoon vanilla extract
1 cup flour	1 tablespoon milk
2 tablespoons sugar	6 tablespoons softened
¼ cup cocoa	butter
1 egg yolk	

Filling: ¼ cup sugar
1 cup cocoa   1½ cups canned candied
¾ cup melted butter   chestnut spread
1 teaspoon vanilla extract   sour cream
4 egg whites   triangles of small
                                                 Toblerone

Sift the flour with the sugar and cocoa. Add the remaining ingredients and work quickly with the fingers until the dough forms a smooth ball. Chill for 30 minutes. Roll out the dough on a lightly floured board to ⅛-inch thickness and use the dough to line the tart pans. Chill.

For the filling, mix the cocoa with the melted butter and the vanilla. Beat the egg whites until stiff. Gradually beat in the sugar 1 tablespoon at a time until stiff and glossy. Mix the chestnut spread with the cocoa mixture. Fold in the egg whites. Blend well. Spoon the mixture into tart pans. Chill. When ready to serve, decorate with a spoon of sour cream and a piece of Toblerone. Makes 6 to 8 tarts.

COCOA LACE WAFER CONES WITH CHESTNUT WHIPPED-CREAM FILLING

Les Cornets à la Crème aux Marrons

1 cup sifted all-purpose   ½ teaspoon orange
    flour   flavoring
¼ cup cocoa   ½ teaspoon almond
⅔ cup sugar   flavoring
⅛ teaspoon salt   Chestnut Whipped-Cream
½ cup honey   Filling
½ cup butter

Sift together the flour, cocoa, sugar and salt. Heat the honey to the boiling point. Remove from the heat, and add the butter and flavorings. Stir until the butter is melted. Add the sifted dry ingredients and blend well. Cool. Drop dough by teaspoonfuls, about 4 inches apart on a lightly greased cookie sheet. Bake in a preheated moderate oven (375°) for 5 to 7 minutes. Cool about 1 minute on a rack, then remove the wafers from the cookie sheet with a spatula. Shape into cones with your fingers. Let stand on a rack to harden. Do not fill until ready to serve. Keep the filling refrigerated until the cones are ready to be filled. Makes about 4 dozen cones.

Chestnut Whipped-Cream Filling

1 pint heavy cream,	*1 can (1 pound, 1 ounce)*
whipped	*candied chestnut spread*

Whip the cream until stiff. Fold in the candied chestnut spread. Blend well. Chill.

FUDGE CAKE SQUARES WITH FUDGE FROSTING

Schokolade Schnitten

½ cup butter	*¾ cup all-purpose flour,*
2 tablespoons cocoa	*sifted with*
2 eggs	*¼ teaspoon salt*
1 cup sugar	*Fudge Frosting*
1 teaspoon vanilla extract	
1 cup chopped nuts	

Melt the butter and blend in the cocoa. Beat the eggs and gradually beat the sugar into the eggs. Stir the eggs into the first mixture. Add the sifted flour and salt, and mix well. Add the vanilla and nuts. Pour into a greased and floured 8-inch square pan and bake in a preheated moderate oven (350°) for about 30 minutes. Cool in the pan. Spread with Fudge Frosting, and cut into squares to serve.

Fudge Frosting

¼ cup butter
½ cup heavy cream
½ cup cocoa

1 ½ cups confectioners'
sugar
1 teaspoon vanilla extract

Combine all the ingredients and blend well. Beat until they are smooth and fluffy, adding more confectioners' sugar if necessary. Spread on the cooled cake.

FILLED CHOCOLATE CUPCAKES

Petits Gâteaux au Chocolat

⅔ cup butter
1 ½ cups sugar
3 eggs
2 cups sifted all-purpose
flour
1 teaspoon baking soda

½ teaspoon salt
½ cup cocoa
1 cup milk
1 teaspoon vanilla extract
Raspberry-Almond Filling

Cream the butter until it is light and fluffy. Gradually beat in the sugar. Beat in the eggs, one at a time. Sift the flour with the baking soda, salt and cocoa, and add alternately with the milk. Stir in the vanilla. Line muffin cups with cupcake papers and fill them two thirds full. Bake in a preheated moderate oven (350°) for 25 minutes or until the cake springs back when lightly touched. Cool on racks. With a sharp knife, cut out a small cone of cake at the top. Fill the hole with Raspberry-Almond Filling. Replace the top and sprinkle with confectioners' sugar. Makes about 24 cupcakes.

Raspberry-Almond Filling

1 ½ cups raspberry jam   *blanched almonds*
½ cup chopped

Combine the ingredients and blend well. Use the mixture to fill the cupcakes.

ST. GALL MONASTERY TORTE

St. Gallner Klostertorte

Traditional.

¾ cup butter
⅔ cup sugar
⅔ cup blanched almonds,
  ground
⅔ cup cocoa
1 egg

1 ½ teaspoons baking
  powder
2 ¾ cups all-purpose flour
1 teaspoon cinnamon
1 cup apricot jam

Cream together the butter and the sugar, preferably using an electric beater. Beat in the ground almonds and cocoa. Blend thoroughly. Beat in the egg. Sift together the flour with the cinnamon and baking powder. Add flour to the first mixture and stir to form a soft, well-blended dough. (This is best done with the hands; the dough should form a ball.) Butter and flour an 8-inch spring-form pan. With floured fingers, pat two thirds of the dough into the bottom of the pan and up the sides to the height of 1 inch. The sides will form the rim of the torte. If desired, score the rim with the tines of a fork. Spread jam over the bottom. Divide the remaining third of the dough into six parts. With floured fingers, roll each part into 8-inch strips. Arrange the strips over the jam to form a lattice, pressing the strips down at the rim. Bake in a preheated moderate oven (350°) for 50 minutes to 1 hour or until firm. Cool in pan. Serve in small wedges. Makes 12 to 16 servings (the torte is very rich).

JAPONAIS TORTE

Traditional. Makes one 8-inch torte.

5 egg whites
¼ teaspoon cream of
   tartar
½ cup granulated sugar
¼ cup instant flour or

sifted all-purpose flour
⅞ cup blanched almonds
   (4 ounces), grated,
   about 1⅓ cups grated
   almonds

Frosting:
½ pound (2 sticks) sweet
   butter or unsalted
   margarine

2 cups sifted
   confectioner's sugar
2 tablespoons instant coffee
½ cup hot water

Nougat:
3 tablespoons granulated
   sugar

⅓ cup coarsely chopped
   blanched almonds (1½
   ounces)

Decoration:
whole blanched almonds
   dipped halfway into

melted bittersweet
   chocolate (optional)
whipped cream

Have the egg whites at room temperature. Beat the egg whites until very stiff. Fold in the sugar mixed with the flour. Fold in the grated almonds. Line two cookie sheets with foil and mark out four 8-inch circles on the foil. Butter the foil. Divide the egg white mixture equally between the four circles. Spread out the egg-white mixture to the edge of the circles, keeping the layers of egg white as even as possible and keeping the edge of the layers thick. Bake in a preheated hot oven (425°) for 8 to 10 minutes or until the tops of the layers are brown. Cool for 2 to 3 minutes on the cookie sheet. Turn the layers upside down on a rack and carefully strip off the foil. Cool the layers on the rack.

To prepare the frosting, cream the butter or margarine until soft and fluffy. Gradually beat in the sugar and instant coffee. Then slowly beat in the hot water, a few tablespoons at a time. Spread the frosting between the layers and top with the fourth layer. Spread the sides and top of the cake with the frosting.

To prepare the nougat, melt the sugar in a small skillet until the sugar liquefies and turns golden brown. Stir in the nuts. Spread the mixture on waxed paper and let it stand until it hardens. When cool, crush with a rolling pin into a fine powder. Sprinkle the nougat over the top and on the sides of the frosted cake. Chill the torte until ready to serve.

Decorate, if desired, with blanched almonds dipped halfway into melted bittersweet chocolate and add rosettes of whipped cream.

Note: The layers of a Japonais Torte are often used combined with other kinds of layers, such as *bisquit*, to makes the composite *torten* the Swiss like so much.

SCHWARZWÄLDER KIRSCHTORTE

Traditional. Makes one 8-inch torte.

1 recipe Japonais layers (see page 314)	*1 tablespoon Kirsch bittersweet chocolate shavings*
1½ cups cherry preserves	
1 cup heavy cream, whipped	*maraschino cherries with stems*
¼ cup confectioners' sugar	*angelica*

Prepare the Japonais layers as directed in the recipe. Cool the layers. Spread the cherry preserves between three of the layers and top with the fourth layer. Whip the cream with the confectioners' sugar and Kirsch. Frost the sides and top of the torte with whipped cream. Sprinkle the top of the torte with chocolate shavings. Garnish the bottom and the center of the top with well-drained maraschino cherries with stems. Cut a few leaves of angelica and add to the cherries.

ZUGER KIRSCHTORTE

Traditional and very famous. Makes one 8-inch torte.

½ recipe Japonais, using 2 extra large egg whites (page 314)
sponge layer
2 large eggs
7 tablespoons granulated

sugar
dash of salt
⅔ cup instant flour or sifted all-purpose flour
1 teaspoon grated lemon rind

Frosting:

½ pound (2 sticks) sweet butter
2½ cups sifted confectioners' sugar
1 whole egg plus 1 egg yolk

1 teaspoon vanilla extract
½ cup Kirsch
red food coloring

½ cup chopped toasted unblanched almonds

Prepare the Japonais layers according to recipe directions. Cool the Japonais layer and the sponge layer. Beat the 2 large eggs until thick and lemon-colored. Gradually beat in the sugar 1 tablespoon at a time until the mixture is pale yellow and thick. Fold in the salt, flour and the grated lemon rind. Line an 8-inch layer cake pan (bottom and sides) with foil. Spoon the batter into the pan, spreading it evenly into the pan. Bake in a preheated slow oven (325°) for 20 minutes or until the top springs back when lightly touched. Let the cake cool in the pan for 5 minutes. Remove from the pan and carefully strip off foil. Cool the layer.

To prepare the frosting, cream the butter until soft and fluffy. Gradually beat in the confectioners' sugar. Beat in the egg, egg yolk, vanilla and 2 tablespoons of the Kirsch. Tint the frosting a soft pink with the red coloring. Sprinkle the remaining Kirsch over the top and bottom of the sponge layer. Spread one third of the frosting over one of the Japonais layers. Top with a sponge layer. Spread with frosting and top with the second Japonais layer. Spread the sides and top of the torte with the frosting.

Sprinkle toasted almonds in the center of the torte and press almonds into the sides of the torte.

PINE CONE

Tannzapfen

5 egg whites
dash of salt
¾ cup granulated sugar
1 cup instant flour or sifted

all-purpose flour
2 teaspoons grated lemon
  rind

Frosting:
½ pound (2 sticks) sweet
  butter
2 cups sifted confectioners'
  sugar
3 squares (3 ounces)
  baking chocolate,
  melted

1 tablespoon instant coffee
⅓ cup hot water

2½ cups blanched
  almonds, separated into
  halves and toasted
sprig of pine branches
confectioners' sugar

Have the egg whites at room temperature. Beat the egg whites with the salt until they are stiff but not dry.

Gradually beat in the sugar, 1 tablespoon at a time. Fold in the flour and grated lemon rind. Line a 15 x 10 jelly-roll pan with aluminum foil. Butter the foil and spread the cake batter evenly over the bottom of the pan. Bake in a preheated slow oven (325°) for 15 to 20 minutes or until lightly browned. Remove the cake from the pan and carefully strip the foil from the cake. Cool on a rack. Cut the cake into five 10-inch strips—one strip 5 inches wide, one 4 inches wide, one 3 inches wide, one 2 inches wide and one 1 inch wide. With scissors or a sharp knife cut each strip into a shape resembling an elongated iron. The first strip should be the full 10 inches long, the second 9½ inches long, the third 8½ inches long, the fourth 7½ inches long and the fifth 6½ inches long.

To prepare the frosting, cream the butter until light and fluffy. Gradually beat in the sugar, melted chocolate and instant coffee. Beat in hot water until the frosting has a good spreading consistency. Spread the first four layers with frosting and stack them, starting with the largest layer and placing the next layer in the center. Top with the last layer. Frost the entire cone with frosting.

Starting at the point of the cone, put overlapping layers of the toasted almond halves on the frosting to resemble the scales of a real pine cone. Garnish the top of the cone with a real pine branch and sprinkle the cone lightly with confectioners' sugar to resemble snow on the pine cone.

OPEN-FACED TARTS

Wähen oder Fladen

These very popular tarts resemble pizza pies, but they are filled with vegetables or with fruit. *Wähen,* with *café au lait* or tea, often are the whole lunch or supper. When I was a child, *Wähen* were wash-day and moving-day food since they could be prepared the day before.

Apart from the Onion Tart (page 272), I think that fruit *Wähen* are more suited to the American taste. I give the more elegant version, though a simpler one can be made by omitting the cream beaten with the sugar and eggs, and sprinkling the pie with sugar instead. Both plain and richer *Wähen* are made at home, but plain ones are also sold by the bakeries and the finer ones in the pastry shops.

The fruits best suited for the purpose are apples (peeled, cored and sliced), ripe but still firm peaches or apricots (stoned, sliced or cut into halves), pitted cherries and stoned, halved plums.

BASIC FRUIT TART

Fruchtwähe

1 ¼ cups flour	*cut into small pieces*
2 egg yolks, plus 1 egg yolk	*6 cups (approximately) sliced fruit*
sugar	*½ cup ground filberts or*
grated rind of 1 lemon	*unblanched almonds*
½ cup butter, softened and	*½ cup heavy cream*

Sift the flour into a large bowl and make a well in the middle. Put 1 egg yolk, 1 tablespoon sugar, the lemon rind and butter into the well. Stir together with a fork. Work the dough with your hands until all the ingredients are blended and the dough is smooth. Pat the dough with the fingers into the bottom and sides of a deep 9-inch pie plate. Chill for at least 2 hours. Sprinkle the bottom of the dough evenly with the ground nuts. (This will keep the cake from becoming soggy with fruit juice.) Arrange the fruit slices in slightly overlapping circles on top of the nuts. Sprinkle with ⅓ to ½ cup sugar, depending on the sweetness of the fruit. Bake in a preheated oven (350°) for 10 minutes. Beat together the remaining egg yolk, the cream and the egg. Dribble over the fruit. Continue baking about 15 to 20 minutes or until the pastry is golden brown. Serve warm. Serves 6 to 8.

RICH EGG BREAD FROM BERNE

Berner oder Emmentaler Zopf

Traditional. Makes one braided loaf.

*1 package active dry yeast,
    or 1 cake compressed
    yeast*
¼ cup lukewarm water
½ cup lukewarm milk
1 tablespoon sugar

1 teaspoon salt
*1 whole egg, plus 2 egg
    yolks and 1 egg white*
*3 cups unsifted all-purpose
    flour*
melted butter

Add the yeast to the lukewarm water and let it stand for a few minutes. Stir to dissolve the yeast. Cool the milk to lukewarm and add the sugar, salt, egg yolks and whole egg to the milk. Stir in the dissolved yeast. Beat in the flour. Turn the dough out on a heavily floured board and knead until the dough is smooth and elastic. Put the dough into a greased bowl and grease the top. Cover and let rise until double in bulk. Punch the dough down and cut it into 3 equal pieces. On a lightly floured board shape each piece of dough with the hands into a 14-inch-long rope. Put 3 ropes on a greased cookie sheet and braid them as you would hair. Brush the braid with melted butter. Let the loaf rise until double in bulk. Beat the egg white with 1 tablespoon water and brush the mixture over the risen loaf. Bake the loaf in a preheated moderate oven (375°) for 25 to 30 minutes, or until the loaf is deeply browned.

ALMOND COOKIES

Mandel Guetsle

Traditional for Christmas.

1 cup soft butter	*blanched almonds,*
4 eggs	*grated*
1 cup sugar	*4 cups sifted flour*
grated rind of 1 lemon	*1 egg yolk, beaten with 1*
1 cup plus 2 tablespoons	*tablespoon cold water*

Cream the butter. Add the eggs, one at a time, beating well after each addition. Add the sugar and lemon rind; mix well. Add the almonds and flour, mixing thoroughly. Chill overnight. Roll on a floured board to ⅛-inch thickness. Cut into desired shapes, and put the cookies on greased cookie sheets. Brush with the egg yolk and water. Bake in a preheated slow oven (325°) about 15 minutes. Makes about 12 dozen small cookies. Store airtight. Will ship well.

ANISE SLICES

Anisbrot

Traditional.

5 *eggs plus 2 egg whites*   1 *cup cake flour*
1 *cup sugar*   2 *tablespoons aniseed*

Beat the eggs and egg whites until they are thick and lemon-colored. Gradually beat in the sugar, 1 tablespoon at a time. Fold in the flour and aniseed. Butter the bottom of a 9 x 5 x 4 loaf pan. Bake in a preheated slow oven (325°) for 30 to 40 minutes or until the cake springs back when lightly touched. When the loaf is cool, cut it into ½-inch slices. Place the slices in a preheated hot oven (400°) about 5 minutes or until golden brown.

ALMOND COOKIES FROM
THE GRISONS

Totenbeinli

Traditional. These cookies are baked for All Souls' Day, November 2, in commemoration of the dead.

2 *cups almonds*   3 *eggs plus 2 egg yolks,*
½ *cup butter*   *beaten*
1 *cup sugar*   1 *tablespoon rose water*
1 *teaspoon ground*   2½ *to 3 cups all-purpose*
  cinnamon   *flour*
                                ½ *teaspoon salt*

Blanch the almonds. While they are still warm, cut them into slivers. Cream the butter with the sugar and the cinnamon. Beat in the 3 whole eggs, one at a time, beating well after each addition. Stir in the rose water. Beat in 2½ cups of the flour and the salt. The dough will be sticky, but if it is too sticky to handle, beat in the remaining flour, a little at a time. Knead the dough on a lightly floured baking board. Knead in the almonds. Chill the dough for 2 hours. Shape the dough into finger-length rolls. Place the cookies on buttered and floured baking sheets. Paint the cookies with the egg yolks. Bake them in a preheated moderate oven (375°) for about 10 to 15 minutes or until golden brown. Cool for 2 minutes on baking sheets, and remove the cookies with a spatula. Makes about 40 cookies.

ANISEED COOKIES

Chräbeli

Traditional. These resemble in taste the German *Springerle,* though they are not molded.

2 eggs	*rind (optional)*
1¼ cups sugar	*1 tablespoon Kirsch*
2 to 3 tablespoons	*(optional)*
crushed aniseed	*1½ to 1¾ cups sifted*
1 teaspoon grated lemon	*all-purpose flour*

Beat the eggs until light. Gradually beat in the sugar, 1 tablespoon at a time. Beat well after each addition. Long beating is essential; Swiss cookbooks say the eggs and sugar should be beaten by hand for 40 minutes, but 15 minutes with an electric beater at medium speed will do. Stir in the aniseed, the lemon rind and the Kirsch. Add the flour to make a stiff dough and knead well. Cut the dough into four pieces. Roll out each piece into 1-inch strips. Cut the strips into 3-inch lengths. Nick each strip 3 times to the depth of ½ inch. Bend the strips slightly into a U-shape, keeping the nicked side on the outside. Put the *Chräbeli* on buttered and floured baking sheets. Let them stand overnight at room temperature to dry out. Bake in a preheated slow oven (300°) for 15 minutes, or until a very pale yellow. The nicks in the cookies expand during the baking into little feet.

BROWN COOKIES FROM BASLE

Basler Brunsli

Traditional.

2 egg whites	*blanched (about 2⅔*
3 to 4 tablespoons Kirsch	*cups) and finely ground*
sugar	*7 tablespoons cocoa*
½ pound semi-sweet	*1 teaspoon ground*
chocolate, grated	*cinnamon*
1 pound almonds,	*1 teaspoon ground nutmeg*

Beat the egg whites until very stiff. Beat in the Kirsch and 1 cup sugar, one tablespoon at a time. Add the remaining ingredients. Knead on a lightly floured baking board until smooth. Sprinkle the baking board with sugar. Roll out the dough to the thickness of ¼ inch. Cut out shapes with cookie cutters. Bake on a lightly buttered baking board in a preheated slow oven (300°) for 10 to 15 minutes. The cookies must not rise nor split, and if they are cooked in too warm an oven, they will harden. Like meringues, they should dry out rather than bake.

BASLER LECKERLI

Traditional honey cookies from Basle, and famous the world over.

2 ⅔ cups clear honey
¾ cup Kirsch
2 cups sugar
½ cup finely chopped
  candied lemon peel
½ cup finely chopped
  candied orange peel
1 pound (2 cups) shelled
  unblanched almonds,
coarsely ground
grated rind of 2 lemons
2 tablespoons cinnamon
2 teaspoons cloves
8 to 10 cups all-purpose
  flour (approximately)
Confectioners' Glaze (see
  below)

Pour the honey into a large saucepan. Bring to a boil. Remove from the heat. Add the Kirsch, and stir in the sugar. Return to medium heat. Stir in the remaining ingredients except the flour and glaze. Remove from heat. Stir in the flour gradually, until the dough cleans the side of the pan. This should take about 15 minutes. If the dough is still sticky, add more flour, a little at a time. Roll out the dough on a lightly floured baking board to about ½-inch thickness. Cut the dough with a special *Leckerli* or *Springerle* mold, or into 2 x 3-inch bars. Place the cookies closely together on a heavily greased and floured baking sheet. Let stand overnight at room temperature. Bake in a preheated moderate oven (350°) for 20 to 25 minutes or until golden brown. While hot, brush with Confectioners' Glaze, and dry. Makes about 10 dozen 2 x 3-inch cookies.

Note: These cookies ought to ripen before eating. Pack them in airtight containers and keep, if possible, for 3 to 4 weeks. Stored this way, they will keep almost indefinitely.

CONFECTIONERS' GLAZE

Beat together for 10 minutes ¾ cup confectioners' sugar and 2 unbeaten egg whites. If more glaze is needed, make up several batches rather than doubling recipe.

BERNER LECKERLI

A traditional cookie from Berne, and an excellent one.

½ *pound (1 cup) shelled unblanched almonds*
½ *pound (1 cup) shelled filberts*
2 *cups sugar*
½ *cup flour*
2 *teaspoons cinnamon*
½ *cup candied orange peel, ground or finely chopped*
1 *tablespoon honey*
5 *egg whites*

Glaze:
1 *cup confectioners' sugar*   2 *tablespoons orange juice*

Grind the almonds and filberts in a nut grinder or in an electric blender. Combine all the ingredients except the egg whites and mix well. Beat the egg whites until stiff. Fold the egg whites into the nut mixture. Blend to a stiff dough. Chill overnight. Roll out the dough to ½-inch thickness on a lightly floured board. Press the dough into cookie shapes with floured *Springerle* molds or a flower-carved rolling pin. Cut the shapes apart and place them on greased cookie sheets. Bake in a preheated moderate oven (350°) for 5 or 6 minutes or until golden brown. Glaze while hot. To make orange glaze, combine confectioners' sugar and orange juice and beat to desired consistency.

Note: These cookies will keep well in an airtight container. In Berne, they are often made with century-old, prettily carved wooden molds. They can be shaped with any mold, provided it has been dipped in flour to prevent the dough from sticking.

CHRISTMAS BUTTER COOKIES

Mailänderli

Traditional. The most popular Christmas cookie. Swiss bakers sell the dough so that the housewife has nothing to do but bake them.

½ cup butter
¾ cup sugar
grated rind of 1 lemon
juice of 1 small lemon or 1
   tablespoon Kirsch

2 eggs plus 1 egg yolk,
   beaten
2½ to 2¾ cups
   all-purpose flour

Cream the butter. Gradually beat in the sugar, beating well after each addition. Beat in the grated lemon rind, the lemon juice and the 2 whole eggs. Blend thoroughly. Stir in the flour, beginning with 2½ cups. Knead the dough with the hands until it is smooth and clears the fingers. If it is too sticky, add the remaining flour. Wrap the dough in waxed paper and chill for 4 hours or over-night. Roll out the dough between two sheets of waxed paper to the thickness of ¼ inch. Cut it with small fancy cookie-cutters, such as stars, hearts and crescents. Place them on a buttered and floured baking sheet 1 inch apart. Brush with the beaten egg yolk. Bake in a preheated moderate oven (350°) for about 15 minutes or until golden. Keep in a tightly closed container. The cookies will taste best after 2 days.

CINNAMON STARS

Zimmetsterne

Traditional. There are two varieties of these Christmas cookies which are of German origin. One is simply a butter cookie flavored with cinnamon, and not nearly as interesting as the one that follows.

3 egg whites	*1 tablespoon lemon juice*
3 cups confectioners' sugar	*1 tablespoon cinnamon*
3 cups unblanched grated	*¼ teaspoon mace*
almonds	*sugar*

Beat the egg whites until stiff. Beat in the confectioners' sugar, 2 tablespoons at a time. The mixture should be stiff and glossy. Reserve 1 cup of the mixture. Beat the almonds, lemon juice, cinnamon and mace into the remaining egg-white mixture. Let it stand for 30 minutes to 1 hour; it should dry out and be firm. Sprinkle a baking board with sugar. Carefully roll out the dough to the thickness of ½ to ¾ inch. If the dough sticks, sprinkle more sugar on the baking board. Cut out the dough with star-shaped cookie-cutters. Paint each cookie carefully and neatly with the reserved egg-white mixture. Place the cookies on a buttered and floured baking sheet. Bake in a preheated slow oven (275°) for about 15 minutes or until set. The icing must remain white.

ZURICH FRIED CARNIVAL COOKIES

Zürcher Eieröhrli, or Fastnachtküchlein

Traditional and very old. These cookies, golden in color and resembling a crumpled plate, are eaten during

Carnival, the three days preceding Lent. Similar fried cookies are found throughout Switzerland.

2 eggs	2 to 2½ cups all-purpose
5 tablespoons cream	flour
½ teaspoon salt	deep fat for frying
2 tablespoons sugar	confectioners' sugar

Beat the eggs with the cream, salt and sugar. Beat in flour to form a stiff dough. Knead well on a lightly floured board until the dough is satin-smooth and filled with air bubbles—about 5 minutes. Cover the dough and let it rest in a warm place for 30 minutes. Cut dough into pieces the size of a whole walnut. Roll out each piece of dough on a lightly floured board. Roll it as thinly as possible, into a round. With fingers, stretch out the dough even further until it is paper-thin. Place the dough on a lightly floured kitchen cloth and let it dry for 15 minutes. Fry in deep fat at 380° (on the thermometer) for 5 minutes or until golden brown. While the dough is frying, push the circle together with two wooden sticks (such as the handles of wooden spoons) to give the cookie a crumpled appearance. Drain well on absorbent paper, and serve hot or cold, sprinkled with confectioners' sugar. Good with coffee or a glass of Swiss or Alsatian white wine.

FILLED COOKIES FROM ST. GALL

Weisse St. Gallner Kräpfli

Traditional.

Dough:

2¼ cups sugar	4½ cups sifted all-purpose
4 eggs, well beaten	flour (approximately)
grated rind of 1 lemon	

Filling:
¾ *pound unblanched*   *cinnamon*
   (*about 2 cups*) *almonds,*   *1 teaspoon ground nutmeg*
   ground   ½ *teaspoon ground cloves*
1 cup sugar   ¼ *cup milk*
1 tablespoon ground   (*approximately*)

Combine the sugar, eggs, grated lemon rind and enough flour to make a stiff dough. Roll out on a lightly floured board to ¼-inch thickness. Cut into 2½-inch rounds. Blend the almonds, sugar, cinnamon, nutmeg and cloves with enough milk to make a paste. Place a small spoonful of filling on half the rounds. Top each round with another round. Press the edges together. Let stand at room temperature overnight. Brush with water and sprinkle with sugar. Bake in a preheated moderate oven (350°) for 10 to 15 minutes or until golden brown. Makes about 3 dozen.

FRIED COOKIES

Strüzeli

Traditional from Berne. Similar fried cookies are found in all of German-speaking Switzerland.

4½ *cups all-purpose flour*   ¼ *cup butter*
1 teaspoon salt   ¼ *cup currants*
2 teaspoons baking powder   *2 eggs, well beaten*
½ *teaspoon baking soda*   *1⅓ cups milk*
sugar   *deep fat for frying*

Sift the flour with the salt, baking powder, baking soda and ⅓ cup sugar. Cut in butter until the particles are like cornmeal. Add the currants, and stir until they are well coated. Combine the eggs and milk. Add to the flour mixture. Stir until a soft dough is formed. With a spoon, divide the dough into balls the size of walnuts. On a lightly floured board, form each ball of dough into a horseshoe shape. Fry in deep fat (380°) for 4 to 5 minutes, turning once to brown both sides. Sprinkle with sugar. May be eaten hot or cold.

JAM COOKIES

Spitzbuben

Traditional.

1 cup sugar	*flavoring*
1 ¼ cups butter	*3 ¼ cups sifted all-purpose*
2 ¼ cups ground blanched	*flour*
almonds	*apricot jam*
2 teaspoons vanilla	*confectioners' sugar*

Beat the sugar and the butter together until light. Beat in the almonds and the vanilla flavoring. Add the flour. Knead until smooth. Roll out the dough on a lightly floured baking board to the thickness of ⅛ to ¼ inch; the thinner, the better the cookie. Cut with small round, star- or diamond-shaped cookie cutters. Place the cookies on lightly buttered and floured baking sheets. Bake in a preheated slow oven (325°) for about 15 minutes, or until golden. Remove the cookies from the baking sheet. Spread half the cookies with apricot jam. Top with the remaining cookies. Dip the edges into confectioners' sugar.

NUT COOKIES

Rugenkuchen

Traditional. Prepare half the recipe for a family-size portion; the full recipe for holidays or company.

4½ cups all-purpose flour
2¼ cups sugar
1¼ cups shelled almonds or filberts, finely chopped

2¼ cups butter, melted and lukewarm
1 teaspoon cinnamon
10 unbeaten egg whites

Blend the flour with the sugar and nuts. Beat in the melted butter and cinnamon. Fold in the egg whites. Beat well. Spread the dough about ½ inch thick on a well-buttered and lightly floured cookie sheet. With the back of a knife, mark the dough lightly into diamonds. Bake in a preheated moderate oven (375°) for 5 to 10 minutes until golden brown. Break into pieces. Store in an airtight covered container to keep crisp.

ST. GALL ALMOND BARS

St. Gallner Brot

Traditional.

¾ cup butter
1 cup and 2 tablespoons sugar
2 large eggs, plus 1 egg white, slightly beaten
3¼ cups flour (approximately)

½ pound (about 1⅓ cups) unblanched almonds, chopped
2 teaspoons cinnamon
1 teaspoon cloves
grated rind of ½ lemon

Cream the butter and sugar. Beat in the 2 whole eggs. Add the remaining ingredients except the egg white. Stir until the dough cleans the bowl. Knead on a lightly floured board. Roll out to ½-inch thickness in the shape of an oblong. Brush with beaten egg white. Place on a greased cookie sheet. Bake in a preheated moderate oven (350°) for 20 to 30 minutes or until golden brown. Cut into bars and serve. Makes about 3 dozen, depending on the size of the bar.

XXIII

Other Desserts

SWITZERLAND abounds in desserts, both plain and fancy. The fancy ones—creams and puddings rich with eggs and cream, and handsomely decorated with swirls of whipped cream—are definitely company or special-occasion fare. Among the plain family desserts are the usual cornstarch puddings, rice puddings and, above all, stewed fruits, fresh-fruit desserts and just plain fruit. Swiss fruit is excellent, especially the cherries, plums, apples and pears, which come in many varieties.

Orchards are part of the Swiss landscape, and their fruit provided food, not luxury, to the Switzerland of the past. The large open fruit tarts, still served as the main dish of a meal, page 318, are proof of this. So is the extensive use of dried fruit, especially apples and pears, which are still home-dried in the rural districts. Dried fruit is used in compotes, in baking, and in combination with a vegetable such as potatoes or cabbage. In the old days, dried fruits were the major source of vitamins during the winter months, when an orange was a child's special Christmas treat.

Swiss eating has become lighter, as eating has become

lighter all over the world. In many Swiss families, dessert has become the exception rather than the rule, the children being given fresh or dried fruits and raisins instead. Interestingly, yoghurt—served as is or used instead of cream with fruits—has become extremely popular among both urban and rural people.

APFELBRÖISI

Traditional. A good dish for children.

6 slices stale white bread, broken into small pieces	*peeled, cored and cut into thin slices*
½ cup butter, melted	*½ cup sugar*
3 large green apples,	*⅓ cup raisins*

In a skillet brown the stale bread pieces in the melted butter. Add the thinly sliced apples. Cover, and let simmer until the apples are tender. Stir in the sugar and raisins. Serve hot.

APPLE CHARLOTTE I

Schiterbigi

A traditional dish from Berne, a good hot apple pudding.

1 medium loaf thinly sliced firm white bread	*2 tablespoons milk*
4 cups cooked or canned apple slices, drained	*2 tablespoons sugar*
	grated rind of 1 large lemon, or ½ teaspoon
2 eggs, well beaten	*ground cinnamon*

Trim the crusts from the bread. Cut each slice into 3 finger-lengths. Place under a broiler and toast until golden brown. Or toast whole slices of bread in a toaster and then cut them into 3 finger-lengths. Butter heavily a 7-inch spring-form pan. Line both sides and the bottom of the spring-form pan with some of the toast fingers. Pour half the apple slices over the bread. Cover with a layer of toasted bread fingers. Pour the remaining apples over the toast. Top with another layer of toast. With the back of a spoon, firmly press the whole pudding together. Beat eggs, milk, sugar and lemon rind or cinnamon together. Carefully spoon this mixture around the edge of the spring-form pan. Bake in a preheated moderate oven (350°) for 30 minutes or until the top is browned and the egg mixture firm. Turn out onto a platter. Serve hot, with cream, a fruit or wine sauce.

APPLE CHARLOTTE II

Apfel-Tschu

A very old Zurich recipe.

6 green apples, peeled and cored
½ cup sugar plus 2 tablespoons
¼ cup raisins

¾ cup butter
¼ cup sugar
12 thin slices firm white bread

Cut the apples into ½-inch slices. Add the sugar and raisins. Cover, and simmer until the apples are firm but tender. Brush an 8-inch square pan with 2 tablespoons of the butter. Sprinkle ½ cup sugar over the bottom and sides of the pan. Melt ½ cup of the butter, and use to brush both sides of the slices of bread. Line the pan with the bread slices, reserving 4 slices for the top. Pour the drained cooked apple slices and raisins into the bread-lined pan. Top the apples with the remaining bread slices. Sprinkle with 2 tablespoons sugar and dot the top with pieces of butter (2 tablespoons in all). Cover the pan with foil and bake in a preheated moderate oven (350°) for 30 minutes or until the top is golden brown. Cut into squares and serve warm with cream.

APPLE FRITTERS FROM BASLE

Pfnutli

Traditional. The apples should be tart, or the dish will be undistinguished.

1 cup white or red dry wine	*3 eggs, well beaten*
¼ cup butter	*2 large tart apples, peeled, cored and cut into*
¼ cup sugar	*½-inch cubes*
2 cups all-purpose flour	*deep fat or oil*
½ teaspoon salt	

Heat the wine. Add the butter and sugar. Stir until the butter melts. Mix the flour and salt with the wine mixture. Beat to a smooth paste. Fold in the beaten eggs and cubed apples. Drop by spoonfuls into hot deep fat (380° on the thermometer) for 5 to 6 minutes or until golden brown. Drain and serve, sprinkled with additional sugar. Makes about 18 *pfnutli*, depending on size.

UNCOOKED APPLESAUCE

Rohes Apfelmus

Desserts of uncooked fruits are very popular.

juice of 3 to 4 lemons	*½ cup heavy cream, plain or whipped (optional)*
2 pounds firm apples	
sugar or honey to taste	

Put the lemon juice into a bowl. Stem and core the apples, but do not peel them. Grate or shred the apples directly into the lemon juice. Stir them frequently so that they will not discolor. Sweeten to taste with sugar or honey. Fold in the cream if desired. Serve immediately.

APPLE MERINGUE

Äpfel mit Meringue

An unpretentious but very pleasant and easy dessert. The apples must be tart.

2 pounds green apples, peeled and cored	*⅔ cup sugar*
¼ cup melted butter	*2 tablespoons fresh lemon juice*
⅓ cup yellow raisins, plumped	*3 egg whites*
	½ teaspoon salt

Cut the apples into ¼-inch slices. Place the apples in a well-buttered shallow baking dish. Pour the melted butter over the apples. Sprinkle with the raisins, half of the sugar and the lemon juice. Cover with foil. Bake in a preheated moderate oven (350°) for 20 minutes or until the apples are tender but still shapely. Beat the egg whites with salt until stiff. Gradually beat in the remaining sugar to make a stiff meringue. Spread the meringue over the apples, to the edge of the dish. Bake for an additional 10 minutes or until the meringue is golden brown. Serve warm, with heavy cream, if desired.

APPLE PANCAKE

Äpfelomelette

Traditional.

1 cup sifted all-purpose, flour	*½ teaspoon ground cinnamon*
½ teaspoon salt	*⅓ cup wine*
⅔ cup milk	*2 apples, peeled and cored*
2 eggs, well beaten	*¼ cup butter*
3 tablespoons sugar	*2 tablespoons sugar*

Sift the flour and salt. Stir in the milk. Beat until smooth. Add the beaten eggs, sugar, cinnamon and wine. Beat until smooth. Let stand 15 minutes. Cut the apples into ¼-inch-thick slices. Melt the butter in a large skillet. Sprinkle the skillet with the sugar. Pour the batter into the skillet. Top with the apple slices. Fry until golden brown. Turn and brown the other side. Cut into wedges and serve hot.

BLUEBERRY GRUNT

Heitisturm

A traditional supper dish from Berne, and good for a simple American lunch or supper.

1 quart blueberries	*¼ cup melted butter*
¼ cup sugar	*1 cup cold milk or cream*
4 slices bread	

Pick over the berries; wash, drain and crush them with a potato masher or a fork. Sprinkle with the sugar. Trim the crusts off the bread and cut the bread into ¼-inch squares. Sauté the bread in melted butter until crisp and golden. Add to the blueberries and toss together. Add milk or cream, and serve immediately in deep bowls.

BAKED CHERRY PUDDING

Chriesitotsch

A traditional dish from Zurich.

6 tablespoons butter	*1 cup finely grated*
7 tablespoons sugar	*zwieback*
4 eggs, separated	*1 cup milk or cream, or*
½ cup blanched almonds,	*juice drained from*
finely ground	*cherries*
grated rind of ½ lemon	*2 cups pitted black*
	cherries, drained

Cream the butter. Add the sugar, and cream until the mixture is light and frothy. Add the egg yolks, one at a time, beating well after each addition. Grind the almonds in a nut grinder or blender. Add the almonds, grated lemon rind, zwieback crumbs and milk or cream or cherry juice. Blend well. Beat the egg whites until stiff. Fold into the batter. Pour half of the batter into a buttered 8-inch spring-form pan. Bake in preheated moderate oven (350°) for 10 minutes. Remove from the oven and top with the drained cherries and the remaining batter. Continue baking in a 350° oven for an additional 20 to 30 minutes or until golden and firm. Serve hot, with cream if desired.

FRIED CHERRIES

Chriesitütschli

Traditional. Switzerland is a great cherry country.

2 eggs, well beaten
⅔ cup milk
2 tablespoons oil or melted
 butter
1 cup all-purpose flour
¼ teaspoon salt

2 tablespoons sugar
fresh Bing cherries, small
 size
deep fat for frying
ground cinnamon and
 sugar, mixed

Beat the eggs with milk and oil or butter. Stir in the flour, salt and sugar. Beat with a rotary egg beater until smooth. Tie 5 or 6 cherries into bundles, using the stems. Dip the bundles into the batter. Fry in deep fat at 380° for 5 or 6 minutes or until golden brown. Roll in a cinnamon and sugar mixture.

HEIDI'S CHERRY PUDDING

Heidi's Chriesibrägel

Traditional, from Zurich. The recipe comes from Heidi Albonico's family, who have lived in Zurich for many generations. Children like this dish very much, and it can easily be doubled.

1½ cups hot milk
1½ cups stale white bread,
 broken into very small
 pieces
¼ cup butter
¼ cup sugar
2 eggs, well beaten
½ teaspoon cinnamon

1 teaspoon grated lemon
 rind
½ to 1 pound dark sweet
 cherries, unpitted or 1 to
1½ cups pitted canned
 dark cherries, well
 drained

Add the hot milk to the bread. Beat until smooth. Cream the butter and beat in the sugar. Beat in the eggs. Blend thoroughly. Stir in the cinnamon, lemon rind and cherries. Pour the mixture into a well-buttered 1½-quart baking dish. Bake in a preheated slow oven (325°) for 30 minutes. Serve warm.

CHERRIES IN RED WINE FROM THE TICINO

Le Ciliege nel Vino Rosso

Switzerland is rich in superb cherries, and this is one of the best and simplest ways of cooking them. The cherries should be sweet, red and juicy.

Stone the cherries with a cherry pitter or with the rounded part of a hairpin. Put them into a saucepan. Sprinkle sugar over the cherries—the amount depends on the sweetness of the fruit. Sprinkle a little cinnamon and ground cloves over the cherries, or a little grated lemon rind. This is optional. Let the cherries stand at room temperature for 30 minutes. Pour a good dry red wine over the cherries to cover. Bring to a quick boil and remove from heat. Chill before serving.

FIGS IN CREAM FROM LUGANO

Fichi alla Crema

The figs grow in the gardens of this famous lake resort town in southern Switzerland.

12 ripe figs
1 cup Marsala or
semi-sweet sherry

1 to 1½ cups heavy cream,
whipped

Peel the figs and cut them into quarters. Put half the figs into a glass serving dish. Sprinkle with ½ cup Marsala or sherry. Top with the remaining figs. Sprinkle with the remaining Marsala or sherry. Chill for 1 hour. Top with whipped cream. Chill for 15 more minutes. Serve with plain sugar cookies.

MELON WITH WHITE WINE

Melon au Vin Blanc

Any good ripe melon, such as cantaloupe, honeydew, Persian, etc., may be used.

Peel and seed the melon. Cut it into 2- to 3-inch slices. Put a layer of melon slices in a glass serving dish. Sprinkle with sugar and lemon juice. Top with more melon and repeat the process until all the melon is used. Pour a dry or sweet wine over the melon. There should not be too much wine or the dish will be soupy. Chill for about 1 hour. Serve with cookies.

PEACHES COOKED IN WHITE WINE FROM SION

Les Pêches au Fendant du Valais

A simple and excellent dessert which depends for its flavor on a good dry white wine, such as the Fendant du Valais. Sion, a ravishing and relatively un-touristy medieval town, is the capital of that fascinating canton, which, oddly enough, resembles Spain in the valley where the Rhône flows toward the Lake of Geneva.

1 cup sugar
1 cup dry white wine
½ cup water

6 ripe peaches (the fruit
    must not be bruised)
boiling water

(343)

Combine the sugar, wine and water. Cook uncovered over low heat for 5 minutes. Scald the peaches in boiling water. Peel and cut into thin slices. Drop a few slices at a time into the boiling syrup; they should not crowd each other. Cook for a few minutes, depending on the ripeness of the fruit (it must be still firm). Remove with a slotted spoon and put in a glass serving dish. Pour the remaining syrup over the peaches. Chill before serving.

Note: Peeled sliced apples or stoned dark cherries may be cooked in the same syrup. Cooked peaches and cherries may be combined for a compote, but apples should be served by themselves, since their flavor does not blend with that of other fruit.

FRESH PEARS WITH CHESTNUTS AND CREAM

Les Poires aux Marrons

A simple and delicious dessert.

6 *ripe Bartlett pears*
½ *lemon*
1½ *cups chopped marrons glacés or candied chestnuts, drained*

3 *tablespoons Kirsch or pear brandy*
1½ *cups heavy cream candied violets*

Peel and core the pears, but leave them whole. As soon as a pear is peeled, rub it with the cut side of a lemon to keep it from darkening. Combine the *marrons glacés* with 2 tablespoons of the Kirsch or pear brandy. Stuff the pears with the mixture. Place the pears on a silver serving dish or on individual plates. Whip the cream lightly. Flavor with the remaining tablespoon of Kirsch.

Coat each pear with whipped cream. Place a candied violet on the stem end. Chill before serving.

COOKED PEARS WITH CREAM SAUCE

Gekochte Birnen mit Nidel

Traditional from Zurich.

6 *firm Bartlett pears*	1 *teaspoon cinnamon*
1/3 *cup butter*	

#1	#2
1 1/2 *cups cream*	3/4 *cup butter*
1/3 *cup sugar*	1/3 *cup sugar*
	1 1/2 *cups cream*

#1—Peel the pears. Remove the cores and stems. Cut into halves or quarters. Melt the butter. Sauté the pears until firm but tender. Add the cream, sugar and cinnamon. Reheat but do not boil. Serve hot.

#2—Peel the pears. Remove the cores and stems. Cut into halves or quarters. Sauté the pears until firm but tender. Melt the butter; add the sugar. Cook over a low flame until the sugar turns brown. Add the cream. Reheat slightly. Pour the sauce over the cooked pears.

FRESH PRUNE COMPOTE

..Pflaumenkompott

Traditional.

1/2 *cup sugar*	1 *lemon, cut into thin slices*
1 *cup water*	1 1/2 *pounds fresh Italian*
	prunes, sliced

Combine the sugar, water and lemon slices in a sauce-pan. Stir until the sugar is dissolved. Heat to the boiling point. Wash the prunes, cut in half and remove pits. Add to the syrup, and cook 2 to 3 minutes. Serve warm or chilled.

FRESH PRUNE CRUMB PUDDING

Pflaumenpudding

3 pounds fresh Italian
   prunes
1 ¼ cups sugar

1 ⅓ cups sifted all-purpose
   flour
¼ teaspoon salt
½ cup butter

Wash and cut the prunes into quarters. Measure; there should be about 6 cups. Combine ¾ cup of the sugar, 4 tablespoons of the flour and the salt, and mix with the prunes. Turn into a 10 x 6 x 2 baking dish. Mix the remaining sugar and flour together. Add the butter, and cut into crumb consistency. Sprinkle over the prunes. Bake in a preheated moderate oven (375°) for 1 hour or until the prunes are tender and the crumbs are brown.

CHESTNUT CREAM

Vermicelles aux Marrons

A standard Swiss dessert or teatime sweet, eaten in the *confiseries*, where it is served in small individual paper cups. *Vermicelles* means "little worms," since the chest-nut purée is shaped into spaghetti-like strips by being piped through a pastry tube.

2 pounds chestnuts
water to cover chestnuts
4 cups milk
1 vanilla bean, split into
  halves lengthwise
½ cup sugar, or sugar to
  taste

3 tablespoons butter
2 tablespoons Kirsch
  (optional)
1 to 2 cups heavy cream,
  whipped with sugar to
  taste

Cut a gash in the flat side of the chestnuts with a sharp knife. Cover the chestnuts with water and boil them for about 15 minutes. Remove the chestnuts, a few at a time, from the hot water and take off the outer shell and inner skin. (They are easier to peel when hot.) Scald the milk with the vanilla bean in the top of a double boiler. Drop the chestnuts into the hot milk. Cook, covered, over boiling water until the chestnuts are soft and mealy. Stir occasionally. Drain the chestnuts, and save the milk for a custard or pudding. Force the chestnuts through a fine sieve or a food mill while they are still hot. Beat in the sugar, butter and Kirsch. (Older chestnuts are sweeter and need less sugar.) Put the purée into a pastry bag equipped with a small tube. Press the mixture into the individual serving dishes or a large dessert dish. Hold the pastry bag about 1 inch away and pile the purée lightly so that the chestnut strands remain fluffy. Wash out the pastry bag or use another pastry bag for piping the whipped cream in decorative swirls over and around the chestnuts.

CHESTNUT CREAM GARNI

Vermicelles à la Crème

Make 2 cups of cooked vanilla pudding with the milk left over from the Chestnut Cream or with 2 cups of light cream. Beginning with a layer of chestnuts, make alternate layers of chestnut purée and pudding in individual serving dishes or in a large dessert dish. Decorate with whipped cream and glacé cherries or candied violets.

CHESTNUT SOUFFLÉ

Castagnaccio

A traditional dessert from the Ticino, where there are many chestnut trees. It can be made with fresh chestnuts, chestnut flour, or, easiest for the American kitchen, imported canned chestnuts.

¾ *cup drained canned*
   chestnuts
½ *cup sugar*
3 *tablespoons melted*
   butter
2 *tablespoons Maraschino*
   liqueur or Kirsch
½ *teaspoon vanilla extract*
5 *eggs, separated*
granulated sugar
candied violets (*optional*)

Press the chestnuts through a fine sieve. Combine with the sugar, butter, Maraschino, vanilla and egg yolks. Beat well. Beat the egg whites until stiff. Fold into the chestnut mixture. Pour into a well-buttered 1-quart soufflé dish. Bake in a preheated moderate oven (375°) for 30 to 40 minutes. Sprinkle with the granulated sugar and candied violets, if desired, before serving. Serve immediately.

CHOCOLATE CRINKLE CUPS

Coupes au Chocolat

These showy cups are served in many Swiss hotels and pâtisseries, filled with *vermicelles*, vanilla or chocolate

pudding or whipped cream. They are surprisingly easy
to make.

6 squares semi-sweet chocolate	*2 tablespoons butter*

Heat the chocolate and butter over hot water in a
double boiler until the chocolate is partially melted.
Then remove it from the hot water and stir rapidly until
the chocolate is entirely melted and has blended with the
butter. (The mixture should be thick.) With a teaspoon,
swirl the mixture around the insides of 10 large baking
cups, covering the entire surface with a thin layer. Place
in muffin pans and chill until firm. About 10 minutes
before serving, fill the cups with any desired filling and
place in the refrigerator. Peel off paper just before serving. Garnish with grated semi-sweet chocolate.

CHOCOLATE MOUSSE

Mousse au Chocolat

This is a rich, dark mousse which must be chilled for
at least 8 hours.

2 cups dark-type cocoa	*1 teaspoon vanilla*
½ cup melted butter	*flavoring or 2*
½ cup strong coffee	*tablespoons rum,*
5 eggs	*brandy or Kirsch*
⅔ cup light cream	*whipped cream, sweetened*
¾ cup sugar	*to taste*

Blend the cocoa with the butter, coffee, egg yolks and
heavy cream in the top part of a double boiler. Heat over

hot water, stirring constantly until thick. Cool. Beat the egg whites until stiff but not dry. Gradually beat in the sugar, 2 tablespoons at a time, until the mixture is stiff and glossy. Fold in the chocolate mixture and flavoring. Pile lightly into small individual white soufflé dishes (*pots de crème*), sherbet glasses or in a glass dish. Chill 8 hours or overnight. Serve garnished with whipped cream sweetened to taste.

CHOCOLATE PUDDING

Schokoladekopf

Traditional.

½ cup rice flour or
   cornstarch
⅛ teaspoon salt
½ cup sugar
1 cup milk

½ pound dark sweet
   chocolate
3 cups light cream
sweetened whipped cream

Combine the rice flour or cornstarch with the salt and sugar. Add the milk gradually, stirring to get a smooth mixture. Melt the chocolate over hot water in a double boiler. Add the chocolate slowly to the cornstarch mixture. Slowly stir in the cream. Cook over low heat, stirring constantly, until the pudding is smooth and thick. Pour into a wet 1½-quart mold. Let stand until cold. Chill in refrigerator. Unmold and serve with whipped cream.

Note: The pudding may also be put into a glass dish, instead of a mold.

CRÈME CARAMEL FROM GLARUS

Karamelcreme nach Glarner Art

The caramel is in the *crème*, and not on the top as usual.

2 tablespoons cornstarch	1 to 2 tablespoons brandy
¼ cup milk	1 cup heavy cream,
7 tablespoons sugar	whipped
2 cups hot milk	⅔ cup chopped toasted
4 egg yolks, well beaten	almonds or filberts

Mix cornstarch and milk to a smooth cream. Reserve. Put sugar into a heavy saucepan, and cook over the lowest possible heat, stirring constantly, until the sugar has melted and is golden and bubbly. Do not brown or scorch. Remove from the heat and stir in the hot milk. The sugar will lump, but the lumps will dissolve. Stir mixture until the sugar has dissolved; if necessary, stir over low heat. Beat the egg yolks with 3 tablespoons of the hot milk mixture. Stir the egg yolks into mixture in the saucepan. Gradually stir in the cornstarch mixture. Cook over low heat, stirring constantly, until smooth and thickened. Cool; stir in the brandy. Chill. Fold in the whipped cream. Spoon into a glass serving dish or into individual dessert dishes. Sprinkle with toasted nuts. Serve with plain, crisp cookies.

PARFAIT AU GRAND MARNIER

A favorite hotel and restaurant dessert, excellent for a party. This version is from the Mövenhof in Zurich.

14 egg yolks
2 cups cold sugar syrup
    (see below)
6 tablespoons Grand
    Marnier
grated rind of 2 oranges
juice of 2 oranges

2 cups heavy cream,
    whipped
fresh or candied orange
    sections
whipped cream for
    decorating

Put the egg yolks in a heavy saucepan. With a wire whisk or an electric beater, beat until they are thick and lemon-colored. Place the saucepan over very low heat. Gradually add the sugar syrup, beating all the time. Continue beating until the mixture is thick and smooth. Remove from the heat and beat until the mixture is cold. To speed this process, place the saucepan into a bowl with water and ice cubes. Stir in the Grand Marnier, orange rind and juice. Fold in the whipped cream. Pour into a 3-quart rinsed mold. Cover the mold with its own cover. (You can make a cover with aluminum foil doubled and cut to the shape of the mold. Tie this cover to the mold with string.) Freeze, without stirring, until solid. Unmold on a platter, preferably a silver one. (Unmold by wrapping around the mold a towel that has been dipped in hot water and wrung out. Place the platter on the mold and reverse. If the ice cream still won't come out, repeat the hot towel process.) Decorate with fresh or candied orange sections. Pipe swirls and rosettes of whipped cream around the parfait. Makes 12 to 15 servings.

Note: The recipe can be halved.

Sugar Syrup

Combine ¾ cup water with 2½ cups sugar. Cook together over low heat for 5 minutes. Cool before using.

CREAM CANDY

Nidel-Zeltli

A traditional candy made by children.

2 cups cream   *1 ¼ cups sugar*

Place the cream in an enamel saucepan. Bring to a boil. Add the sugar. Cook over medium heat, stirring constantly, until golden brown. Pour on a greased and then floured warm cookie sheet. Spread with a wet knife to a ½-inch thickness. Let cool 10 minutes. Then cut into squares or into various shapes with a cookie-cutter.

XXIV

Odds and Ends

HERE IS a small posy of miscellaneous recipes meant for my readers' random interest. I have purposely chosen them for their Swiss nature, omitting recipes of a similar kind for drinks, preserves, etc., which are similar to those of the countries that surround Switzerland.

BRAZILIAN CHOCOLATE

Chocolat Brasilien

½ cup cocoa
¼ cup sugar
1 cup water
3 cups milk

1 tablespoon grated orange rind
¼ teaspoon almond extract
cinnamon sticks

Blend the cocoa with the sugar. Gradually stir in the water and the milk. Heat to the boiling point. Add the orange rind and almond extract. Chill. Before serving, beat with a rotary egg beater until frothy. Serve with a cinnamon stick in each cup. Makes 1 quart.

CHOCOLATE RUM DELIGHT

La Délice au Chocolat

¾ *cup cocoa*	*1 cup Kirsch or brandy*
⅔ *cup sugar*	*1 cup heavy cream,*
4 cups milk	*whipped with 2*
1½ cups strong coffee	*tablespoons sugar*

Blend the cocoa with the sugar. Gradually stir in the milk. Heat to the boiling point. Remove from the heat and add the coffee and Kirsch. Chill until ready to serve. Pour the cocoa mixture to make a glass two thirds full. Add about ¼ cup whipped cream for each serving. Blend well and serve at once. It makes about 8 cups.

OLD WOMAN'S LIQUEUR
FROM
THE TICINO

Latte di Vecchia

An old household nostrum.

2 cups milk	*grated rind of 1 lemon*
2 cups brandy	*1 vanilla bean, cut into*
2 pounds sugar	*halves lengthwise.*

Combine all the ingredients in a large jar or pitcher. Close the jar or cover the pitcher and shake thoroughly to mix well. Let stand for 14 days, shaking once a day. Strain through cheesecloth into bottles. Seal. Makes about 1 quart of liqueur.

HONEY WATER

Acqua di Miele alla Luganese

When I was a child in Lugano, this used to be given to me—and to anybody else who needed a strengthening drink—for a cold, or before going swimming in Lake Lugano.

1 quart dry red wine   *1 cinnamon stick*
1 cup honey

Combine the wine and the honey in a bowl and mix well. Add the cinnamon stick. Cover, and let stand in the sun for 3 days. Stir occasionally. Remove the cinnamon. Pour into bottles or glass jars and seal. Let stand 3 more days in the sun. Makes about 1¼ quarts.

MULLED WINE

Wiwörm

New Year's Drink.

2 cups water   *3 cloves*
⅓ cup sugar   *½ teaspoon nutmeg*
2 cinnamon sticks   *3 cups wine*

Combine the water, sugar, cinnamon sticks, cloves and nutmeg. Bring to a boil and simmer 10 minutes. Remove whole spices. Add the wine. Reheat slightly and serve hot. Makes about 5 cups.

SWEET-SOUR PLUM RELISH

Saure Pflümli

Traditional. An excellent old-fashioned relish for any kind of roast or boiled meat and fowl, and for cold cuts.

3 pounds purple Italian plums	*2⅓ cups sugar*
1½ cups dry red wine	*15 whole cloves*
1½ cups wine vinegar	*1 4-inch stick cinnamon*

Wash the plums. Prick each plum several times with a needle, and put them into a bowl (do not use an aluminum bowl). Combine all the other ingredients and bring them to a boil. Simmer, covered, for 5 minutes. Cool the mixture and pour over plums. Let stand overnight. The next day, drain the syrup from the fruit. Bring it again to a boil. Let it cool and pour it over the fruit. Let stand overnight. The third day, transfer the plums and the juice to a heavy saucepan. Cook over the lowest possible heat until the plums' skin begins to tear in one or two places. Remove from the heat. Take out the plums with a slotted spoon and put them into jars. Boil the remaining syrup until it is the consistency of heavy cream. Cool, and pour the cold syrup over the plums to cover them. Seal the jars in the usual manner. Makes about 2 quarts.

Index

---◄◆►---

Nika Standen Hazelton

---◄◆►---

Born in Rome, Nika Standen Hazelton spent her early years traveling to the capitals of Europe with her father, who was a diplomat. She studied under Harold Laski at the London School of Economics and wrote for the *New Statesman* before coming to the United States to join the staff of *Fortune*. She then worked successfully in advertising for many years. She began writing cookbooks during World War II and has been a cookbook expert for several magazines, including *Ladies' Home Journal*, *House and Garden*, and *National Review*, and for *The New York Times Book Review*. Mrs. Hazelton is the author of *Reminiscence and Ravioli*, *The Art of Cheese Cookery*, *Continental Flavor*, *The Art of Danish Cooking*, *The Art of Scandinavian Cooking*, *The Best of Italian Cooking*, *The Picnic Book*, and *The Belgian Cookbook*.